Contents

Introduction

Today's new parents have many advantages over their predecessors, but they also face many new challenges. Knowledge of the way babies grow and develop both before and after birth has increased enormously in the past few years. This knowledge in itself creates new pressures, worries, and anxieties for parents. If you are a couple thinking of starting a family, how do you know where to turn? I hope that this book will help you to find out what best suits you, and what makes you feel comfortable and confident enough to follow your own instincts.

There's much evidence to indicate that the unborn baby benefits from having a relaxed, calm mother who can take obstacles in her stride. Other research demonstrates that the most important factor in determining whether a pregnant woman is tranquil or not, is a caring, interested, supportive partner. And here we have come to the reason for my writing this book. It is not just for first-time mothers, but for couples – mothers and fathers. I've included basic advice on caring for your baby during his first year of life, but it's just as important to emphasize how a baby will affect your relationship.

The impact on your relationship

Few couples think about the impact their new baby will have on their lives, their work, their emotions, and their feelings for one another. With the care of their baby as the top priority, parents can easily give too little consideration to looking after themselves.

Both new mothers and new fathers will find their world turned upside down by the advent of a baby. This may create tensions and strains, which, if unspoken and unresolved, could drive a wedge between them. It's a huge leap from being a couple to becoming a family. A man is very different from a father, and different things are expected of him. If they're honest, most men admit to experiencing difficulties in making the transition to fatherhood. By the same token, a mother is a very different person from a woman, who was probably self-confident and independent before she became pregnant. Now she may be apprehensive and come to feel isolated. She has to cope with a baby who is completely dependent upon her, which can bring with it a perceived loss of identity. This in turn may lead to confusion, resentment, and irritation towards her partner.

The good news is that it's possible for both of you to pick your way through this minefield of new feelings and responsibilities. But it isn't always easy and it requires a lot of give and take to smooth the path. Perhaps now, more than at any other time, each of you has to be aware of and sensitive to the needs of the other and actively look for ways of showing you care.

Advice and reassurance

While my main aim is to give new parents the confidence to follow their own instincts in fashioning their particular brand of family life,

first-time
parents

first-time
parents

what every new parent needs to know

Miriam Stoppard

LONDON, NEW YORK, MELBOURNE, MUNICH, DELHI

For Ed and Amie

Editors: Jinny Johnson, Elise See Tai
Designer: Phil Gamble

Senior Art Editor: Helen Spencer
Managing Editors: Jemima Dunne, Penny Warren
Managing Art Editors: Lynne Browne, Marianne Markham

Picture Researcher: Liz Moore
DTP Designer: Traci Salter
Production: Maria Elia
Special Photography: Ruth Jenkinson

First published by Dorling Kindersley in 1998
This revised edition published in Great Britain in 2006 by Dorling Kindersley Limited, 80 Strand, London WC2R 0RL
A Penguin Company

A CIP catalogue record for this book is available from the British Library.

ISBN-13: 978-1-40531-060-4
ISBN-10: 1-40531-060-X

Reproduced by Colourscan, Singapore.
Printed and bound in Singapore by Tien Wah Press

Discover more at
www.dk.com

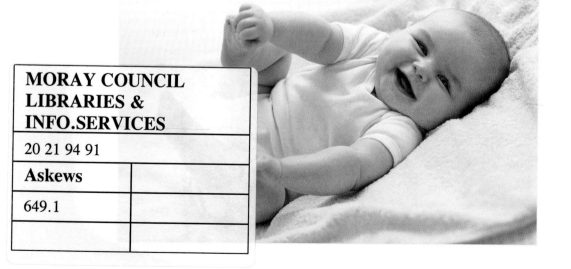

and to be open and loving with one another so that their relationship is enriched by their new baby, there's no doubt that first-time parents find bits of advice quite useful. So I've tried to be helpful in matters with which most young families have problems.

Issues such as how to stay healthy during pregnancy, where to have your baby, what to expect during labour, how to establish breastfeeding and cope with broken nights or an inconsolably fretful baby are all covered. While love for your baby can begin from the moment of birth, his care is a skill that you'll be learning throughout his first year, and understanding how he develops is a crucial part of it. All new parents feel anxious and inept to begin with, but if you share the worries as well as the joys, you're less likely to strain your relationship.

Making room for fathers

Throughout the book, I approach pregnancy, birth, and babycare as a joint venture. Fathers figure on every page because mothers and babies need involved, active fathers. Men are as good at fathering as women are at mothering; there's no qualitative difference between the two. Fathering instincts are strong and only need a little encouragement to flower. Babies love being nurtured by fathers as well as mothers; it follows that parenting should be equal and shared.

On the face of it, following this principle may seem fraught with obstacles, but it need not be so. Parents can share all the elements of babycare with a little planning and a generous heart. After all, babycare means loving and encouraging your baby, teaching your baby, watching your baby grow and develop, and establishing bonds with your baby that in all probability will be the strongest you ever make with anyone. Who in their right mind would miss out on it?

Men should try not to allow themselves to be deprived of this unique relationship. And when they're fully involved with their baby, a little miracle occurs along the way: their relationship with their baby's mother flourishes, too.

Making parenting a partnership

To help both parents become fully involved, I've included special panels that give the mother's point of view on one side of the page and the father's point of view on the other. Arranging information in this way has a special purpose: it can help you gain insight into what your partner may be feeling about a particular topic, or might want to say but is reluctant to make demands. Looking at this information together may help you to get a discussion going. Communication is the key to a successful relationship, so hopefully these panels will enable you to talk things through and be generous about the other's way of looking at things.

Above all, couples whose relationship is on a sound footing and who enter into parenthood as a true partnership are doing the best for their baby, who will grow up secure in the love of both parents. Shared care means there'll be time for your baby, time for yourselves and time when, as well as being a family, you're just a couple – but with the knowledge that together you have produced and nurtured a wonderful baby.

DR. MIRIAM STOPPARD

Deciding on
parenthood

When you decide to have a baby, you're also making the decision to become a parent. This is probably the most important step you'll ever take in your life, because bringing a child into the world isn't something that you can simply add on to your current lifestyle. You're creating a completely new person, and taking on a responsibility that is lifelong. You're also creating a new unit – from being two individuals, you're becoming a family – something that both cements and puts strains on your existing relationships with each other, your friends, and your family. This is equally true if you're a lone parent and, even if you have children from a previous relationship, your new baby is going to create a new family grouping. So it's well worth looking at all the implications of parenthood and the different forms that the modern family takes, and to ask yourselves some searching questions about how you see parenting and how it's going to affect your everyday needs and your emotions.

The changing family

How roles are changing

At their most basic, the terms "mother" and "father" describe a range of biological facts. A mother produces eggs and gives birth to children. A father's sperm fertilize the eggs and contribute half his child's genes. But these are obviously not the only differences. Human beings belong to a species with clear distinctions between male and female. Traditionally, the physical differences between men and women meant that men (being bigger and stronger) were seen as protectors of women.

No need for brute strength
For thousands of years, men used their biological role to claim authority over women, but today, the traditional roles of mother and father are no longer relevant. Modern technology has done away with the need for brute strength and nowadays women and children generally don't need men to protect them.

Involving men in parenting
Since the 1970s it has been increasingly recognized that men should be more involved in the upbringing of their children. This is sometimes seen as a spin-off from the women's movement, but this misses the point. The equal sharing between men and women in the upbringing of their children isn't just the result of women's changing thoughts, but also the outcome of men's need to be involved in the nurture, guidance, and upbringing of their children.

Having a baby creates a whole new social unit. Instead of being two people, you become a family. Families give babies constant care and protection and though family groupings may vary, babies know only the quality of care, interest, and love that they receive.

How it used to be

Until two or three generations ago, the family was usually based on the extended model. People were part of a large grouping of three or four generations, extending outwards to include cousins. When people's lives were less mobile, and they lived and worked in one small area, face-to-face contact was possible on a daily basis. This larger family unit could act as a support group for its members, particularly in the case of child rearing.

The extended family
Four generations were gathered together for this photograph – an example of the traditional extended family that was already becoming a rarity by the 1920s, when this photograph was taken.

The family today

In the past 50 years, the extended family has largely broken down. Rapid technological change produced a labour market that demanded mobility; people wanted to go where the jobs were, or were forced to do so through economic necessity. Leaving home meant leaving the extended family network and possibly settling where there were no relations at all to lean on for financial and emotional support. At the same time, increased prosperity allowed people to set up their own homes, whereas in the past they may have remained in the family home, even when married. This broad social movement saw the rapid spread of the isolated nuclear family – just mother, father, and children. Even when embedded within an extended family, this unit can be a hothouse of troubled emotions; on its own, its long-term survival is more likely to be precarious.

New family groupings

Since the 1960s, women have increasingly developed a degree of financial independence that made them less likely to hang on to the last remnant of a marriage just because they didn't think they could provide for

The nuclear family
The majority of modern families plan the number of children they have, and both parents want to become involved, to a greater or lesser degree, in childcare.

themselves and their children on their own. Liberal attitudes to welfare have also played their part in the transformation of the traditional family; as the nuclear family – detached from its older members or more tenuous branches – became the norm rather than the exception, so the divorce rate increased, giving rise to less orthodox family structures.

Divorce and remarriage

Many divorced or separated people haven't turned their backs on marriage or partnership as such, but only on the one they found intolerable. A good proportion of them is prepared to have another try, thus often creating a stepfamily (see p. 142). As with the nuclear family, the stepfamily has been around for a long time (and hasn't always had a very good press), but its recent growth has been quite dramatic.

Single parents

The one-parent family is a much maligned institution. It's true that it has often grown out of unhappy situations and the pressures, not least financial, on the lone parent are great. But many single-parent families are thriving and vigorous units that are bound by particularly close ties and offer the children involved continuity, stability, and happiness (see p. 140).

A new kind of parenting

Not only has the composition of the traditional family changed in recent times, but also how it functions. Fathers used to be seen as protectors, having little direct involvement in day-to-day childcare, but their importance as equal partners is now being recognized – side by side with women's increasing role as equal or even primary financial provider. And in some families the father cares for home and family by choice, while his partner earns the daily bread (see p. 176). One reason why such families are often strong and successful units is that they take account of both partners' talents and, generally, are a result of careful discussion and planning. But whatever the practicalities of any individual family unit, providing a stable, loving, and open environment in which to bring up children is probably the only important constant.

What is a father?

No one has a problem defining a mother's role. A mother's role is to care for children: mothers feed, comfort, and dress; they encourage, teach, carry, undress, and put to bed. We know this because it's what we experienced as children. Defining the father's role can be more difficult.

Finding a role model

Much as you may love your father, you may want your relationship with your own children to be different to the one that you had with your father. Men are constantly encouraged to become fully involved in nurturing their children, but few have any role model to demonstrate what this actually means. What we really need is for fathers to be more like mothers.

Babies don't mind

Babies and young children don't mind whether they are cared for by their mother or father. They experience comfort, warmth, and security from their parents and, though they soon learn to tell them apart, they don't make value judgments based on what mothers and fathers ought to do. Apart from breastfeeding, there's nothing a man can't do for his baby.

The need for parenting

Babies don't need mothering and fathering, they need parenting. They need the most important adults in their lives to be models of what parents do for their children. A child will only separate her expectations of each parent if this is what she learns from her experiences.

Why be a parent?

Mother

It's worth questioning your own ideas about parenthood, and whether what you think of as a mother's role isn't just as applicable to fathers.

Attitudes to fathering

■ Traditionally, fathers came home from work expecting the home to be clean, the children ready for bed, and a meal on the table. Today, it's hard to believe that many modern mothers would entertain this.

■ Some women still expect their partners to handle all the family finances, sometimes to their disadvantage. It's a good idea if couples can find a fair way to share their financial burdens.

■ It's often assumed that men do all the heavy work. However, while a man must do this when his partner is pregnant and the baby is young, women are fitter and stronger than they used to be and these tasks can be shared.

■ Women still tend to take on the chores while their partners play with the baby, even when both parents work. It's much better, though, if both of you play with your baby, and share the housework equally.

■ Some women leave discipline to their partners, but this is both outdated and a cop-out. Try to agree attitudes to discipline and apply them consistently (see p. 181).

You may never do anything more important than bring up a child. However satisfying your career, whatever sporting or leisure goals you've achieved, you'll find parenthood is a role that is rewarding in a way that is unlike anything else.

Following your instincts

The instinct to bear children is a strong one, and luckily the joy and fulfilment felt by most parents far outweigh some of the inconveniences and compromises that they may have to accept. Although this isn't always so, making the decision to have a child usually comes from within a close, loving relationship between two people who decide that they would like to express their mutual affection in having a baby. This is just as well – you're unlikely to make the decision because you're attracted by the idea of reduced free time, never being able to put yourself first, sleeplessness, and forking out for designer infant trainers! If you think carefully about the changes brought about by parenthood, you'll realize that it's your genes that are pushing you relentlessly towards recreating yourselves in the form of children. Nowadays, people don't like to admit that they might be at the beck and call of basic urges and tend to dress them up as something more refined. That's fine, so long as we remember that we can also push back and say no to parenthood. For some, that can be the best decision, because having a baby is a commitment like no other.

More than just nature

Aside from biological reasons, people also want to have a baby for fulfilment and personal achievement. Human beings are social animals, and the way they think and act always has a social element. This is shown most clearly in human parenthood in the case of adoption where (usually) two people voluntarily make a commitment to assume all the rights and duties of natural parents, while being genetically unrelated to the child (see p. 142). Adoption also illustrates the depth of the emotional need that people feel to nurture, educate, and, above all, love a child. What you give to your children in time, love, understanding, and example will constantly be repaid as you watch them grow and develop over the years. Every child is genetically the sum of his parents, but he is also a unique personality in his own right, and knowing that you have been the primary influences and educators in allowing that personality to take shape and mature is deeply enriching as well as being a major achievement.

Social and economic pressures

In a society where everyone goes to school, everyone expects to go to school. Similarly, when everyone except a small minority has children, people expect to have children. It's as though a person has to have a reason for remaining childless, rather than the opposite. In the past, when families tended to live close together, in the same street or village if not actually in the same house (see p. 10), there were quite important economic reasons for having children. As soon as they were old enough to work, children made a vital contribution to the family's economic welfare, and parenthood was also a guarantee of being cared for in old age.

Changing demands

In the much more fragmented society in which we live today, children aren't expected to contribute to the family income (at least not until they have finished their education), and the state has taken over some of the basic responsibilities for the elderly, or people make their own provision for old age. As a result, the economic demands of the family are now directed downwards, from parents to children, instead of the other way round. Bringing up children today can be a costly business, and not just financially. For the first time in history, large numbers of women can achieve a whole range of satisfactions outside parenthood and the home; and with safe methods of contraception, they can also choose when and whether they want to have children. This doesn't mean that large numbers of women are opting out of motherhood, though some are; but what they are doing is fitting having and bringing up children into lives where work and a career are also seen as theirs by right.

A question of upbringing

Having begun to consider parenthood seriously, the first thing to realize before you go further is that having a baby is just the overture to bringing up a child. It isn't too difficult to imagine having a baby – the excitement, the celebrations, the delighted grandparents, the supportive friends and family. It's almost impossible to visualize bringing up a child if you haven't done it. The demands in time, energy, and emotion are almost limitless, unless of course the first thing you're going to teach your toddler is how to use the remote control for the TV and video. This isn't an option for most people because, even before you become parents, you'll have some idea of the kind of people you hope your children will grow up to be, and of the upbringing that will make this idea a reality.

A firm foundation

Upbringing begins from the moment of birth. For a baby or young child, everything is a learning experience, so how you care for your baby is influential from day one. It's worth looking at the background of someone you know who is independent but has a large capacity to love and interrelate with others, who is effective and confident, who recognizes that there is such a thing as the general good, and wants to contribute to it. You'll probably find that person found the world an accepting, loving, encouraging, reasonable, and respectful place from birth. His parents made him feel that way, and the foundation for everything he has become was provided by them in his first year of life.

Sidebar:

Father

It's a good idea to be clear about your own attitude to parenting to make sure it doesn't reinforce traditional stereotypes about mothers and fathers. What you may think of as a mother's role can be just as applicable to fathers.

Attitudes to mothering

■ While it's still true that it's mostly women who stay at home, many are now returning to work within months of the birth. Also, more and more men are becoming stay-at-home dads (see p. 176).

■ Recent surveys show that women, even full-time working mothers, still do most of the chores in the home. Ask yourself if this is fair – there's no reason why cooking and cleaning can't be shared.

■ Tasks, such as dealing with carers and teachers and taking and fetching from school, used to be seen as a mother's responsibility. But more fathers are fitting daily activities like the school run or taking their child to the doctor into their working day.

■ It used to be thought that mothers put children to bed, but most fathers enjoy the bedtime routine, especially if they've been away from their children all day.

■ The idea – prevalent not so long ago – that it was somehow demeaning for a man to push a pram is now laughable. Men are pleased to be seen doing this and are also more than happy to take their children out without their partners.

Timing it right

Your attitude to parenting

Parenting is not an exact science. However right the decision to have a child may seem at the time, it may be helpful to ask yourselves the following questions. If you answer "yes" to more than five, you may need to think about your attitude to parenting:

■ Do you already have ambitions for your children's future?

■ Are you uncertain about how parental actions affect children?

■ Have you still got to work out some of your views on parenting?

■ Do you think that after the birth, instinct will take over and you'll know exactly how to behave towards your child?

■ Are you worried that you and your partner have different ideas about parenting?

■ Do you believe in a strict routine for a newborn baby?

■ Do you think a baby would benefit from such a routine?

■ Can you spoil a young baby?

■ Do you believe that babies cry for no reason?

■ Will you leave investigating childcare until after the birth?

■ Are your views on baby care at odds with those of your partner?

■ Will you find it hard to tolerate all the disorder of a new baby?

■ Do you foresee any conflict with family members about the way you intend to care for your baby?

It's rare for a couple to feel that everything is just right and that the perfect moment has arrived to have a child, but now that we have control over our fertility, it gives time for all the options to be considered carefully.

Making the decision

For many people, finance and accommodation may be the most pressing issues when making the decision whether or not to become parents. Others may look at their personal freedom, and how having a child may affect it. In today's society, where more and more women are finding satisfaction in the progress of their careers, making the decision to break off and have a child can be extraordinarily difficult. Although many companies – and countries – are providing increasingly generous maternity leave and benefits, this may not compensate for the fact that having a baby could delay your career prospects, especially if you want to spend more than a few months at home with your baby. This is one reason why many women, particularly those with satisfying or high-powered jobs, are waiting to start a family at least until their thirties, when they feel that they've reached a level of achievement that enables them to stand back from their careers with confidence.

Making space for parenthood

Men also need to think about how their work commitments may impact upon their relationship with their children. Many older men who become parents for a second time in a new relationship have acknowledged that they regretted having missed out on their first family's childhood because pressures of work effectively separated them from their children. Childhood passes quickly and you only have one chance with any child, so think about how much time you will be able to give to her.

Practical considerations

You can bring up a child in anything upwards from a two-room apartment – if there's a separate space for the baby, that's ideal. If you're thinking of moving into a larger home to accommodate future children, try to move before you become pregnant; otherwise it's best to wait until after your baby is born. You don't want the double pressure of a new baby and moving house. No one pretends there isn't a financial implication in parenthood, but the cost of having a baby is largely dependent on what a couple sees as essential. Be assured that no baby in a carrycot with one or two loving parents ever lay awake wondering why she didn't have a smart crib with Brahms' lullaby wafting from the attached electronic musical box. Nevertheless, it makes good sense to make the best of what's on offer. Look at your likely overall income and expenditure once the baby is born, taking account of benefits available (see p. 184), and plan accordingly. Whenever your purse allows you to shop, invest in the basic minimum (see p. 74); leave luxuries until you can really afford them.

Partnership or marriage

If you're in a long-term stable relationship, but are unmarried, you probably had good reason for choosing this kind of partnership. Now that you're considering parenthood, is there a case for reconsidering your position? Have either or both of you anything to gain from marrying and, more importantly, has your prospective child? One of the reasons most commonly given by prospective parents for marrying before the baby is born is that it ensures the father is the legal parent of his child. The legal situation may vary from country to country, so formal marriage may not necessarily be the only option for you, but clearly neither of you would want to encounter problems in gaining access to your child in the event of your relationship breaking down and leading to a split. However unlikely this may seem at present, no one can foretell the future and most couples would want to guarantee that their baby always has the equal benefit of both parents, even if at some time they may not live together any more.

Changing relationships

Sometimes new parents haven't bargained for the fact that their relationship with family and friends will change. More importantly perhaps, the dynamics of their own relationship will also change. No time is better spent before you even start trying for a baby than in exploring together what these differences might be (see p. 128).

Grandparents You both know the personalities of the grandparents and you may see difficulties ahead because their views may not be the same as yours. You'll find later that agreement with grandparents about how you're going to set limits for your child is invaluable. It's also a good idea to agree that you'll both gently but firmly resist any attempt by them to dictate methods of parenting to you. You can, however, ask them to help you to implement yours. But it's also wise to listen to their views or you may be passing up good advice based on real experience.

Your friends Once you have children you may not be available to your friends as much as you were before, so they'll appreciate it if you retain your identity as a friend rather than a parent while you're with them. Bear in mind also that you'll meet other people with babies with whom you'll forge friendships, based on the shared experience of new parenthood.

The impact at work Try also to rehearse in advance what difference the advent of the baby may have at work. You may never have clock-watched in your life before now, but it's difficult not to when you're aching to get back to your baby – and this is just as true for fathers as it is for mothers. However, your colleagues, no matter how sympathetic, have the right to assume that you'll be as good value as you were before. If you can see possible pitfalls, be up front and negotiate; you won't always be a new parent and lost trust is difficult to re-establish.

Questioning your reasons

Even if you think you both really want a baby, it's still sensible to think about all the issues. The following questions don't have right or wrong answers, but provide what I hope will be a useful starting point for you:

■ Does the idea of having a baby seem to be the instinctive next step for you both?

■ Have you always taken it for granted that you would have children?

■ Do you just want a child, or do you want a child specifically with your partner?

■ Does one of you want this baby more than the other? If so, what effect has this had on your relationship?

■ Do you want to have a baby because you think it will strengthen your relationship with your partner?

■ What images do you see when thinking about life with your baby? Do they include sleepless nights and dirty nappies?

■ What will you miss most about being a couple rather than a trio?

■ Have you any firm personal ambitions that could be compromised by having a baby?

■ Do you want a baby to make up for areas in you life that you find unsatisfactory?

■ Is any part of your motivation to please family members, such as grandparents?

■ Are you and your partner quite clear about the commitment each of you will make to the baby?

Preparing for
parenthood

Pregnancy is an exciting time for you both, but your excitement can also be tinged with apprehension, uncertainty, and – if the pregnancy is a surprise – even dismay. Each person's reaction to the knowledge that he or she is going to become a parent is different, but luckily nature has made sure that there is plenty of time to get used to the idea during the 40 or so weeks from conception to birth. Pregnancy is not an illness, but it does put a lot of strain on a woman's body. So if you're planning to become parents it makes sense to think about your fitness well before you conceive and to look after yourself during the pregnancy. Once the pregnancy is confirmed you will both feel happier if you follow its progress by attending antenatal checks and finding out as much as possible about how your baby develops in the womb. It will help you both to understand the minor discomforts and emotional ups and downs that a pregnant woman sometimes feels, and to face up to the slight possibility of something unexpected happening.

Plan for pregnancy

Mother

Your due date will be calculated as 40 weeks from the first day of your last period, so you need to take that into account when planning pre-pregnancy fitness.

Why fitness is important
There are a number of physical changes during pregnancy. Here are a few: the womb increases in volume (muscle) 1,000 times; the womb increases in weight (protein) 30 times; the work done by a mother's heart increases 50 per cent; the volume of her blood increases by one third; her kidneys filter 50 per cent more blood.

Preventing anaemia
If you're anaemic, your heart is overworked, which can affect your baby. A blood test would reveal anaemia and it may be necessary to take iron supplements.

Avoiding birth defects
Folic acid reduces the risk of some birth defects like spina bifida. It's a good idea to start increasing folic acid intake three months before you stop contraception, and for three months after you conceive. Good food sources are green leafy vegetables, cereals, and bread, or, you can take supplements.

If you have a medical problem
If you take regular drugs for a medical condition, let your doctor know before you try for a baby, as the dose may have to be changed once you're pregnant (see p. 35).

When you decide to become parents, it makes sense to prepare yourselves in advance. To have a healthy baby, research shows that by far the most important factors are your own and your partner's fitness and nutrition.

Timing of the birth

If you're serious about starting a family, ideally you should begin to think about it at least a year before the time you'd like your baby to be born. It's a good idea to allow at least three months to get your bodies to peak pre-conception fitness (see opposite). There are other issues you may want to take into account as well. If you're planning to move house, or know that work commitments are going to take you away from home at a specific time of year, you'll want to avoid allowing these to clash with the possible arrival of your baby. Some parents may even want to take account of whether their baby is born in winter or summer. Most education systems involve an autumn start to the academic year and there is evidence to suggest that some children born in the summer, the youngest in their school year group, may not achieve as well academically as the older and more mature children who are born in the winter. This doesn't just affect the early years; it can sometimes last well into the teens.

Delaying parenthood

More women are now delaying childbearing into their thirties or even early forties. A pregnant woman over 35 will be monitored more closely, but women's general health and fitness have improved so much that the older pregnant mother is no longer likely to have the same risks of earlier generations. In addition, couples starting a family in their thirties are more likely to have planned the baby, be in a stable relationship, and be financially secure. But leaving conception until later does increase the time you might have to wait to conceive – an average of six months when you're 35, as opposed to four months when you're 25 (see p. 20).

When to stop contraception

If you've been using straightforward barrier methods, such as the condom or diaphragm, you can safely conceive as soon as you stop using them. However, most doctors recommend at least one normal period after ceasing other forms of contraception, before you try to conceive.
The pill It's best to stop the pill three months beforehand, but a month would do, so long as you have one normal period before conceiving.
Intra-uterine device (IUD) The same timescale would apply to an IUD, so have it removed three months before you intend to get pregnant. Have at least one normal period before stopping all contraception – use a barrier method in the meantime.

Routine health precautions

WHAT TO LOOK AT	WHAT TO DO
Smoking	Smoking reduces fertility, especially in men as it lowers their sperm count. Give up before you try for a baby; smoking during pregnancy – direct or passive – harms your unborn child.
Alcohol	Alcohol can damage both sperm and the ovum, so prospective parents should consume no more than five units a week for women, ten for men. (One unit = one small glass of wine or a half pint of beer.)
Drugs and medication	Many medicinal and street drugs affect fertility. In particular, cannabis reduces sperm production; the effects can take months to wear off. Consult your doctor if you're taking regular medication.
Pre-pregnancy screening	Well before trying for a baby, check for rubella (German measles) immunity and get immunized if necessary; have a cervical smear test and any treatment; check for sexually transmitted diseases.
Environmental factors	Before conceiving, and once you stop contraception, make sure you avoid X-rays, hot saunas, and pollutants such as dioxins and PCBs (found in many garden and household products).

Father

Your partner's fitness and lifestyle obviously has a bearing on her ability to conceive, but your own fitness is also a crucial factor. If you aren't fit, you may not donate the best genetic material to your child in your sperm.

Why your lifestyle matters
Male fertility not only depends on the number of sperm produced, but also on the health of that sperm. This is affected by all sorts of lifestyle factors, such as smoking, alcohol, and drugs (see left), and also stress. Try to re-order your life if it's stressful, and look at your diet and fitness.

How fitness helps you both

As a prospective mother, your body undergoes a great deal of physical change (see box opposite). The fitter you are, the more easily your body will cope. But fitness and lifestyle may also change a man's ability to father a child, by affecting sperm production (see box above). Think about your health and lifestyle at least three months before you plan to stop contraception. As well as improving your fitness, it will increase your chances of conceiving without delay and of having a healthy baby.

A healthy diet

Adjusting your diet shouldn't require uncomfortable changes. Your staple diet should include good quality carbohydrates, such as wholewheat bread, rice, and potatoes. Keep your animal fat intake down by changing to skimmed milk and low fat cheeses, and use olive or sunflower oil for cooking. Eat lots of fresh fruit and vegetables every day (see p. 36). Don't skip meals, avoid processed foods, outlaw the liquid lunch, and eat a hearty breakfast, though not a fried one.

Taking exercise

Exercise makes a contribution to becoming a healthy potential parent, so if you don't already do so, start a gentle exercise programme together, such as jogging, swimming, or gym sessions. Try for 20 minutes' exercise that increases your heart rate at least three times a week. However, bear in mind that very strenuous training or dieting may reduce fertility.

Genetic counselling

Seek advice and have tests in advance if a genetic disorder, such as cystic fibrosis, muscular dystrophy, thalassaemia, or haemophilia, runs in your family.

What happens in counselling
The counsellor explains the condition and your family background and shows you the pattern of inheritance through past generations. Not all carriers of a defective gene get the condition. If it's recessive it can be masked by a healthy version, whereas a dominant gene will always show up. With a dominant gene, the chances of your baby being affected are one in two, with a recessive gene they are one in four.

Conception

Increasing chances of conception

The following tips might help you conceive more quickly:

■ Try to have intercourse during your most fertile period (see right). This period is signalled by the texture of your cervical mucus, which becomes clear, thin, and slippery, making it easier for the sperm to swim up through your cervix. Ovulation usually occurs 24 hours after this type of mucus is at its most profuse.

■ Avoid love-making for a couple of days before your fertile period to help build up to an optimum number of sperm.

■ The "missionary position" (man on top) may be most effective for conception, particularly if you lie down for half an hour afterwards.

■ Cut down on caffeine. It's possible that it interferes with the embryo's ability to implant in the wall of the uterus.

Conceiving a baby is the ultimate expression of a loving sexual relationship between partners. You could conceive within a few months of deciding to have a baby, especially if you have intercourse when you're most fertile.

When you're fertile

A woman is fertile only when she is ovulating – when an egg has been released from her ovary. This is nearly always 14 days after the first day of the last menstrual period. You can therefore predict ovulation by tracking your periods in a diary, or you can do an ovulation test on your urine, which may be helpful if you don't have a regular 28-day cycle. Three-quarters of all couples who have unprotected intercourse will conceive within nine months, and 90 per cent in 18 months, but from the age of about 25, the fertility of both men and women does start to wane.

What happens when you conceive

As the egg can survive for 36 hours and sperm for 48 hours, your fertile period can last for about three days. When ovulation and intercourse overlap, sperm swim up through the cervix and uterus to meet the egg, and fertilization with one sperm usually happens in the upper end of the Fallopian tube. It then takes three to four days for the fertilized cell (called a zygote) to reach the uterus and implant in the endometrium – the specially prepared uterine lining. The process of implantation is called nidation; the fertilized egg, now called a blastocyst, burrows into the lining and quickly forms a primitive placenta; seven days after fertilization, the blastocyst is embedded and growing.

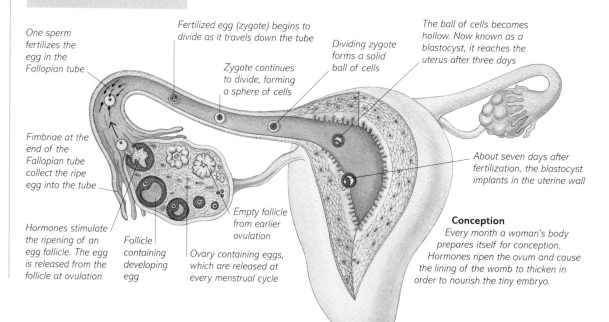

One sperm fertilizes the egg in the Fallopian tube

Fertilized egg (zygote) begins to divide as it travels down the tube

Zygote continues to divide, forming a sphere of cells

Dividing zygote forms a solid ball of cells

The ball of cells becomes hollow. Now known as a blastocyst, it reaches the uterus after three days

Fimbriae at the end of the Fallopian tube collect the ripe egg into the tube

About seven days after fertilization, the blastocyst implants in the uterine wall

Hormones stimulate the ripening of an egg follicle. The egg is released from the follicle at ovulation

Follicle containing developing egg

Empty follicle from earlier ovulation

Ovary containing eggs, which are released at every menstrual cycle

Conception
Every month a woman's body prepares itself for conception. Hormones ripen the ovum and cause the lining of the womb to thicken in order to nourish the tiny embryo.

Finding out if you're pregnant

Many women suspect that they are pregnant within days of conception, but the single most obvious indicator is a missed period, and anyone who has a regular menstrual cycle will realize something has happened once they are three or four days late. Other women may not realize for two or three weeks, especially if they continue to have so-called "withdrawal" bleeding, where pre-pregnancy hormones still present in the body cause a weak menstrual bleed. They may, however, suspect that they are pregnant from other physical signs (see below). Either way, you'll probably want to confirm it as soon as possible with a pregnancy test.

Pregnancy tests

You can buy pregnancy test kits that confirm whether or not you are pregnant from the day your period is due. If you can wait a day or two longer, you'll get a more reliable result; you may wrongly test negative if you try too early. You can also ask your doctor to do the test.

Other signs of pregnancy

■ Tender, heavy breasts that may tingle a little. Your bra may seem a touch too tight, the veins on your breasts more prominent than usual, and your nipples and areolae may seem redder than usual.
■ A feeling of nausea. Although often called "morning sickness", it may happen at any time of the day.
■ A super-sensitive sense of smell, and a metallic taste in your mouth.
■ The need to pass urine more frequently than usual.
■ Feeling incredibly tired, especially in the evening.

Waiting a long time to conceive

If you've been trying to conceive for 12 months without success (or eight months if you're over 35), you could approach your doctor to talk about being referred for investigations into your fertility. Finding out that you are unable to conceive without help can be very stressful, but many couples discover that taking this first step is in itself an antidote to stress and they may go on to conceive before talking to the specialist.

Preparing yourselves for fertility investigations

The test process can be long and difficult, so both partners must enter willingly into the investigation. Before you embark on it, you should think carefully about the strain (including perhaps financial) of what you are about to do. Many relationships have crumbled under the stress of infertility investigations, and living with the uncertainty, and the unpleasant and invasive tests, can be extremely hard.

Sharing the responsibility

Be aware that your ability as a couple to conceive – your fertility – is the sum of both your fertilities. Investigations may indicate a problem that will probably be treatable, and it's worth remembering that in as many as half of infertile couples, the problem lies with the man. Infertility is nobody's fault, you share the problem. Don't apportion blame, feel resentment or guilt, or you'll drive a wedge between you that may make conception even more elusive.

Boy or girl?

Nature does well in maintaining a balance of about 103 boys to 100 girls and I'm not in favour of trying to interfere with that. With ultrasound and fetal cell investigations, you may be able to find out the sex of your baby during pregnancy – if you want to.

What determines a baby's sex?

Men produce sperm with 22 chromosomes plus either one X (female) or one Y (male) sex chromosome. Women's eggs also have 22 corresponding chromosomes, but they only produce an X sex chromosome. A zygote fertilized by an X sperm grows up to be a girl; a Y sperm results in a boy.

Is it possible to influence a baby's sex?

Although no method with any scientific validity has been developed, by noting the different characteristics of X and Y sperm, it's possible to suggest a way of increasing your chances of conceiving the gender you want:

■ X sperm are larger and slower than Y sperm and X sperm live longer than Y sperm.

■ To increase the chances of a girl, intercourse should be two to three days before ovulation, as only X sperm survive long enough to meet the egg when it's finally released.

■ There's a higher chance that a Y sperm will fertilize an egg on the day of ovulation because it will reach the egg more quickly, and the baby will be a boy.

■ Frequent ejaculation lowers the proportion of Y sperm, so a girl is likely. Infrequent sex increases the proportion of Y sperm and the chances of a boy.

Adjusting to pregnancy

Pregnancy after miscarriage

A miscarriage, stillbirth (see p. 35), or even a termination in the past, can affect how you both feel about your current pregnancy.

Rekindling grief
Even if your earlier pregnancy or pregnancies were some time ago, being pregnant again may rekindle your grief. Talk things over with your partner or a close friend.

Reliving the past
If you had a miscarriage, you'll both find it difficult to be relaxed about the new pregnancy. Take heart from the fact that most women who miscarry go on to have a healthy child the next time.

After a termination
If you had a termination due to abnormality, you're likely to be offered diagnostic tests in this pregnancy as soon as practically possible. Again, take heart from the fact that many such problems are extremely unlikely to recur. If your termination was for other reasons, you may suffer feelings of guilt that you're going ahead with this pregnancy. It's important to talk about this rather than bottling up feelings that may affect your relationship with your new baby.

After a stillbirth
If you had a stillbirth, you'll probably be wondering whether or not this baby is alive and find the end of your new pregnancy almost unbearable. Although you'll be monitored carefully, talk to your consultant – you may be able to have the baby some days or even weeks before the due date.

Becoming a parent is one of the most profound experiences you'll ever have. It's an essentially positive and deeply satisfying experience – but you're going to find it shattering, exhausting, and incredibly hard work too.

Thinking ahead

Your pregnancy is a time to ponder on the changes ahead – for each of you as individuals and for you as a couple. In many ways it's impossible to describe exactly what's ahead in pregnancy until you're there, but it's certainly true that you can be as prepared as it's possible to be by asking questions, reading, and talking to friends who've already gone through it.

Your differing reactions

Men and women often respond differently to the news of pregnancy; elation may fade into fear, anxiety, or depression at the thought of the responsibilities looming, and the changes that are unavoidable. Changes in relationships can be threatening at the best of times. Those that take place in early pregnancy are particularly taxing because they have to be played out when the mother is feeling tired and possibly anxious, and the father may be feeling ambivalent about the new situation (see p. 24). Use the months ahead to prepare, as much as possible, for what's in store, but try to enjoy your pregnancy, too. Life will, after all, never be the same again. If you can, go away for a weekend or have a holiday when you're between four and seven months pregnant – it will give you plenty of time and space to share your feelings together.

Feelings about pregnancy

At first, the physical changes common to most pregnant women may colour your view of the pregnancy. Many women find the physical discomforts of the first three months – tiredness, nausea, tender breasts – begin almost as soon as the pregnancy has been confirmed, sometimes within a few days of missing a period (see p. 21). This can take couples by surprise, turning initial delight into apprehension and uncertainty. However, this reaction is usually temporary, lasting about 12 weeks; after this you'll suddenly realize that you're not waking up with nausea and a fuzzy head, that you're full of energy and that instead of just looking thicker around the waist, you're developing a recognizable "bump" that announces your pregnancy to the world, and of which you can be proud!

Planned or unplanned

Whether the pregnancy was planned or not has a bearing on your attitude to it. An unplanned pregnancy may be welcomed by one partner more than the other (and this is often the father rather than the mother), or both of you could be ambivalent about it, especially if you have financial worries. Whether your pregnancy is planned or unplanned, there may well be implications for your career, especially if you work for a company that doesn't have a sympathetic attitude to parenthood. This is more important for working women than men, but experience shows that it is possible to resume a career even when you've had a long break for birth and childcare (see p. 170). Once you know you're pregnant, talk to your employer about the options as soon as possible to find out what maternity leave is on offer (see p. 184). This will help to allay any fears you have about your career prospects.

If your pregnancy was assisted

Your attitude to your pregnancy is bound to be affected if you've had to wait a long time to conceive, and perhaps had treatment to assist conception. You'll feel an enormous sense of relief that your longed-for baby is at last on the way, but may worry about doing anything that may lead to miscarriage, so there may be a tendency to treat the pregnancy like an illness. Try to avoid this; most specialists in assisted conception will hand their patients over to the normal maternity services once the pregnancy is established – if anything is going to go wrong, it is most likely to happen in the first eight to ten weeks, and you'll have been warned about this. Even if you've had to endure quite lengthy and invasive treatments to achieve the pregnancy, try not to dwell on them and look forward instead to the birth of your healthy baby.

Giving the news

You might want to tell everyone straight away that you're having a baby; on the other hand you might want to hug your secret to yourself for a while. You may surprise yourself at how it comes out, depending on who you're telling, because many people find admitting they are about to become parents to a third party seems to make it real for the first time. The support of friends and family can help to overcome any feelings of doubt; alternatively you may find yourself confessing to your closest friend your ambivalence to the whole thing, even though on the surface you appear to be delighted. Bear in mind that in the event of a miscarriage, the more people you've told, the more distressing it may be for you if you have to explain that you've lost the baby (see p. 35).

Pre-birth bonding

Although it's wonderful to be able to see your baby moving when you have your first scan (see p. 29), most women feel that the bonding process really begins once they feel it. Though this may not happen until about 20 weeks in a first pregnancy, it's an advantage you have which your partner lacks – so share your feelings as much as possible and encourage him to feel your tummy. First sensations of movement often coincide with a change in energy levels, so you'll probably be feeling better about yourself and the baby than you ever thought possible to start with.

Father

The physical changes of pregnancy can affect how your partner feels about it. Preparing for this should help you deal with any low moments she may have.

Your partner's feelings

■ Exhaustion is common in early pregnancy – it's probably caused by all the hormones the body suddenly has to deal with. Encourage your partner to take things easy, and look forward to the middle months when she'll probably feel incredibly energetic and wide awake. The "bloom" of pregnancy at this time will make your partner look wonderful – so make sure you tell her!

■ The effect of pregnancy hormones combined with the whole idea of becoming a parent could make her much more emotional than usual. Be supportive and sympathetic.

■ She may worry about the fact that she'll inevitably be gaining weight. Don't draw attention to this. Be positive about how she looks and compliment her. It's a very bad idea to diet in pregnancy, but she doesn't need to eat for two either. Encourage her with the fact that most of the fat gained in pregnancy is stored to nourish breastfeeding, and is burnt off remarkably quickly once she starts feeding (see p. 78).

■ Your partner may feel that she's lost control of her life because there's always someone else with ideas on what's best for her. Don't add to this – she knows her body best and when it comes to decisions, she has the last word.

The expectant father

Mother

Your relationship with your partner will change before the baby is born, so it'll help to be prepared for this.

Understanding your partner
■ It's very easy for men to feel left out so make sure you involve your partner as much as possible.

■ Expecting a baby is an external experience for your partner and it may be very difficult for him to empathize with the invisible changes taking place within you. Remember, his day-to-day life will stay much the same until after the baby is born.

■ Talk to your partner about how you're feeling. You may have big mood swings and go through periods of feeling insecure and unattractive. Sit down with your partner and explain how you're feeling.

Affection and sex
■ Your partner may be anxious about your wellbeing and treat you as if you're ill. This kind of attention can be suffocating so tell your partner if you don't like it. Also, remind him that you're as keen as he is not to do anything to harm the baby. Equally, if your partner isn't giving you enough attention, tell him.

■ Your desire to have sex may change at different stages of your pregnancy. If you don't want intercourse, tell your partner.

One of the most exciting moments of your life will probably be when you find out that you're going to be a father. The emotional impact is just as real for you as for your partner so talk about your feelings and get involved in the pregnancy and birth plans.

Understanding your conflicting emotions

The pregnancy may not seem real for the first couple of months – not least because your partner will physically look the same. Don't worry if you feel differently from her about the pregnancy; it's an internal experience for her and an external one for you, and you don't suddenly become one person with one set of feelings just because you are having a baby together. However, once you see that your partner's body has begun to change and, later, when you have felt the baby move, the idea of having a baby will become more real. It is at this time that your feelings of joy and excitement may be replaced by fears and worries; whatever your family set-up, it's normal for a man to begin to worry about being able to provide for his family. Having a child can be an extra financial burden, especially if your partner is going to give up her job, but try not to make life-changing decisions, such as getting a new job or seeking promotion. It's difficult to know whether you'll want extra responsibility a year down the line, once you are a parent. Remember, as a father, you have more than just material possessions to offer your child.

How you can participate

Being an expectant father is the one time in your life when you're quite likely to feel out of control. This feeling of being an outsider will not be helped by the way other people treat you – well-meaning female friends and relatives may unconsciously push you out of what they see as their territory. You may also find that the professionals, such as obstetricians and midwives, direct their conversations at your partner more than you.

Take the initiative

Don't step back and allow your female relatives and friends to be more involved than you. Tell your own friends and colleagues – you may be subject to a certain amount of teasing, but people may also view you as more responsible and mature. Try to find out as much as you can about the pregnancy so that you can understand the changes taking place in your partner's body.

Plan for the birth together

You will need to discuss with your partner the type of birth that she wants (see p. 26) and decide what your involvement will be. If possible, go with her to the scans so that you can see your baby developing, talk about the

Taking an active role

WHAT TO DO	HOW IT CAN HELP YOU
Talk to your partner	The best way to understand how your partner is feeling, and what is going on in her body, is to talk to her. Ask her what it feels like to feel the baby move; discuss your plans for the birth together; find out if she's got particular discomforts. She'll appreciate your interest.
Go to antenatal classes	If you go to antenatal classes (especially father-only sessions), you'll have an opportunity to learn about the birth and talk through your own concerns. This will help you to work out the best way to support your partner and enable you to be more involved in birth choices.
Talk to other fathers	Get to know the other expectant fathers at antenatal classes – they will probably be feeling the same as you and be glad to have someone to talk to. Talk to friends and colleagues who have babies; find out what their experiences were like and ask their advice.
Read about pregnancy and parenting	Read pregnancy and parenting books and any leaflets you're given. The more you understand about what's going on during the pregnancy, the more familiar it will become and it can help you to understand how your partner is feeling. It will also enable you to ask the right questions.
Ask questions	Go to antenatal appointments with your partner so that you can meet the professionals and be present at the examinations. As a first-time parent, there will be things you don't understand and need to know about. If you ask questions of professionals, they are more likely to involve you.

Prenatal bonding

Babies can hear sounds outside the womb by five or six months; if you talk to your baby, he will bond to your voice and, in fact, he can hear your low-pitched voice more clearly than his mother's. To help you to bond with your baby:

■ Gently massage your partner's tummy and feel your baby move.

■ Talk to your baby, and nuzzle him through your partner's skin.

■ Use inner tubes of toilet rolls to listen to the heartbeat.

■ Go to scans with your partner to see your baby develop (see p. 29).

Being involved

It's your baby too, so:

■ Be open about your feelings.

■ Express your concerns without fear of misinterpretation.

■ Talk candidly to your partner about sex so that it doesn't become an issue.

■ Be involved in all arrangements and plans for the birth.

■ Go to antenatal classes.

■ Go to antenatal appointments so that you can hear your baby's heartbeat and see him move on the ultrasound monitor.

■ Visit the hospital and delivery room with your partner.

■ Contribute to the birth plan.

fact you're going to be a father, and ask as many questions as you want – most of all, enjoy it! You will also need to talk to your employer about taking time off to go to the antenatal appointments as well as the birth.

The birth plan

Discuss the issues raised by the birth plan (see p. 27) with your partner, but don't impose your views. If your partner feels strongly about certain issues such as a drug-free labour (see p. 43), try to respect her feelings, but talk about the advantages and disadvantages too. Look forward to being present at the birth. Remember, being at your child's birth is probably one of the most precious things you will ever experience and holding your baby in the first few seconds of life is proven to help you bond with your child.

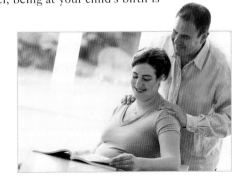

Share the planning
Get as involved as you can in the planning of the birth and give your partner plenty of love and support.

Options for antenatal care

There's now a huge choice in maternity care, although how wide the choice is will depend on what's available in your area. Looking at your antenatal options also means looking at your birth options.

Who can deliver care?

Once you know you're pregnant, your first call will probably be to your family doctor. He or she may confirm the pregnancy with another test, take your blood pressure, and ask you about when your last period was to work out the due date. Your doctor will tell you the different options for antenatal care available in your area and you can also talk through where the baby will be born as these are often linked. Don't feel you have to make your mind up on any of these issues immediately – go away and think about the possibilities before finalizing details.

Shared care Antenatal care may be offered by your doctor, in association with community midwives and the hospital. Routine checks will be done by your doctor and the community midwife, and you'll go to the hospital for specialist checks, such as ultrasound. This type of care is helpful if you live some way from the hospital. However, you may not meet the midwife who delivers your baby in the hospital before the event.

Midwife care In some places, antenatal care is given almost entirely by community or hospital midwives working in teams, or under the "Domino" system (see opposite). They are based either at a local health centre or hospital and can also arrange home births. You'll be able to build up a relationship with the midwives who will also deliver your baby.

Independent midwives If you want to be cared for solely by midwives, you might want to consider hiring an independent one. This is expensive, but it does allow you to arrange your care, labour, and birth exactly as you want it.

Hospital care You'll be cared for by hospital-based doctors and midwives. The care may lack the informality of other options, but if you have any complications, have an existing medical condition, or are having twins, it's probably the wisest choice.

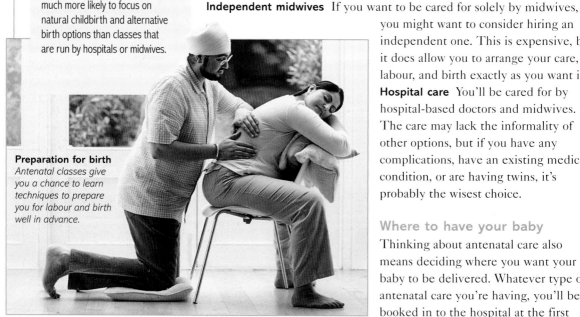

Preparation for birth
Antenatal classes give you a chance to learn techniques to prepare you for labour and birth well in advance.

Where to have your baby

Thinking about antenatal care also means deciding where you want your baby to be delivered. Whatever type of antenatal care you're having, you'll be booked in to the hospital at the first appointment (see p. 28). If you want to have a home birth, it may need a certain amount of discussion with your doctor or midwives. Either way you need to look at the options side by side with those for antenatal care.

Hospital birth

Having a first baby in hospital feels right to many couples. There's plenty of backup on hand if things aren't straightforward, and in most hospitals there's access to the full range of pain relief.

Advantages Having your baby in hospital doesn't necessarily mean opting for high-tech – many hospitals have special low-tech birthing rooms where you'll be free to walk around in labour and where intervention will be kept to a minimum. Many hospitals have pools for pain relief (see p. 43), though it's difficult to ensure you'll get to use one as you can't usually pre-book them. In some areas, under a scheme known as "Domino", a midwife comes to your home once you're in labour, accompanies you to hospital, delivers your baby, and returns with you to your home as little as four hours later. If you like the idea of being back with your family at home as soon as possible, but want the medical backup for the delivery itself, this option could be ideal for you.

Disadvantages Having a baby in hospital does mean agreeing to policies that may cramp your style. You may, for example, be given electronic fetal monitoring, at least for a time, which may make it difficult for you to stay active and upright throughout if this is what you want, but this is no longer routine for low-risk mothers.

Home birth

If you feel you would like a home birth, talk to your midwife. Most midwives are happy to attend a home birth unless there are good reasons why it may not be safe. Alternatively, you can consult an independent midwife (see opposite).

Advantages Home is a more relaxed place to have a baby than hospital. You're far less likely to need emergency treatment if you remain active as far into labour as you can. Your chances for a straightforward, problem-free delivery at home are good, even if this is your first child.

Disadvantages You don't have immediate access to emergency treatment, so if anything untoward happens or your labour fails to progress, you might need to be transferred to hospital. You also won't have access to pain relief, such as an epidural, and, in some countries, pethidine (see p. 43).

Delivery in a birth centre

Birth centres are usually sited near hospitals, but are completely self-contained and designed to have a less medical feel. They may be staffed by family doctors and community midwives or run solely by midwives. Staff often don't wear uniforms, and you'll probably be given your own room in which to spend your labour, give birth, and then remain after the delivery. These centres can provide an excellent halfway house, giving you the informality of a home birth with the safety net of high-tech care nearby.

Your birth plan

Once you've considered all your antenatal care and birth options, it's worth preparing a simple birth plan in consultation with your doctor and midwife. This should be kept with your hospital notes. Wait until you're about 32–36 weeks pregnant, as by that time you'll probably have discovered whether there are any special factors in your pregnancy that might affect some of your requests. You also need to be prepared to be flexible because things may not go according to plan on the day. Your birth plan might include the following:

■ Who you want to be present at the birth with you.

■ Your views on interventions, such as induction, the artificial speeding up of labour (see p. 50), and fetal monitoring (see p. 44).

■ Your views on active labour, and whether you would like the possibility of using a birthing pool (see p. 43).

■ Your preferences for pain relief (see p. 43), and the use of breathing and relaxation techniques.

■ Whether you mind student doctors or midwives being present during your labour and birth.

■ What position you might adopt to deliver your baby (see p. 46).

■ Whether you would prefer not to have an episiotomy (see p. 46).

■ Whether you mind if the delivery of your placenta is speeded up with syntometrine or whether you'd prefer it to be delivered naturally (see p. 48).

Your antenatal care

The physical examination

At every antenatal appointment, various checks will always be done to rule out potentially dangerous medical conditions.

Blood pressure
A rise in blood pressure could mean you're at risk of pre-eclampsia (see p. 34).

Urine test
Your urine will be tested for the presence of protein, which could mean an infection or, later, pre-eclampsia; glucose or sugar, which could signal diabetes; and ketones, chemicals that indicate you're not eating enough.

Abdominal check
The midwife will feel your abdomen to check the size of your uterus. She'll also listen to your baby's heartbeat, using either a Pinard stethoscope or a sonicaid, an electronic stethoscope that amplifies the baby's heartbeat so you can hear it (see below).

In general, antenatal checks are to ensure that all is going well with your pregnancy – that you are healthy, and that your baby is growing properly.

Your first appointment

Often known as the booking-in appointment, your first antenatal session may be quite long, lasting as much as an hour. It may be at your home, at the local health centre, or doctor's surgery, or at a hospital clinic. A midwife will take a detailed medical history, and will ask questions about your general health, your family's health, and your gynaecological and obstetric history. She will also ask whether or not this baby was planned, how long ago you stopped using contraceptives or what contraceptive you were using when you got pregnant, and the date of the first day of your last menstrual period. The midwife will also ask you how you feel and talk to you generally about your pregnancy. She'll offer advice on issues like diet, exercise, and maternity benefits. You can discuss what kind of delivery you'd like, though you don't have to decide at this time unless you're absolutely sure (see p. 27). You'll probably be asked to bring a urine sample to each appointment.

The blood test

You'll probably have some blood taken, which will be sent to the laboratory for analysis. Ask the midwife exactly what your blood will be checked for and why; it's routinely checked for iron content, blood group and rhesus status, rubella immunity, blood sugar levels, and sexually transmitted diseases. Other tests, such as one to check whether you've been exposed to toxoplasmosis (a parasitic disease that may affect your unborn baby) may also be available. Blood isn't usually tested at every appointment, but in certain situations you will be asked to give blood again at later appointments (see opposite), and most hospitals test at 28 weeks for anaemia, blood group antibodies, and diabetes.

Future appointments

Your routine antenatal checkups will generally be shorter than your booking-in appointment. Between appointments, it's a good idea to write down any questions you may have and keep them with your maternity notes.

Your baby's heartbeat
It's a thrill the first time you hear your baby's heartbeat amplified through a sonicaid.

Ultrasound scans

Ultrasound is now offered routinely to almost all pregnant women, as it enables the baby's age to be measured very accurately and can also detect visible abnormalities. Many hospitals offer two scans, one at about 12 weeks and the other at 16 to 20 weeks. The scans are carried out at the hospital, and your partner should be allowed into the examination room with you; this is a wonderful opportunity for a father to relate to his growing baby as you'll be able to see it moving about. The operator slowly scans across your abdomen with a hand-held instrument called a transducer that detects sound waves bounced off your uterus and baby's body. These are transmitted to a computerized monitor for visual interpretation.

Having an ultrasound scan
The transducer is passed gently to and fro across your abdomen and an image of your baby is transmitted to a monitor.

Thinking ahead

If you're offered any of the tests for abnormalities (see chart below), it's helpful to ask yourselves what you'd do if you found your baby did have Down's syndrome or spina bifida. If the answer is that you wouldn't do anything, but continue with the pregnancy, it may not be worth having the tests. If you know you would have a termination, or wouldn't be able to decide until you had the information, then you may want to go ahead. Before any test, find out:

■ Exactly what your baby is being tested for.

■ Whether the test involves risk.

■ How accurate it is.

■ What information the test will actually provide.

■ Whether there's an alternative.

Specialist screening and diagnostic tests

TEST	HOW IT IS DONE	WHAT IT CAN TELL YOU
Nuchal scan	A non-invasive scan at 11–13 weeks, measuring the thickness of the "nuchal pad" in the baby's neck. Often combined with a blood test.	A thick nuchal pad may mean a higher risk of chromosomal defects, so you'll be offered a test such as amniocentesis or CVS later.
Triple (or bart's) test	This blood test screens you for the risk of Down's syndrome. It is done at 15–16 weeks along with a scan to confirm dates.	Hormone levels indicate the risk of your baby being affected; if it is greater than 1 in 250, you'll be offered amniocentesis.
AFP test	A screening blood test that checks the level of alpha-fetoprotein (AFP) at about 15–18 weeks.	A higher or lower level than usual may indicate Down's syndrome or spina bifida.
Chorionic villus sampling	A diagnostic test, in which a cannula (tube) is passed through the cervix at about 10–12 weeks to take cells from the developing placenta.	The cells are examined to check the baby's chromosomes for any abnormalities. CVS carries a 1 per cent risk of miscarriage.
Amniocentesis	A diagnostic test done at about 15 weeks. Guided by ultrasound, a needle takes a sample of amniotic fluid through the abdominal wall.	Chromosomes in fetal cells can be checked for abnormalities, such as Down's syndrome. There's a small risk (1 in 200) of miscarriage.
Fetal blood test (cordocentesis)	This rare diagnostic test is carried out after about 18–20 weeks. It takes blood from the umbilical cord.	Blood is tested for abnormal chromosomes or infections. There's a miscarriage risk of about 1–2 per cent.

The progress of pregnancy

Mother

Coping with common complaints

■ Feeling sick is most common in the first three months. It may happen in the morning, but by no means always, and you may also vomit. Eating little and often rather than big meals helps. If you're vomiting incessantly, consult your doctor.

■ You're more likely to get cramp in your legs or feet. It's not known exactly why, but you can relieve it by pulling your toes up hard towards your ankle.

■ Constipation is a common problem, caused by the presence of hormones that slow down the workings of the large intestine. Eat plenty of fibre, exercise regularly, and drink plenty of water. Iron pills may make it worse.

■ Later in pregnancy, you may suffer from indigestion or heartburn, because your enlarging womb is pressing on your stomach. Prevent this by eating smaller meals more often, sitting up straight when eating, and avoiding spiced foods. Sipping milk, especially at night, can help if you have heartburn.

■ Haemorrhoids – swollen varicose veins that protrude from the back passage – occur in pregnancy due to pressure from the baby, especially if you're constipated. Eat plenty of fibre and avoid standing for long periods. Check with your doctor if they become very painful .

Having a baby growing inside you is like being part of a real-life miracle. Sometimes you'll pat your bump and feel you can hardly believe your child is in there. Take time to ponder on the wonder of what's happening; you'll both be laying the foundations for a baby who feels secure and wanted.

Following your pregnancy

No part of a woman's body escapes when she's carrying a baby, and you both need to keep that in mind. For instance, tender breasts that are getting ready for breastfeeding need to be treated gently by a father when he caresses them; the growing uterus pressing on your internal organs means that you must never be too far from a toilet during the last three months of pregnancy. The guide that follows is only a brief outline of the complex changes going on inside your body.

What's happened by three months

The first three months of pregnancy (the first trimester) are tremendously important in laying the foundations of your baby's healthy development, although there are few visible signs of your baby's phenomenal growth.

You at three months Your pregnancy is well established now:
■ You'll really start to gain weight regularly; any morning sickness will soon disappear.
■ The uterus is rising out of the pelvis and can be felt.
■ The risk of miscarriage is almost zero by this time.
■ Your heart is working flat out and will continue to do throughout the rest of your pregnancy.

Your baby at three months She is fully formed, but needs to mature.
■ She has a fully formed body, complete with fingers, toes, and ears.
■ Her eyes move, though her eyelids are closed.
■ Her body is covered with fine hair.
■ She wriggles if poked – her muscles are growing.

At three months
You'll start to gain weight and the visible signs of your pregnancy will begin to appear.

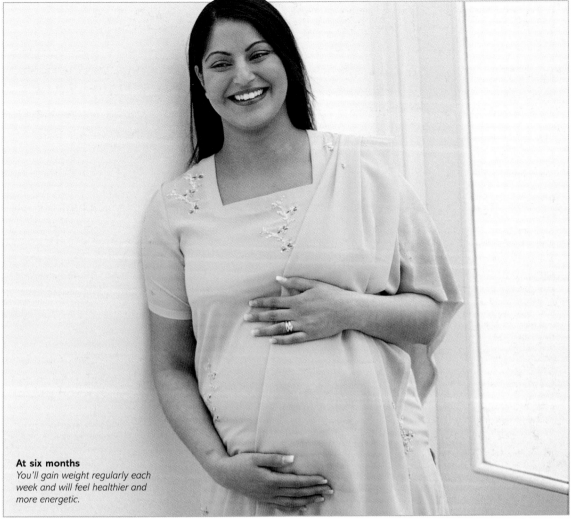

At six months
You'll gain weight regularly each week and will feel healthier and more energetic.

What's happened by six months

The period from about the third to the sixth month (the second trimester) is when pregnancy sickness ends, your baby really grows, and you begin to feel her move. You're brimming with energy, vitality, and well-being.

You at six months You'll notice the following signs:
- You're putting on about 0.5 kg (1 lb) in weight per week.
- Your uterus is a good 5 cm (2 in) above the pelvis.
- You may have bouts of indigestion.
- From about 20 weeks, you'll feel your baby move.

Your baby at six months She's well developed and growing:
- Her hearing is acute, she can recognize your voice.
- She's becoming better proportioned – her body is catching up with her head.
- She's well muscled but thin. She'll put on fat now.
- Her lungs are growing and maturing fast.

Feeling your baby
You should be well aware of your baby's movements now.

Full term
Not long to wait now. Soon you and your partner will meet your new baby for the first time.

What's happened by nine months (full term)

The final 12 weeks or so of pregnancy, known as the third trimester, are when the baby puts on fat in preparation for birth and the brain and lungs mature in preparation for independent life.

You in the last weeks of your pregnancy You may have to visit the antenatal clinic more often and you may notice the following signs:

■ You may feel a "lightening" as your baby's head drops into the pelvis.

■ It's more difficult to find a comfortable position for sleep.

■ Your breasts secrete clear-coloured nutritious colostrum.

Your baby in the last weeks of your pregnancy He's preparing to be born:

■ He weighs about 2.7–3.5 kg (6–8 lb) and he measures 35–38 cm (14–15 in) from crown to rump.

■ His head is "engaged", lying just on top of your cervix.

■ The placenta is 20–25 cm (8–10 in) across, 3 cm (1 in) thick and there is 1.1 litres (2 pt) of amniotic fluid.

■ His breasts may be swollen due to the action of your hormones.

Pregnancy at a glance

It's useful to be able to visualize what is happening by the end of each of the three phases, or trimesters, of pregnancy, so that you understand what is happening. By the end of the first trimester your baby is recognizably human but tiny. The second trimester is a period of rapid growth and during the third the baby gets longer and heavier.

Father

Although you're experiencing the pregnancy secondhand, following its progress helps you to become emotionally attached to your unborn baby.

The progress of pregnancy

■ Accompanying your partner to antenatal appointments (see p. 28) enables you to find out together how your baby is growing.

■ Remember that the baby is part of you as well as your partner. It's amazing to think that a single cell created from your sperm and your partner's ovum (see p. 20) can develop so rapidly.

■ Understanding and learning about the impact of the growing baby and uterus on your partner's body helps you to be sympathetic when she suffers the inevitable discomforts caused by the pregnancy (see p. 30).

At three months
Your uterus is about the size of a grapefruit and can just be felt above the pubic bone. All your baby's organs are formed and virtually impervious to the potential dangers, such as an infection and medication.

The fetus is recognizably human, and all his internal systems are in place

At six months
Your baby's organs are fully formed, his face is that of a newborn, and he sucks his thumb. Your uterus is poised for labour. You may notice Braxton Hicks contractions (see p. 42).

Hearing is developed; he may respond to noise. Skin is red and thin, with little fat beneath it

Below: Size of the baby's hand in relation to your hand at six months.

At nine months (full term)
You'll find you get breathless because your baby is now so big. His eyes are open and he's fat and healthy. If your baby is a boy, his testes have descended.

By full term, the baby is usually positioned head downwards

Below: Size of the baby's hand in relation to your hand at full term.

Difficult pregnancies

"Small for dates"

After reviewing the date of your last period and your expected date of delivery, both your heights, and scans of the baby, your pregnancy may be pronounced "small for dates". Don't worry, but doctors will keep an eye on you by:

■ Giving you scans every two weeks for a while to ensure all's well and to check the placenta.

■ Checking on the baby's heart rate for any sign of strain.

■ Discussing with you the possibility of inducing your baby or delivering by Caesarean (see p. 52), to prevent the baby having to go through a vaginal delivery.

Pre-eclampsia

This is a potentially serious condition that can affect one in ten women, especially first-time mothers and women carrying more than one baby. It can start at any time in the second half. It's not known precisely what causes it, but it tends to run in families.

How it affects you
There are no symtoms, but raised blood pressure and protein in the urine, may signal its presence. It affects the placenta and so the baby may grow more slowly than normal. The pregnancy can't be restored to normal, but delivery of the baby and placenta ends the disease. Delivery may be arranged before serious complications arise. For most mothers, delivery reverses all the effects.

Although the majority of pregnancies proceed without incident, occasionally things don't go according to plan. When something unexpected happens or there's cause for concern at your antenatal checkup, you're both going to feel extremely concerned about it, especially if all has gone well up to this point. Until now you may have been confident that all would be straightforward. Now, suddenly, the pregnancy seems to be in question, and you may feel apprehensive and confused. It helps enormously to face what's ahead together and to get as much information as you can.

Causes for concern

Some worrying development, like vaginal bleeding, may strike out of the blue; a "small for dates" baby (see above left) or high blood pressure (pre-eclampsia – see below left) may be diagnosed at a routine antenatal check. Whatever the cause for concern, your midwife or doctor should give you a full explanation.

Vaginal bleeding

Never ignore vaginal bleeding at any stage of your pregnancy. Although it's always worrying, close medical supervision can help avoid serious problems.
Bleeding in the first three months Bleeding in early pregnancy doesn't mean you'll lose your baby. You may not yet have high enough hormone levels to subdue your periods. You may have a condition such as cervical erosion or polyps, neither of which are likely to interfere with your pregnancy. Contact your doctor or hospital as soon as possible so you can be referred for a scan; if the heart is beating well, bleeding will probably stop and the pregnancy will continue normally. You'll need to rest and forego sex for a while.

Placenta

Placenta praevia
The placenta embeds close to or across the cervix. Pressure from the baby may cause bleeding.

Bleeding in later pregnancy It's rare to bleed late in pregnancy, but it's serious since it may indicate problems with the placenta, such as placenta praevia or approaching placental abruption. Placenta praevia means the placenta is positioned in the lower part of the womb, possibly across the cervix (see left). Placental abruption means that the placenta is beginning to separate from the uterine wall. Both conditions can be confirmed by ultrasound scanning, and hospital admission for observation and subsequent Caesarean delivery (see p. 52) will be necessary.

Multiple pregnancy

Carrying more than one baby will undoubtedly mean you have more professional attention and more antenatal appointments during your pregnancy. The diagnosis of twins, triplets, or more will be confirmed with an ultrasound scan, and the news may take a lot of getting used to, but there's a lot of help and support for you both.

If both twins are head down, it's more likely that both will be delivered vaginally

How twins lie
Twins normally lie both head down, or one head down and one breech. How they lie may affect the way your delivery is managed (see p. 51).

If the first twin is breech, a Caesarean is more likely

How you may feel
Nausea Multiple pregnancies often cause severe nausea, even vomiting, in the first three months. Eat little and often, and drink plenty of fluids – drinks containing glucose or glucose tablets may boost energy levels if you feel too sick to get calories from food.
Increasing size You get bigger faster than a mother with one baby because, as well as carrying two babies, you produce more amniotic fluid.
Backache Be careful about posture and avoid carrying or lifting heavy weights, because the additional levels of pregnancy hormones mean your pelvic ligaments can soften and stretch, and become painful.
Fatigue You'll tire very easily, and this may be made worse by anaemia. Rest, eat meat, and take folic acid and iron supplements.
Indigestion This may be worse than in a single pregnancy (see p. 30) because your stomach is squashed against your diaphragm. Have nourishing drinks and soups and eat frequent small meals.

Pregnancy and pre-existing medical conditions

Any existing medical condition means that your pregnancy will be carefully monitored. Medical conditions like asthma, epilepsy, heart disease, or kidney disease don't in themselves make pregnancy and labour difficult. If you take care of yourself, have meticulous antenatal supervision, and prepare yourself for in-patient hospital care in the last ten weeks of pregnancy, the chances are you'll have a normal birth.

Diabetes

Sugar – a sign, but not proof, of diabetes – may appear in your urine at any time in pregnancy. The most common reason for this is a change in the way the kidney handles sugar in pregnancy: no treatment is needed. "Latent" diabetes can do the same thing and can be controlled with diet alone, though you'll be checked more frequently at the antenatal clinic. Pre-existing diabetes needs strict supervision because your insulin needs may change. Babies of diabetic mothers tend to be large so you may be induced early or you may need to have a Caesarean section (see p. 52).

Losing your baby

No one can imagine the grief of losing a baby. Seek counselling so that you can grieve fully and come to terms with your loss.

Early miscarriage
A miscarriage in the first few weeks is more common than you might think – in fact one in three of first pregnancies. It usually happens because there was something amiss with the fetus or perhaps it had not implanted correctly. Early miscarriage may not be accompanied by much pain, although you may suffer severe period-like cramps. You'll both feel let down, and a woman has to deal with sudden hormonal changes that can make her very emotional.

Late miscarriage
This occurs between 13 and 24 weeks, usually because of placental problems or a weakened cervix that opens due to the weight of the growing fetus. It can also be the result of infection. You have a mini-labour to expel the fetus with whatever pain relief you choose.

Stillbirth
Losing your baby at or close to full term is very hard to bear, but nowadays you'll be given a chance to hold and name your baby and to have a funeral.

Dealing with your loss
Your distress needs careful handling: it's a bereavement that may be complicated by feelings of guilt and blame. Talk about your feelings to each other and to your doctor; ask her to explain the reasons for your loss, but accept that no one may know exactly why your baby died. Above all, look forward to the future; most couples who have lost a baby go on to become proud parents of healthy babies.

Taking care of yourself

Balancing your diet

Try to follow these tips:

■ Eat complex carbohydrates, such as pasta, potatoes, or pulses (beans and lentils), for energy.

■ Eat fish, poultry, dairy products, wholegrain cereals, seeds, pulses for protein, for the baby's growth.

■ Don't cut out fats altogether, but don't eat too much either.

■ Get vitamin C daily from raw fruit and vegetables, and the B complex from wholegrains, nuts, pulses, green vegetables, dairy products, eggs, oily fish, and meat.

■ Eat red meat, fish, egg yolks, apricots, and cereals for iron, to maintain red blood cells.

Food safety

Take extra care with food hygiene:

■ Listeria is a rare bacterium found in products made with unpasteurized milk, liver, pre-cooked meals, and undercooked meat. Avoid these as infection may result in miscarriage or stillbirth.

■ Salmonella is a bacterium infection found in eggs and chicken that causes fever, severe diarrhoea, and abdominal pain. Cook food thoroughly to destroy it.

■ Toxoplasmosis is caused by a parasite in cat and dog faeces, and in raw meat. It can cause birth defects. Cook meat thoroughly, wash hands after handling pets, and wear gloves when gardening.

Pregnancy is natural and women's bodies are designed to accommodate it. However, your body does have to work hard, so it's important to eat well and keep active to help it to cope.

Weight and diet

Your body uses up a lot of energy during pregnancy and you need to eat well to fuel your requirements and those of your growing baby. You could reasonably increase your intake of food by 200–300 calories a day and expect to put on 9–15 kg (20–30 lb) in weight, much of which is accounted for by the baby, uterus, and amniotic fluid. Pregnancy is not a time to go on a diet, but you should also forget the myth about "eating for two"; the rule is to eat to satisfy your hunger, and no more. Later in pregnancy you may find you simply can't take in much food at any one time so eat little and often. Keep healthy snacks, such as dried fruit, rice cakes, crispbreads, and hard fruits in your bag, car, or office.

Body maintenance

The pregnancy hormones have profound effects on teeth, hair, nails, and skin, so don't be surprised by some temporary changes.
Teeth Progesterone makes the gums soft so they may bleed more easily. Take care of your teeth and gums, and visit your dentist at the start of your pregnancy. Make sure you tell him you are pregnant in case he wants to take X-rays, as these may be dangerous to the developing embryo.
Hair and nails Straight hair can become curly, and vice versa. Hair grows and falls in phases – pregnancy often prolongs the growth phase, making thin hair thick and glossy, whereas thick hair may become dry and unmanageable. The downside is that you'll experience hair loss after the birth, although it'll grow back eventually. Although they grow faster, nails also become brittle. Keep them short and use creams to keep them moist.
Skin Oestrogen gives your skin the legendary bloom of pregnancy, but dry skin becomes drier and greasy skin more oily. Patches of brown pigment (chloasma) may appear on your face and neck but will eventually fade. All skins deepen in colour with browning of the nipples and a line down the abdomen. Tiny dilated capillaries (spider naevi) on the face are common but disappear later. Stretch marks on the breasts, thighs, and abdomen are very common; they're related to the breakdown of protein in the skin by the high levels of pregnancy hormones. Most marks will fade after the birth.

Dealing with fatigue

Fatigue is a periodic problem during pregnancy, especially during the first three months and the last six to eight weeks. Its extent may take you by surprise, especially during the first few weeks – it's the kind of tiredness where you feel you don't even have the energy to blink. You're sleepy in the early stages of pregnancy because you're sedated by the high levels of progesterone. Your metabolism speeds up to deal with the demands of your baby and the extra work all your organs are called on to do. Later on in pregnancy you're tired because your whole body is working flat out 24 hours a day, and you're having to carry extra weight around that puts a strain on your heart, lungs, and muscles.

Ways of coping

- Never stand when you can sit, never sit when you can lie.
- If possible, put your feet up whenever you sit – if you're in the office invert a wastebin or box under the desk.
- Sleep anywhere; put your head down on your desk during your lunch break; close your eyes on the bus or train home after work.
- When you're at home, plan specific rest times and let nothing interfere with them; some people like to lie down after lunch, others find they need to rest in the late afternoon or early evening.
- Lie in every weekend.
- Go to bed early at least three times a week.
- Find ways to help you drop off, such as watching TV or reading.
- Lie down and listen to music – not too loud as your baby can hear it.
- Find different comfortable resting positions for instant relief of tiredness. Try lying on the floor on cushions with your feet on a bed, sofa, or chair and your knees at right angles, or take up the first-aid recovery position with cushions under your knees and upper body (see below).

Relaxation Use whatever technique you can to relax – you're going to need at least 30 minutes a day from now on and it will be so refreshing if you teach yourself to let go in seconds. You'll probably be taught relaxation techniques at your antenatal classes (see p. 26), and there are plenty of books and CDs to guide you.

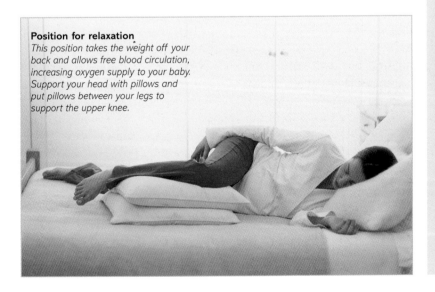

Position for relaxation
This position takes the weight off your back and allows free blood circulation, increasing oxygen supply to your baby. Support your head with pillows and put pillows between your legs to support the upper knee.

On your own

Some women decide to have a baby on their own without the baby's father. However, most women on their own didn't make that choice. If being on your own wasn't your choice, you need to allow yourself to work through your feelings of disappointment and even outrage.

Coping with your feelings
At a time when women naturally expect support, comfort, and the shared pleasure of contemplating parenthood, you are experiencing the very opposite. Ideally, explore your feelings with a friend or, even better, a professional counsellor who will help you to isolate each issue and deal with it.

Being positive
Avoid those people who may not take a positive view of either you or your condition. Since you don't have the most obvious form of support – a partner – the last thing you need is negativity, no matter where it is coming from.

Looking after yourself
Try not to neglect your health. When you're on your own, it's only too easy to skip meals or opt for easy snacks. Make sure you go to all your antenatal checkups. The health professionals are there to help you and if you need extra support, they will help you find it.

Feelings towards your baby
If you are feeling hostile towards the baby's father, try not to associate this feeling with your unborn baby; it's not her fault. By deciding to have her without the support of a partner, you have already demonstrated how committed you are to her.

Pelvic floor exercises

The pelvic floor consists of muscles and fibrous tissue suspended like a funnel from the pelvic bones. The layers of muscle are thickest at the perineum, where there are openings for the urethra, vagina, and anus, which the pelvic floor muscles also support. To locate your pelvic floor muscles, stop your urine flow in midstream – the muscles used here are pelvic floor muscles.

Exercising your pelvic floor
The pelvic floor is put under strain by pregnancy, when the presence of hormones causes it to soften and relax. Keep it toned by doing these exercises five times a day:

■ Pull in your pelvic floor muscles, then let them go quickly; do this five times.

■ Pull the muscles in and hold for a count of five, then let them go slowly; repeat this five times.

■ Finally, do the first, quick exercise five more times.

Restart these exercises after your baby is born to minimize the risk of prolapse.

Precautions

Before any exercise, do some stretches to warm up. Keep your back straight, breathe evenly, and flex your feet. Your ligaments are softened through the action of the pregnancy hormones so take it easy and don't twist suddenly. Stop if you are breathless, dizzy, overheated, or feel pain. Avoid dehydration by drinking lots of water, and cool down afterwards with more gentle stretches.

Exercise in pregnancy

Both you and your baby benefit from exercise: your blood starts circulating freely; there's a blast of oxygen to your baby's brain; exercise hormones, such as endorphins, give you both a wonderful high; and your baby loves the swaying motion. Exercise increases your strength, suppleness, and stamina, which will make pregnancy easier and equip you for the rigours of labour. Exercise also helps you to understand your body, to believe in its power, and it gives you the key to relaxation so that you can cope with fatigue and prepare yourself for the actual birth.

Whole-body exercise

Try to do some exercise every day, beginning gradually, at a pace that is comfortable. Always stop if you get out of breath or feel pain. Whole-body exercise is best as it tones up your heart and lungs, so walking and swimming are excellent. Dancing is good too as long as it's not too energetic. Yoga is ideal because it stretches tight muscles and joints and also relieves tension. Yoga methods help with labour and pain relief too.

Exercise to avoid

Pregnancy is not a time to start learning an energetic contact sport; however, you can continue sporting activities for a while if you're already fit and play often. Don't engage in sports like skiing, cycling, or horse riding after 20 weeks because balance may become a problem from that time. Take it easy on very energetic sports like tennis or squash and don't do heavy workouts at the gym, especially tough abdominal exercises.

Preparing for labour

Help yourself to prepare for labour and birth by introducing your body to some exercises and postures that will help when the baby is coming. You'll be taught different techniques at your antenatal classes (see p. 26), but it's a great help if both of you can learn the exercises so that your partner can help and encourage you to practise at home.

Postures to prepare for birth

Tailor sitting Sit up with your back straight (lean against a wall if you like), with the soles of your feet together. This opens up the hip joints.
Squatting Squat down on your haunches as low as possible, supporting your back against a wall or sofa – or lean against your partner while he is sitting in a chair. Squatting stretches and relaxes the birth canal, and when it comes to the delivery you may well find that this is the position that you adopt naturally, since it will help you to bear down (see p. 46).
All fours Getting down onto all fours is very helpful during pregnancy when you have a bad back, especially if you combine it with a few gentle pelvic floor exercises (see above left). Put a pile of cushions in front of you so you can rest on them with your head on your arms, and ask your partner to massage your back. Many women also find this a comfortable position for backache during labour, and for the actual delivery (see p. 46).

Looking after your back

The hormones of pregnancy soften your ligaments in preparation for the birth; the problem is that this also makes them more susceptible to strain during pregnancy, and your back is the most vulnerable.

Standing correctly

As pregnancy progresses, good posture becomes increasingly important, otherwise you'll have a tendency to bend your spine to balance the bump in front, leading to an arched back and slumped shoulders. Try to avoid this by keeping a straight back, tucking your buttocks under and tilting your pelvis forward (see right). Try to drop your shoulders to avoid tensions in your neck.

Carrying and lifting

Avoid carrying a heavy bag for long periods; this can put a strain on your shoulders and neck. If you need to lift something from floor level, always bend your knees and keep a straight back, lifting the object high against your chest. Never bend down or twist from the waist; you could damage your lower back. After lying down, always get up by pushing yourself up onto your hands first and then move into a kneeling position if you're on the floor, or swing your legs over the edge of the bed.

Sitting correctly

Sitting badly for long periods can be as bad for your back as poor posture when standing. If you have to sit for a long time, make sure you use a firm, straight-backed chair and sit well back with your feet raised slightly on a footstool or flat on the floor (see left). Sitting badly, slumped in your chair, forces your baby up against your diaphragm and stomach, constricts your lungs, and causes breathlessness and indigestion.

Father

Looking after your partner's wellbeing during pregnancy is good for your unborn baby, good for your relationship, and essential to your partner's long-term physical and emotional health. Try the suggestions below, but don't treat her like an invalid:

How you can help

■ Your partner's hair and skin will look marvellous, especially during the middle trimester, from four to seven months. Tell her how good she looks to boost her self-esteem. Towards the end of the pregnancy she may begin to get very bored and feel uncomfortable and unattractive; encourage her to go out and treat herself at this time.

■ Encourage your partner to eat and drink well. Get involved in the shopping and cooking, if you haven't done so before. You can both follow the basic advice on diet (see p. 36) – it will be beneficial for both of you.

■ Give your partner opportunities to rest: bring her breakfast in bed at weekends; make sure visitors aren't invited when she normally likes to rest, whether it's after lunch or early evening. Put the television in the bedroom, if there isn't one there already, so she can watch in bed.

■ Do the heavy lifting so that your partner doesn't strain her back or other muscles softened by pregnancy hormones (see left). If she does lift something, make sure she bends her legs, rather than bending from the waist. Carry the shopping and other heavy items.

Your new baby, your new life

The birth of your first baby is one of the most amazing moments of your whole life. It's the sort of event that parents remember in minute detail years later, even when other memories have faded. Although no birth experience is exactly like another, your first is special simply because you have never done it before. But just because you can't predict exactly what it will feel like either physically or emotionally, doesn't mean that you can't be prepared for most eventualities. Knowing how a normal labour progresses, what your pain relief options are, and what can be done if things don't go according to plan, means that together you can approach labour and birth positively. The importance of how you experience the birth and the first few precious moments you spend together with your baby cannot be overestimated. At this time, the bonds of interdependence and love begin to form and tie you together as a family. Don't be perturbed if it doesn't happen immediately. Rest assured the bonds will strengthen gradually as your body recovers and your confidence builds during the first few days after the birth.

Countdown to birth

Mother

Labour can start any time from 36 weeks, so be prepared. Keep telephone numbers of your partner, your midwife, and hospital delivery ward to hand. Have your bag (see below) or everything for a home delivery ready (see p. 46). What you need for hospital:

■ Your hospital notes.

■ A large T-shirt or short, loose nightdress for labour.

■ You may also need a hot-water bottle for backache, bottled water and a natural sponge to suck, a water-spray bottle to cool you, and a hand mirror to see your baby's head as it appears.

■ Socks in case you're chilly immediately after delivery.

■ Two front-opening nightdresses or pyjamas, a dressing gown, and a pair of slippers.

■ Two packets of super-strength sanitary pads and several pairs of cotton pants. Some disposable pants can also be very useful in the early days of heavy blood loss.

■ Properly-fitted nursing bras and disposable breast pads.

■ Toiletries, flannel or sponge, and a couple of bath towels.

■ For your baby you'll need stretch suits or nighties and vests (see p. 96), nappies, and nappy changing equipment (see p. 86–88). You may also need a blanket or shawl for your baby.

As your due date approaches, the days may seem to drag by and you probably feel uncomfortably large. As the expectant father, you'll be waiting for the telephone to ring with the call you've been waiting for.

Getting ready

Although pregnancy is said to last 40 weeks, this is only a convenient method of calculation – it's quite normal for a baby to be born anything between 38 and 42 weeks. If your baby hasn't been born by the official due date, don't worry. Most doctors aren't in a hurry to induce a baby if the mother is healthy and there are no obvious problems, such as raised blood pressure. Keep active and arrange some outings and visits. It's much better for both of you – and the baby – instead of hanging around the house feeling apprehensive.

Packing your hospital bag

It's a good idea to have everything ready for your baby's arrival and your bag packed for hospital three to four weeks before the due date, so that you are prepared for any eventuality. Your midwife will give you a list of what you need to take with you in the way of toiletries and other items, such as sanitary pads, and nappies, bedding, and clothes for your baby. Your tour of the delivery ward (see p. 26) will help you decide what bulkier items you might need, such as extra pillows or cushions.

Getting near labour

In the few days before labour begins properly, you may notice some signs that indicate you haven't got much longer to wait.

Feeling pre-menstrual You may experience similar feelings to those before your period, such as a low, nagging backache.

Braxton Hicks You may become more aware of the painless tightenings of the uterine wall. These are Braxton Hicks contractions, which can begin at around six months, and occur on and off during the last few weeks.

Mild diarrhoea You may have looser bowel movements as your system is affected by the increasing uterine activity.

Abdominal lightening There may be an easing of discomfort under your ribs – a feeling of lightening – as your baby's head engages in your pelvis. This may happen a week or two before the birth with a first baby, but just as often it doesn't happen until labour.

Burst of energy Many women experience a sudden burst of energy even if they have been very tired and sluggish for several weeks previously. You may find you want to rush around making sure everything is ready for your baby's homecoming; this is known as the "nesting instinct".

Irritability Understandably, you may become short-tempered and impatient, with a definite sense that it's time pregnancy was over!

The stages of labour

Labour has three distinct stages. The first stage is when the uterine contractions pull the cervix open; second stage, from full dilation to when the baby is born; and third stage, until the placenta is delivered.

The first stage During the first stage of labour, contractions begin and are established, gradually becoming stronger and lasting longer; this stage can last up to 12 hours, or even longer with a first baby. The first stage has three phases: the latent phase is the longest, lasting around eight hours. This is when the cervix thins. Then there is the active phase, when the cervix is opened up wide; and finally the transitional phase, when the cervix reaches full dilatation, before pushing your baby out. You're most likely to need pain relief during the active phase, and you're likely to feel a burst of energy towards the end to take you through the second stage.

The second stage During the second stage of labour your baby leaves the uterus and is pushed through the birth canal into the outside world. This stage can take anything from a few minutes to two hours with a first baby, and can be exhausting.

The third stage The delivery of the placenta is the third and final stage of labour; it is almost painless, although you may feel some cramping like a severe period pain. It happens within half an hour of your baby's birth, sooner if helped by an injection of syntometrine (see p. 48).

Father

Make sure you can always be contacted easily. If you've got a mobile phone, keep it turned on. What to take to hospital:

- A change of clothes; labour wards are very hot.

- Food and drink — hospital canteens rarely open at night.

- CD player and CDs.

- Camera or camcorder.

- Phone card or change for a payphone, plus important numbers. (Don't use a mobile phone in the hospital.)

Thinking about pain relief

It's sensible to consider options for pain relief before labour starts; discuss what is available a few weeks in advance with your midwife and put your wishes in a birth plan (see p. 27). Many women like the idea of a birth without the need for drugs, but it's good to be prepared, as you can't predict how you'll react when you're in labour.

Gas and air (Entonox)
A mixture of oxygen and nitrous oxide is breathed in through a mask or mouthpiece during a contraction so that it deadens the pain at its height. You start using it as soon as you feel a contraction starting as it takes about 20 seconds to work. The baby is not affected.

Pethidine
A form of pain relief given by injection. Pethidine is quite strong, so you may feel sick or woozy afterwards. It can affect a baby's breathing at delivery (though this can be treated), and makes the baby drowsy, so it isn't given late in labour.

Epidural anaesthetic
Anaesthetic is injected into the spinal column through a catheter via a hollow needle (a canula); it numbs the body from the top of the abdomen down to the toes, but you remain awake and alert. A tube is attached to the needle and taped to your back so that the anaesthetic can be topped up. If you want an epidural, it's best to let the hospital know in advance.

Epidural
The anaesthetist inserts a fine needle into the epidural space – the region around the spinal cord.

TENS
Transcutaneous electrical nerve stimulation (TENS) involves having electrodes taped to your back that connect to a stimulator. You give yourself small, safe amounts of electrical current to stimulate the production of endorphins, or natural painkillers.

Birth pool
Many hospitals now have pools available for use during labour to help relieve the pain. Buoyancy helps reduce the pressure on the abdomen, making your contractions more efficient, and being in water enables you to move easily into different positions. If you want to use a birthing pool, check early on in your pregnancy to make sure that one will be available for you.

What happens in labour

How labour starts

The "show"
This is a brownish/pink discharge that indicates that the mucus plug that has sealed the cervix during pregnancy has now come away in readiness for labour.

Your waters break
Sometimes the amniotic sac ruptures before labour starts, causing fluid to leak slowly or in a gush from your vagina. This is painless. If your waters break, put on a clean sanitary pad and call your midwife for advice. Most doctors would prefer labour to start within 24 hours because of the risk of infection to the baby.

Contractions start
The muscular tightenings of the uterus – contractions – gradually start to pull open the cervix. At first they are sharp cramping pains in the lower abdomen or back that last a few seconds. If they're coming regularly, every 10–15 minutes, you're in labour.

When you go into labour for the first time, it's natural to feel both excited and apprehensive. In spite of all the preparations you've made, for first-time parents labour is a journey into the unknown.

Keeping active

When you realize you're in labour your first reaction may be to rush off to hospital. Try to resist this because the most important thing for a mother in early labour is to keep active. Moving around is a great help in getting and keeping labour established, and most people find it easier to cope with contractions if they're upright. If your partner isn't with you, telephone him so he can join you as soon as possible. The best thing is to potter around at home for as long as possible, trying to be normal; if you have a contraction just stop and breathe through it. You might like to have a shower or bath to relax you. However, it's best to avoid having a bath if your waters have already broken (see left), unless your midwife advises it. Try to eat and drink quite often in small quantities. Have high-energy snacks and warm drinks to keep your strength up.

When to go to hospital

Telephone the hospital when you think labour is established, but unless the hospital is far away, stay at home until contractions are coming every five to ten minutes and lasting for about a minute. However, bear in mind that you've got a journey ahead of you, so don't wait until the idea of getting into a car is beginning to sound like agony. If your partner can't get home in time, don't try to drive yourself; call an ambulance or a taxi.

When you're in hospital

It's now accepted that childbirth is not an illness and most delivery rooms are designed to be as homely as possible. You'll be assigned a midwife when you arrive, and she'll check how far the cervix has dilated, and listen to your baby's heart, repeating these checks throughout your labour. You'll only need to be near the equipment while your baby's heart rate is being monitored, then you can move around. Some medical interventions require constant monitoring, however, so you'll have to stay on the bed.

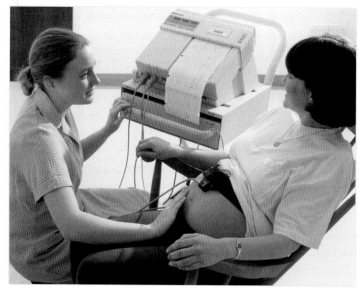

Electronic fetal monitoring
When you arrive at hospital, your baby's heartbeat may be measured during contractions through electrodes attached to your abdomen.

Managing contractions

There are several ways of managing labour pains. Discuss the options with your midwife, including deciding when and if you want to use any pain relief (see p. 43). She'll try to accommodate your wishes and she'll support you both in finding ways of coping with contractions.

Positions for labour

Keeping upright as much as possible helps labour to progress as the contractions work with, not against, gravity. Standing or squatting supported by your partner allows you to control the pain and provides warmth and loving reassurance.

Squatting supported
Squat between your partner's knees while he sits on a chair, taking your weight on his legs

Standing upright
Stand with knees bent, if necessary, letting your partner take your weight

Coping without pain relief

■ Relax as much as possible, especially between contractions – concentrate on the out-breath as you exhale, and drop your shoulders.
■ Keep moving about between contractions, then get into the position that feels right for you. These may include a supported squat, leaning against your partner, on all fours, or kneeling down and leaning forwards on a pillow placed on a chair.
■ Try counting backwards from 100 through a contraction – the concentration needed to do this takes your mind off the pain. Keep your eyes open to externalize the pain; focus on something in the room.
■ Take sips of still water from a sponge if your mouth is dry and ask your partner to massage or knead your back during a contraction.
■ Don't be afraid to say – or shout – anything you like; no one's going to hold it against you afterwards.

Father

Just being with your partner is a huge comfort for her. Trust your intuition as to what's needed, but ask her what she needs too.

How you can help
■ Be loving and intimate: slow and gentle, quiet and reassuring.

■ Be there for her when she wants you, and give her space when she doesn't.

■ Be positive and never criticize; she needs lots of praise, encouragement, and sympathy.

■ Offer practical help, such as a hot-water bottle if she has backache, sprays of water if she's too hot, water if her mouth is dry.

■ If your partner doesn't want pain relief, encourage her while it seems reasonable, but if she asks for it, don't put her off.

■ Talk to the midwife or doctor if you don't understand what's happening, or if you're worried. She's there to help you both, but remember that she is a professional who has your partner's and baby's best interests at heart. At the same time, don't let the hospital staff and their machines become your focus.

■ If your partner shouts or swears at you, seems to get angry, or overwrought, take it in your stride. It's her way of coping with a very stressful situation. This is particularly likely to happen at the transitional phase of the first stage of labour (see p. 43), so be positive, as it's a sign that the second stage isn't far off.

The birth of your baby

Who's who at the birth

For a normal vaginal delivery, you'll probably have one midwife and an assistant. Sometimes, though, the delivery room may seem crowded with people – they may include:

■ Your assigned midwife.

■ An assistant midwife.

■ The obstetric doctor on duty.

■ A paediatrician if there is a potential problem.

■ A paediatric nurse if your baby is premature.

The early stages of your journey to parenthood are now complete. Ahead of you is a shorter, but not necessarily easier, stage: that of pushing the baby out. Together at last you'll meet your new baby.

Coping with second stage

As your baby is gradually pushed down your birth canal, you should try to use gravity as much as possible to help, so keep as upright as you can. Get into whatever position feels most comfortable – it may be sitting up on the bed, squatting on a mat with the support of your partner, leaning against a chair, being on all fours, or using a birthing stool – your partner and midwife can follow your lead. Between contractions use your breathing techniques; in particular, let your pelvic floor, rectum, and anus relax.

Crowning

Your midwife will tell you when your baby's head appears at the vaginal opening – this is called crowning. Listen to your midwife; she'll tell you when to push and when to relax. If you take your time and let your vagina stretch slowly, you may avoid a tear. Once the baby's head crowns your partner can show you by holding a mirror – this is a great encouragement because you know that your baby will soon be born.

Episiotomy

An episiotomy is a surgical cut in the perineum that helps to allow the baby's head to pass through. Given time, you may not need one, but if it's felt you should have one, the midwife or doctor will ask your permission to do this procedure as your baby's head crowns (see above). It's more common to have an episiotomy with a first baby because the vaginal opening may be less elastic and you are more likely to tear. Episiotomies are also performed if your baby is very large, is in the breech position, or you need assistance with forceps or ventouse (see p. 51). If you haven't had an epidural,

Birth at home

More and more women are giving birth at home, though birth in hospital remains the norm because it's difficult to predict how your labour will progress.

Practical preparations
About a month before your due date the midwife will let you know what equipment you need readily available, such as buckets, rubber gloves, and polythene sheeting to cover furniture and carpets. She'll provide all the medical equipment. Decide where in your home you want to have your baby and try to work out your expectations so you can discuss them with your midwife.

When you're in labour
■ Call the midwife, who will come as soon as possible. She'll probably have an assistant.
■ For pain relief, your midwife will provide gas and air and pethidine (obtained on prescription beforehand), so you're likely

to try drug-free ways of managing the pain first (see p. 45). You'll probably be better able to cope at home, anyway.
■ You're more likely to feel in control of events as the midwife is on your territory, and that's an important psychological difference for everyone.

If there's a problem
Talk to your midwife beforehand about when and why she'd recommend a move to hospital. If that were to happen, you would go in an ambulance. In most instances, the same midwives who had attended to you at home would look after you in hospital.

After the birth
The midwife will stay for a couple of hours to make sure that you and your baby are comfortable and healthy, and will return later. You, your partner, and your new baby can spend your first few hours as a family together in your own home.

The moment of birth
You'll never forget the experience of holding your baby for the first time, immediately after he's emerged. It's so emotional that you may well find yourselves weeping with joy and relief.

the pelvic floor muscles will be numbed first with an injection of local anaesthetic. Then the vaginal tissues, plus underlying muscle, are cut at the height of a contraction to extend the opening. The incision is stitched after the placenta has been delivered (see p. 48).

The delivery

The head is the widest part of your baby – it will slowly emerge, and the midwife will check that the cord isn't around the neck and will clear fluid from the mouth and throat. The midwife will ask you to pant, not push at this stage, then with the next contractions she will gently turn the baby so that the shoulders can be born one at a time and the rest of your baby's body will slide out; the pushing contractions stop immediately and you'll feel a wonderful sense of release. Your baby may or may not cry out; some babies whimper, some cry lustily, others begin breathing without any crying.

Meeting your baby

This is the moment for which you've waited nine months, when you can take your baby in your arms together for the first time, the moment that will make everything you've just gone through worthwhile. Your midwife will probably lay your baby on your tummy or give him to you to hold while the cord is clamped and cut; let your baby feel your skin, hold him close to your face and let him look up into yours. Share this moment – you're both his parents – and savour it; this is a meeting that will change both your lives forever. It is also the moment when you claim your new status as parents.

Father

Helping your partner and watching your baby being born is an overwhelming experience. The second stage is hard work for mothers – it's a real effort, but there are ways you can help and be involved.

How you can help

■ Help your partner to get into the position she feels is best, and support her there.

■ Talk to and encourage her all the time. Keep in physical contact so she knows you're with her.

■ If you can see your baby's head as it crowns, describe it to your partner or hold a mirror for her to see – this will be a huge encouragement for her. However, don't get in the midwife's way as she'll need to monitor the baby's progress second by second, and to check the birth of the head.

■ Announce that you have a son or daughter, not just a boy or girl. The words "son" and "daughter" express family feelings.

■ If the midwife agrees, clamp and cut your baby's cord. This is the moment your baby really becomes an individual being.

■ If you feel like weeping, don't hold back. It's one of the most emotional moments of your life.

■ When the baby is born, share with your partner in the first minutes of your child's life.

■ By all means photograph or video your partner and baby, but don't do this to the exclusion of helping them. They are more important than anything else.

After the birth

Bonding

Most newborn animals have an instinct to bond – research has shown that human babies are similarly programmed.

What happens at birth
Your baby can recognize your voice at birth and can focus on your face at 20–25 cm (8–10 in) away. You will be hyper-sensitive to your baby in the minutes after birth. You can bond with your baby for life almost instantly, if you are left alone together without interference – if this private time isn't offered, ask for it. Don't worry if you don't bond at once – you might both just feel utterly exhausted after the delivery. Falling in love will have to wait.

The first hour or so after your baby's birth is a very precious time for all three of you. Although there will be various medical and administrative procedures that need to be carried out, you'll still have time to enjoy your baby.

Your baby after delivery

The midwife will check your baby's condition immediately after the birth by assessing her "Apgar score" (see opposite). Providing she is breathing without difficulty from the start, your baby will probably remain in your arms for the first minutes after birth. If she needs help to start breathing, she'll be put on the delivery room resuscitation table, which has an oxygen mask and a heater to keep the baby warm. Usually she'll soon be pink enough to be handed back to you, but in a few cases she may need to be taken to the special care baby unit for a while (see p. 62). Some time in the first couple of hours your baby will be weighed and measured and every part of her thoroughly examined by a midwife or paediatrician.

Delivery of the placenta

The placenta is usually delivered with the help of an injection of a drug called syntometrine given as the baby's body emerges. The cord is cut and the midwife will then press gently on your abdomen and pull the cord slowly to draw out the placenta. Once the placenta is delivered the midwife will check to make sure that none has remained inside you. If you'd like the placenta to be delivered naturally, without syntometrine, it will take about half an hour and putting your baby to the breast will help the process.

How you will feel

Immediately after the birth, your body temperature drops a few degrees and you may shiver and shake quite violently as your thermostat resets. You'll need to be wrapped in a blanket, and may need to put on a pair of socks. If you are famished after labour, ask for a small, easily digestible snack – a cup of tea and a piece of toast perhaps – and drink plenty if you want to.

Getting to know your baby
Your relationship with your baby begins the second she is born. As you both learn to care for her, your love will deepen and grow.

The Apgar score

The Apgar score is a standard method of assessing the immediate condition of a newborn baby. At one minute and five minutes after the birth, the midwife or doctor does five checks on your baby's heartbeat, breathing, muscle tone, reflexes, and skin colour, and gives them a score of 0, 1, or 2, with a total of 10. A score of 7 or more is normal, and a low first score improving to a normal second score is also fine. This may happen if you had a long second stage, or your baby has been affected by pethidine given during labour (see p. 43). The score is based on the Apgar scale (named after Dr. Virginia Apgar, who devised it).

How the score works
- Heart rate over 100 scores 2; below 100 is 1; no heartbeat is 0.
- Regular breathing or crying scores 2; slow or irregular breathing scores 1; absence of breathing scores 0.
- If your baby is active (good muscle tone), the score is 2; if hands and feet only are moving the score is 1; if the baby is limp, the score is 0.
- Strong reflexes score 2; weak reflexes score 1; no reflexes score 0.
- Pink colouring scores 2; body pink but extremities blue scores 1; blue or pale colouring scores 0. Skin colour shows how well a baby's lungs are working.

Father

You may feel as emotionally exhausted as your partner, but it's important not to underestimate the physical effort of labour and birth on a woman.

How you can help
- You'll probably experience a wave of euphoria now that your baby is born, but if labour has been long and hard your partner may be too exhausted to experience this same "buzz" immediately. It doesn't mean that she isn't as delighted as you are, but after labour, it's not surprising if she finds it difficult to express immediate enthusiasm. Just hold her close and let her know how proud you are of her and of your new son or daughter. Stay with them both for as long as possible after the birth, including settling them in to the postnatal ward.

- Congratulate your partner on her achievement, and let her know how much you appreciate her. Don't belittle your own contribution. You may think you haven't really been much help – this is common for fathers who have seen their partners in labour. However, most mothers will say how beneficial it was to have their partners' emotional support and encouragement.

- Hold your baby while your partner is being stitched, or checked. Go into a quiet corner of the room and get to know your baby. Let her look into your eyes – if you hold her close so that she's just 20–25 cm (8–10 in) away from your face, she can see you and smell you, and she'll learn to recognize you (see p. 156).

If you need stitches

The midwife will examine your perineum and assess whether or not you need stitches. Research shows that minor tears heal better on their own, so it's not necessarily true that any tear will inevitably mean stitches; however, an episiotomy (see p. 46) must be stitched. Depending on the length of the cut or tear, stitching will be done either by a senior midwife or the doctor on duty and you may be given a local anaesthetic. You may be able to cuddle your baby while you're being stitched if you want to, but this is also a good chance for your partner to have time with his baby so that you both get a chance to bond individually.

The first breastfeed

Putting your baby to the breast within an hour of the delivery increases your chances of breastfeeding successfully; many women feel able to put their babies to the breast immediately after the birth, although not all babies want to suck then. Ask your midwife to help you get your baby to latch on, but don't worry if she doesn't want to suck immediately. It doesn't mean she isn't able to breastfeed, just that at this point she doesn't feel like sucking, or she may be tired. She may also be affected by painkillers used during labour, such as pethidine, which leave her rather drowsy and may take a few hours to wear off (see p. 43).

The importance of colostrum

You won't produce milk for three or four days after the birth (see p. 65), but it is very beneficial for your baby to have the high protein "pre-milk" called colostrum that is produced in your breasts at this time. It contains important antibodies from your body that protect a newborn baby from infections, plus a substance called lactoferrin, which acts like a natural antibody. Putting your baby to the breast also helps the uterus to contract.

Special labours

Mother

It's okay to feel disheartened if something happens that means you need an assisted delivery, or even an emergency Caesarean section (see p. 52). Being prepared for the fact that intervention may be needed can help to avoid too much heart-searching after the birth.

Coping with a special labour

■ The medical staff will always tell you why a particular course of action is recommended, whether it's before or during labour. Ask questions or for repeat explanations if you need to.

■ If you're in labour, it may be difficult to concentrate; ask your partner to make sure that all the reasons for certain procedures are clarified so that he can relay the information to you. Remember, unless you're actually unconscious, staff must ask your permission to proceed; they won't accept your partner's opinion.

■ At the end of the day, the most important thing will be that your baby has been born safely. But that doesn't mean your feelings don't matter, and many women can't shake off the idea – however illogical – that they were in some way to blame because things didn't go to plan. If you find yourself in this position, talk to your partner or your midwives or doctor. Having a baby can unleash deep emotions and you may need to work through them before you can enjoy new motherhood fully.

There are many different procedures if labour proves difficult. If a particular procedure is suggested, ask the midwife or doctor to explain why it's necessary, what the risks are, and what would happen if you waited a while before it was started.

When labour is induced

Sometimes labour may need to be induced, which means it is started artificially. If you haven't gone into labour spontaneously by 42–43 weeks, or if there are worries about your own or your baby's health in the last few weeks of pregnancy, induction may be suggested. Similar procedures will be needed if your labour is not proceeding as it should.

How labour may be induced

Induction is often introduced gradually, first with pessaries; then, if necessary, ARM (see below); finally, a syntocinon drip if things are going too slowly.

■ You may be given vaginal pessaries containing prostaglandin, a hormone that should trigger labour.

■ Your membranes may be ruptured artificially (ARM), which can either start or strengthen contractions.

■ You may be given an artificial hormone (syntocinon) into a vein to induce contractions. Syntocinon is started at a low rate and increased gradually so contractions build up slowly. It is also used to speed up labour.

Breech birth

Instead of being born head first, a breech baby is born buttocks first, usually followed by the legs and lastly the head. Breech babies often need to be delivered with the help of forceps or by Caesarean section for the baby's safety, although a natural breech delivery is occasionally possible with the help of an experienced midwife and obstetrician. A breech baby is almost always delivered in hospital; because of the likelihood of intervention you'll probably be offered an epidural, so that you're already anaesthetized if your doctor needs to apply forceps or do a Caesarean (see p. 52). You're more likely to have an episiotomy (see p. 46), because your baby's buttocks may not stretch the vagina enough to let the head out safely, or to allow forceps to be inserted to help lift the head out.

Assistance with forceps or ventouse

Even if you have a normal vaginal delivery, there may be times when you need help, particularly in pushing the baby out during second stage. Depending on the circumstances, your hospital will provide assistance with forceps or ventouse (vacuum extraction). You'll need to have an episiotomy for either of these procedures.

Forceps The two blades of forceps cradle your baby's head, allowing it to be pulled safely through the birth canal without too much compression. Forceps can normally only be used once the baby's head is engaged in the pelvic bones.

Ventouse, or vacuum, extraction This is a more gentle procedure than using forceps and is used in similar circumstances. Your cervix has to be fully dilated and the baby's head must be in the birth canal. The vacuum plate leaves a bruise on your baby's head where the suction was applied, but this will fade within the first two to three weeks.

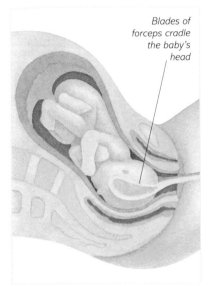

Blades of forceps cradle the baby's head

Forceps delivery
Forceps are instruments that look like the two halves of very large sugar tongs. The blades are inserted one at a time and the baby is drawn out with a few gentle pulls during contractions.

Suction plate or cup is applied to the baby's head by vacuum

Ventouse or vacuum extraction
With ventouse assistance, a small suction plate or cup is applied by vacuum to the lowest part of your baby's head. The doctor will gradually help your baby to be born by applying gentle traction.

Father

A labour that doesn't go to plan can be very scary for you as well as for your partner. Be prepared for any unexpected interventions.

How you can help
■ Well before your baby is due, talk to your partner and make sure you know her views and preferences for any eventuality. Bear in mind, though, that she may change her mind when the time comes.

■ Unless it's an absolute emergency, make sure that any interventions suggested are talked through properly with your partner, and either or both of you ask questions if anything isn't clear. Remember that the medical team must have your partner's consent for any intervention.

■ If something is suggested that you know your partner wants to avoid, try to buy time. For instance, if labour has slowed, suggest a change of position before procedures to accelerate labour are introduced.

■ If the medical team decide the labour needs monitoring with high-tech equipment, try not to be distracted by it. Concentrate on your partner, not the technology.

■ Remember that if something unexpected happens, and intervention is needed, it's never your partner's fault. Everyone will be working in the best interests of your partner and baby.

■ Whatever happens, talk about it afterwards, especially with your partner, but also with friends and, if necessary, health professionals.

If you're having twins

Twins or higher multiples are exciting for everyone, although you're bound to be apprehensive about their arrival. Medical interest in the birth is likely to be much greater if you're expecting more than one baby, and some intervention is more likely to be recommended. Often this becomes necessary, but there's no need to think it's inevitable; many twins, and even triplets, are born vaginally after a normal labour. But continuous electronic fetal monitoring is much more common, and, as with breech birth, you'll probably be offered an epidural because of the likelihood of intervention being needed. This means it's in place in case there are problems with the delivery of the second twin and you have to have assistance with forceps or even a Caesarean. If the first twin is known to be breech, your doctors will probably advise you to have both babies delivered by elective Caesarean.

Mother

You're bound to feel apprehensive about having a Caesarean, and you may feel disappointed if you have an emergency Caesarean after going into labour naturally.

Concerns about Caesareans

■ You may worry about being able to deliver a subsequent baby vaginally, but about 75 per cent of women who have a Caesarean can deliver normally the next time.

■ If you have a general anaesthetic, you'll need longer to recover, so it may be a little while before you feel close to your baby. Don't worry, you will bond with your baby in time, especially when you start breastfeeding (see p. 48).

■ You'll only be left with a tiny scar on your "bikini line".

Why you might need a Caesarean

There are several reasons for a Caesarean delivery:

■ Baby's head is too large for your pelvis (disproportion).

■ Baby is breech (bottom first).

■ Baby takes up a cross-wise position (persistent horizontal lie).

■ Medical condition, such as pre-eclampsia or diabetes.

■ Any problems with the placenta.

■ Your labour is progressing too slowly or has stopped, which might cause fetal distress.

■ If there is fetal distress, even if labour hasn't slowed or stopped.

Caesarean section

In many countries, Caesarean sections are currently on the increase, partly because this procedure in expert hands may be safer than, say, a difficult forceps delivery. Sometimes, however, interventions earlier in labour, such as induction or epidural anaesthetic, may lead to a situation in which a Caesarean becomes more likely. If a Caesarean is recommended, your doctor is obliged to give you clear reasons why, even in an emergency. If it was something you had wanted to avoid, ask whether you could wait or if there is anything else you could try first.

Elective Caesarean

If a Caesarean operation is planned in advance it is known as "elective". This means the reason for it has become apparent before labour started – for example, your blood pressure may have shot up, or your pelvis is so small that delivery is likely to be difficult, or your baby is breech (see p. 50). Your obstetrician will probably discuss this with you two to three weeks before your due date, and a date will be booked for you to come in, so you'll know well in advance exactly when your baby is going to be born.

Emergency Caesarean

An emergency (unplanned) Caesarean happens when events during labour make it preferable to a vaginal delivery. For example, your baby may show distress (measured by heart rate and movements); the labour may not progress despite the use of drugs to speed things up; or your own condition may deteriorate. If you haven't had an epidural anaesthetic, the Caesarean will take place under general or spinal anaesthetic.

Delivery of your baby
If you have a Caesarean under epidural anaesthesia, you'll both be able to share your baby's first moments after delivery.

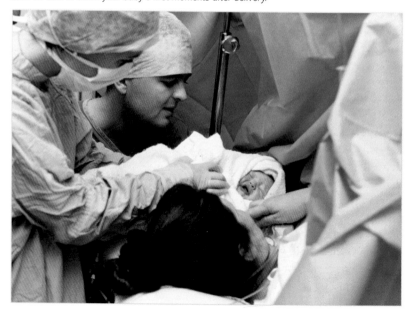

Sudden birth – the father's role

Occasionally labour comes on with such speed that your partner could be overwhelmed by the desire to push before you can get professional help, let alone reach hospital! Although second stage can take a couple of hours, it may not, and babies have been known to be born after a couple of pushes. If this happens, don't panic – babies who come quickly are almost always strong and vigorous and most emergency births are perfectly straightforward.

What to do

■ On no account leave your partner alone for more than a minute or two. Help her position herself where she feels most comfortable.

■ Telephone the doctor or midwife and explain the situation. If it's difficult to get hold of them, call the emergency services and ask for an ambulance as soon as possible.

■ Wash your hands well and have some clean towels ready. Fold one and put it to one side for the baby. If you have time, find some old sheets or plastic sheeting to cover the floor or furniture.

■ When you see the top of the baby's head at the vaginal opening, ask your partner to stop pushing and just pant. This gives the vagina a chance to stretch fully without tearing.

■ Once the head has been born, feel around the neck to see if the cord is looped around it. If it is, hook your finger under the cord and draw it over the baby's head.

■ Hold the baby firmly as he emerges – he'll be slippery – and give him straight to his mother to hold. Wrap him immediately in the spare towel so that he doesn't get cold.

■ Don't touch the cord. If the placenta is delivered before medical help arrives, put it in a dish or plastic bowl so that it can be checked by the midwife or doctor.

Father

Even an elective Caesarean can be worrying, because it's quite a major operation. If it's an emergency, your partner may be feeling distressed, but there's much you can do to help her.

How you can help

■ If an emergency Caesarean is recommended, and your partner is finding it difficult to talk to the doctors, make sure you ask why it is suggested. Although she has to give her permission, your partner may still not be quite clear afterwards why it was necessary, and it's important that you're able to help her understand.

■ Unless your partner wants a general anaesthetic or the operation is too urgent, see if it can be done under epidural or spinal anaesthesia. This means you can share the experience and meet your new baby together.

■ During the operation, sit by your partner's head and reassure her that all is well.

■ You don't have to watch, but if you find it distressing or you feel faint – and many people do – leave the room quickly. Don't hang on; you may cause further difficulties for the medical staff.

■ If the Caesarean is being done under general anaesthetic, your partner may not regain consciousness for an hour or more, and you'll probably be given your baby to hold. Cherish this time. Father-child bonding can be at its best after a Caesarean, because this early time together is so precious.

What happens during the operation

Before a Caesarean, your pubic hair will be shaved and a catheter inserted into your bladder. You'll probably be given a saline drip.

The anaesthetic Most elective, and some emergency, Caesareans are performed under epidural or spinal anaesthesia, because women recover more quickly afterwards. With an epidural, you'll be awake during the operation, but you won't feel anything, and your partner can be with you throughout. You won't be able to see anything because the operating team will be masked by a surgical sheet draped across your chest. Spinal anaesthesia takes effect in five to ten minutes and so it can be used in some emergency situations. If, however, you have a general anaesthetic your partner won't usually be allowed into the operating theatre, but will be able to hold the baby afterwards while you recover.

The operation Your abdomen is opened through a small horizontal incision along the line of the top of your pubic hair, and your baby delivered through a similar cut in the uterus. The amniotic fluid is drained off by suction before the baby is gently lifted out. You may feel some tugs as the operation proceeds. Your surgeon will tell you when the moment approaches when she will lift your baby from your uterus.

After the birth It takes about ten minutes to deliver the baby. You or your partner can then hold your baby while the placenta is removed and you are stitched. A baby born by Caesarean is likely to need help in starting to breathe, but a paediatrician will be on hand to help. Closing the wound can take as long as 45 minutes.

The first day

Hospital routine

Some aspects of the hospital routine can be tiresome, though you may enjoy talking to other mothers.

Keeping your baby close
Almost all hospitals now expect babies to remain in their cots beside their mothers' beds at all times.

Food and drink
The food may be bland, so ask your partner to bring fresh fruit as this will help prevent constipation. Drink plenty of water.

Visits from staff
The midwives will check your stitches, lochia, and uterus (see p. 64). They'll also give advice on cleaning your baby's umbilicus and on breastfeeding. At some point an obstetrician and paediatrician will check you and your baby, and a physiotherapist may visit to advise you on postnatal exercise.

You have both been looking forward to this moment for the best part of a year; your baby is safely delivered and you've experienced a heady brew of strong emotions: relief, pride, elation, excitement, and triumph. Now your baby is lying quietly in her cot by your bed and you both have a chance to take stock.

Your reactions to the birth

Unlikely as it may seem, this could be an awkward moment for you both. It could be passing through either or both of your minds that there is something missing. Where is the rush of love for your baby? It isn't a subject that gets much attention, but it is, nevertheless, a fact that large numbers of parents, quite possibly the majority, don't feel an overpowering attachment to their baby straight after the birth. Most highs, because of their intensity, are followed, not necessarily by a low, but by a diminution of emotion that leaves you feeling somewhat flat in comparison. Having a baby is no exception. It may have been a momentous event for you, but the hospital routine has to proceed as normal and, anyway, a hospital ward isn't conducive to the kind of closeness that you would like to feel for each other on this shared birthday, especially if you're both exhausted.

Looking forward

When you go to the postnatal ward – and this may be two or three hours after the birth – the father goes back to an empty home and the mother is left wondering what her first night as the mother of a baby is going to be like. If it isn't quite what either of you envisaged, be philosophical. In a real sense, life with your baby will actually begin on the day you take her home.

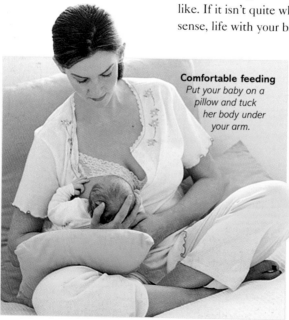

Comfortable feeding
Put your baby on a pillow and tuck her body under your arm.

After a Caesarean

A Caesarean section is major abdominal surgery and you'll feel quite sore once the anaesthetic wears off. As well as asking for pain relief, there are other ways of coping:

- Holding and feeding your baby may be difficult as pressure on your scar may be painful. Try laying her next to you on the bed (see p. 79) or supporting her on pillows in the so-called "football position" (see left).
- Mobility helps you recover so you'll be encouraged to get up and move around as soon as possible after the birth. Support your wound as you walk.

Handling your new baby

It's natural to be nervous about holding and handling your baby for the first time; although she may seem vulnerable, remember that she is really very robust. The main problem is that she has no neck control so her head is very floppy, and her joints are very soft so you need to be gentle when putting on her clothes (see p. 96). Support your baby's head at all times and pick her up as shown here.

1 To lift your baby, slide one hand under her rump and cradle her head with the other. Talk to her all the time.

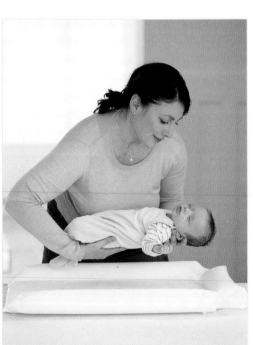

2 Lift her gently but firmly towards you, using a smooth upward movement so that she isn't startled.

3 Swing her body around so that she's resting against your chest and her head and back are cradled by your arms.

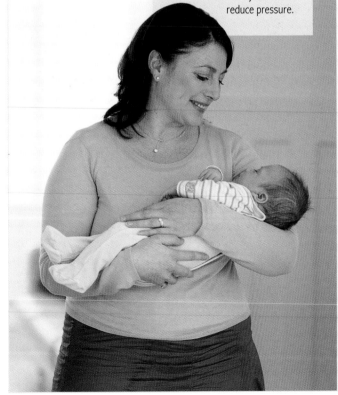

First discomforts

You'll feel a little shaky in the first 24 hours, and there may be some specific discomforts, although these do pass quite quickly:

■ Your perineum will feel bruised and tender, especially if you had stitches. Don't stay in the bath too long as water can harm scar tissue and soften stitches.

■ You may find it difficult or even painful to pass urine. Take a jug of tepid water to the toilet to pour over your vulva as you pass urine.

■ A sore perineum plus stitches may deter you from opening your bowels. Support your vulva with a pad of tissues as you bear down.

■ Sitting upright can be awkward when your abdominal muscles are weak and your vulva and perineum are sore. Prop yourself up with plenty of pillows and half sit and half lie on your side to reduce pressure.

Father

When you go home after the birth you are likely to feel a bit lonely. Use the time to telephone everyone as you'll probably have a huge urge to talk through all that's happened, and your relations will want all the details.

Get some sleep

Although you may feel too excited to start with, make sure you catch up on sleep. You've had an exhausting time too during the labour and you can't support your partner when she comes home if you're tired as well.

Prepare your home

Use your time at home alone to do the washing and cleaning and stock up on groceries and other household items. Fit the straps for the baby seat in the car, if you haven't already done this, so that everything is ready for when your new baby comes home.

Going home early

Some hospitals now encourage mothers to go home as soon as four or five hours after a normal delivery. It may seem very soon after the birth, but you are likely to relax better in your own environment, and recovery will probably be easier at home, where you'll be checked twice on the first day by a visiting midwife. However, remember that going home early doesn't mean you're back to normal. Childbirth leaves you exhausted so try to keep the first day or two virtually visitor-free as you won't have the professional backup that you had in hospital.

Crying and sleeping
Your baby may sleep for much of the first day, although you'll also experience his cry. Pick him up when he cries and take it in turns to hold him when he's sleeping.

Your baby's first day

There's a lot to learn on your baby's first day, and you may feel awkward and anxious about looking after him. On top of trying to get him to feed, you'll have to get to grips with changing a nappy, "topping and tailing" (see p. 90), and dressing your baby. (Most hospitals and midwives leave the first bath for three or four days.) A midwife will show you both what to do; if you're uncertain about anything, don't be afraid to ask.

Reluctance to feed

You may be concerned if your baby is reluctant to feed for the whole of the first day, but this is no cause for worry. Express colostrum (see p. 83) if your breasts feel uncomfortable, so that you will find it easier to feed him as soon as he is ready. Once he feels the need to feed, you may find you are putting him to the breast as often as every two hours.

Your sleepy baby

Your baby will probably have been wide awake and alert for the first hour or two after the birth, but then he may well sleep on and off for much of the first day. Take it in turns to hold him rather than simply leaving him in his cot.

Your baby's cries

Unless he is very sleepy, you'll probably experience your baby crying several times during this first day and you may be astonished both by its force and the fact that you'll recognize it immediately. Neither of these things is accidental. Babies are programmed to signal their needs vociferously and adults are programmed to respond with a feeling of urgency. Always pick him up when he cries; cuddle him in bed with you unless you want to sleep.

Adjusting to parenthood

Mother

Even though you're longing to be home, use your time in hospital to regain your strength and lean on the professional staff for advice. If you're back home within a couple of days of the birth, accept offers of help from friends and relations.

How you can adjust

■ When your partner visits you both in hospital, share anything you've learned about your baby's care with him. If you learn how to care for your baby together, you'll start out on an equal footing and he'll be more likely to take the initiative once you're home.

■ Use these first few days to build on the network of support systems that you will hopefully have set up through antenatal classes before the baby was born. Prepare for time on your own when your partner has gone back to work and friends and family aren't around as much.

■ At some point during the first few days you may experience tearful moments – it often happens just as your milk comes in, three or four days after the birth. The so-called "baby blues" (see p. 132) are your normal reaction to the sudden withdrawal of pregnancy hormones and to the enormity of your new situation. They usually subside in a week to ten days. You'll probably be very tired too, especially if you had a fairly long labour. Be open and share your feelings with your partner.

The first few days of parenthood can be bewildering as you seesaw between intense periods of close attention from health professionals and moments of isolation, when you just have to get on with things by yourselves. You may feel that caring for your new baby leaves little room for your own relationship as a couple, but it will help if you concentrate initially on sharing the simple practicalities of your baby's care and acknowledge rather than hide your natural nervousness and apprehension.

Taking care of each other

When a baby comes to first-time parents, three new relationships begin: mother-baby, father-baby, mother-father. The last is the most complex. Of course a relationship has existed between the parents that pre-dates the baby, but you will not have related to each other before in the roles of mother and father. You have to start thinking of each other in an entirely new way. You have to "redesign" your relationship in the light of your new roles – being more understanding, more patient, more flexible, more long-suffering than you were before. Most of all, you have to be more generous and less self-centred. This can put a strain on your relationship, so you need to be ready to respond to each other (see p. 128).

Help and advice

Use your time in hospital or when you are in the daily care of a midwife or doctor to get the advice you need. Don't feel shy about asking, even if it seems trivial; most health professionals recognize that it's vital to provide reassurance. However, in hospital they may not have enough time to advise you exactly when you need it, particularly with breastfeeding

What a new mother wants from her partner

Recognize her vulnerability	A father needs to recognize how vulnerable a new mother feels, both physically and emotionally, in the days after the birth.
Appreciate the depth of her feelings	A father needs to accept the strength of his partner's overwhelming involvement in the baby and not to construe this as a rejection of him.
Protect her privacy	One of the most important roles for a new father is to make sure that his partner is not overwhelmed by visitors and to give her time and space to establish breastfeeding and recover from the physical stresses of labour and birth.

problems, so it may be helpful to contact a breastfeeding counsellor when you get home. Most counsellors are themselves mothers who have been trained to provide support in a non-medical way and will continue their support for some months. This helps to alleviate the nervousness many mothers feel when they are finally discharged by the midwife, ending a close relationship with the midwifery service that's built up over months.

Advice from family and friends

In the early days of parenthood, your friends and relations may be keen to offer advice. Although it can be irritating if delivered in an overbearing way, the advice that other parents give you reflects their own experience and can be very reassuring. However, if the advice goes against your own beliefs, simply ignore it and do things the way you know is best.

Feeling isolated

After the intense activity of labour and birth, when you were fully involved and couldn't think about anything else, you may both feel quite isolated, disorientated, and lonely for a few days; this could affect how you relate to each other when you do have time together. The new mother may feel bewildered in hospital. Even though she's surrounded by other people, she suddenly finds herself in sole charge of the needs of her tiny new dependant when she's feeling exhausted and possibly in pain. The new father, too, may feel very odd and detached from his new situation when he has to come and go from an empty home.

Talk to each other

When you're together, try hard to talk about how you feel and make sure you tell each other what you have been doing while you're apart. Most hospitals now have unrestricted day and evening visiting for new fathers, so it should be possible to spend quite a lot of time together supporting each other through this short but significant period of separation. It may be difficult to articulate your feelings, but the charts below set out some of the needs of both partners at this difficult time.

Father

As a new father you may feel rather cut off from your partner, particularly while she's in hospital. At the same time, you may feel an intense elation that you want to share with your partner, but she may seem a bit distant as her body recovers from the birth and she tries to establish breastfeeding.

What you can do to help

■ Take the initiative – learn how to do all the practical things your baby needs while your partner is still in hospital.

■ Get to know your baby. Use these early days to establish a close relationship. Even if your partner is in hospital, change your baby, learn to handle her, talk to her, hold her close so that she can focus on your face if she's awake, or simply hold her if she's asleep. Bring her to your partner when she needs to be fed, carry her around, try to be there for her first bath.

■ Be ready for your partner's mood swings. At some point during the first week your partner will probably experience the so-called "baby blues" that come as a reaction to the sudden withdrawal of the pregnancy hormones as well as to new responsibilities. She may also be very tired if the labour was prolonged. The "baby blues" subside after a week to ten days. Your partner may try to hide her feelings from you so as not to worry you or because she fears that you won't take her seriously. Be sensitive to her needs and talk to her about them (see p. 128).

What a new father wants from his partner

Recognize his difficulties	She should be ready to accept that this is also a confusing and emotional time for her partner
Give him some of your time	The baby may be time-consuming, but it is good for your relationship as a couple and as new parents for a mother to reserve some of her time and attention for her partner.
Allow him to make mistakes	After a hospital birth, a new mother necessarily has more time to get used to the baby, but she needs to allow her partner to handle and care for the baby, and not criticize if he fumbles.

Your newborn baby

A newborn's reflexes

A newborn has a set of built-in reflexes that help him to survive. They disappear within a few weeks as he develops (see p. 156).

Grasp
He grasps anything put into his fist; the reflex is so strong that he can take his own weight. The reflex is lost in a couple of weeks.

Step
If his feet touch a firm surface, he will take a step—this has nothing to do with real walking.

"Moro" response
If startled, he throws out his arms and legs in a star shape to stop himself from falling.

Rooting
If you stroke his cheek, he automatically turns his head ("roots") to find the nipple.

Few newborn babies are conventionally pretty, and even though everything is perfectly normal, your baby's appearance may make you slightly apprehensive, so you'll find it hard to resist going over him with a fine-toothed comb, just to make sure.

What your baby looks like

The size of a newborn baby varies enormously—a perfectly normal birth weight could be anything from 5½ lb to 10 lb (2.5 to 4.5 kg). But even a 9–11-lb (4–5-kg) baby will seem tiny and vulnerable when newborn. Your baby may look slightly battered and bruised after the birth, and his head may be rather elongated because of molding in the birth canal, but it will return to a normal rounded shape in a week or so. There may be the odd bruise here and there on his head, especially if your birth was assisted (see p. 50), or there may be a small scar if a fetal monitor was attached to his scalp. Until he has his first bath, his hair may be a bit matted with dried blood and fluid from the birth.

Your baby's head is large compared to the rest of him. The head may have a bump on one side where the skull bones have been molded during birth—the skull bones are soft and can override one another to protect the brain. The skull bones don't fuse completely for a few months, leaving a diamond-shaped soft spot on the top of the head, covered by a tough membrane, called the fontanelle. You may notice a pulse beating there.

Your baby's eyelids may be puffy from the pressure of contractions. A baby's eyes are almost always blue; true eye color develops during the first year. Sometimes there may be a burst blood vessel in the white of the eye, due to pressure during birth. This will go in time.

A pre-term baby's skin may be covered with a protective white substance called vernix. Overdue babies may have dry, flaky skin.

The stump of the umbilical cord usually dries and shrivels within two to three days, and your healthcare provider will remove the clamp. The remainder drops off within ten days.

Your newborn baby's feet are rounded like his hands, and the toes tend to be curled. They may be slightly bluish because of his immature circulation.

Your newborn's hair will usually fall out by three months and grow in a different color later. A pre-term baby may have downy body hair called lanugo.

Your baby's hands will be curled into fists most of the time. Nails may be long and sometimes stained with meconium (see opposite).

Your baby's legs may be so tightly flexed that you can't easily straighten them, but don't apply force.

Your baby's genitals will look large because of the action of pregnancy hormones. For the same reason, both girls and boys may have pronounced breasts, which will shrink, and girls may produce a slight vaginal discharge for a day or two.

Concerns about your newborn baby

YOUR CONCERNS	WHAT IT IS AND HOW IT IS TREATED
Birthmarks	Many babies have birthmarks, most of which fade within a few months, although some, such as the so-called strawberry mark, which is raised, may take much longer. The Mongolian blue spot, a blueish birthmark on the lower back of babies with dark skin tones, is sometimes mistaken for bruising.
Milk spots	Tiny white spots on the bridge of the nose. These disappear after a few weeks.
Neonatal urticaria	A blotchy rash, a bit like a nettle rash. It only lasts a couple of days.
Meconium	At birth your baby's bowel contains a dark green sticky substance called meconium, which is usually passed into the nappy during the first 2–3 days.
Jaundice	Neonatal jaundice is quite common due to a baby's immature liver. It makes the skin yellowish and the urine dark. Your baby may be sleepy so he'll need to be wakened for feeds to ensure he has enough fluid. Persistent cases may be treated with ultraviolet light.
Breathing	Babies snuffle and sneeze a lot, and get hiccups. They may even stop breathing for a second or two, but breathing soon becomes strong and regular.
Lip blisters	Some babies develop a white sucking blister on the lips. It doesn't cause discomfort and will fade in a few days.
Scalp swelling	Some babies develop a swelling on the scalp due to bleeding under the skin during the birth. This is quite normal, but it does take a few weeks to disperse.

Newborn baby check

Your baby is given a top-to-toe check before you leave hospital.

Vision and hearing
The doctor will shine a light into your baby's eyes and will note if they move on hearing her voice. She may also do a hearing test.

Heart and lungs
She'll listen to your baby's heart and check his lungs and breathing.

Ability to suck
She'll put her finger into his mouth to check that he can suck properly.

Internal organs
She'll gently feel his abdomen and check his anus.

Spine
She'll feel his spine to make sure the vertebrae are in place.

Hip manipulation
She'll remove his nappy and check his legs and hips for any sign of congenital hip dislocation.

The Guthrie test
On about the sixth day, a tiny drop of blood will be taken from his heel to test for thyroid function and for phenylketonuria, a rare disorder that may cause mental retardation if undetected.

What your newborn baby can do

SKILL	HOW TO STIMULATE YOUR BABY
Sight	He can see you clearly if your face is 20–25 cm (8–10 in) from his. He's wired to respond – his heart rate rises when he focuses on your face, so talk and smile. He'll react with body jerks and fish-feeding movements of his mouth – that's his first attempt at a conversation.
Hearing	His hearing is acute – he knows both your voices from having heard them in the womb and he'll respond instantly to pleasure in your voice. Start talking, singing, saying rhymes from the moment of birth and never stop.
Movement	He loves physical movement – after all he's been jogging and swaying in the womb for nine months – so carry him around as much as possible. Move his limbs gently while changing him, clap his hands gently, do gentle knee bends. But avoid sudden movements that startle him.

The special care baby

How a pre-term baby may look

If your baby is born prematurely, she may look a little different from what you expect:

■ Her skin will be loose, wrinkled, and red because she hasn't had time to fill out with fat.

■ She'll be covered in downy hair called lanugo hair.

■ Her head will seem very large.

■ She'll be very thin and bony, especially her ribs and buttocks, with stick-like limbs.

■ Her breathing will seem laboured and uneven.

■ Her movements may be jerky.

Feeding special care babies

At first your baby may need to be fed glucose intravenously, or have milk fed through a tube in her nose, but hopefully will soon be able to try sucking. Breast milk is especially good for a premature baby as your body will make milk suited to your baby's gestation, and you may need to express your milk so your baby can be tube-fed.

Introducing breastfeeding
When your baby is ready to try breastfeeding, it may take time and patience to get her used to it. Avoid bottles as far as possible if you want to breastfeed fully when you can, as weaker babies can quickly get used to bottles and may then reject your nipple.

If your baby needs some specialist care, you'll be understandably anxious. However, it will only be done for the best of reasons – to increase your baby's chances of thriving as a normal, healthy baby.

Why do babies need special care?

Although many people think special care only applies to premature births, in fact about one in ten babies need some sort of specialist attention, and by no means are they all born before term. There are several possible reasons.

Prematurity A baby born before 37 weeks is pre-term or premature, and may need close monitoring, as well as help with breathing and feeding.

Low birth weight Any baby who weighs 2.5 kg (5½ lb) or less at birth is considered to have a low birth weight. Low birth weight babies may be either pre-term, or full term but "small for dates" (see p. 34), and may need to spend a short time in a special care unit.

A health risk A baby who may have had difficulties with breathing during the birth, or have picked up an infection, may need special attention for a while. Alternatively, there may be birth defects, such as a "hole in the heart" that may have been diagnosed before or at the birth.

What special care means

If your baby needs special care, her needs can be catered for in a special care baby unit (SCBU) or a special section of the unit called a neonatal intensive care unit (NICU). This may mean she has to be moved to a different hospital. If she was premature or of a low birth weight, she could have difficulty with breathing, be prone to infections, be unable to regulate temperature, or feed properly. Without support, low blood sugar levels can cause brain damage and she may lack iron and calcium. For these reasons, she may need the protection and constant monitoring of incubator care, with intravenous or tubal feeding (see left), until she catches up on growing and learns to feed and breathe without help.

Getting through it

Having a baby in special care is a bit like feeling you've lost a leg. Something is missing; your baby is born, but isn't yet able to be where she should be – in your arms. If she was born early, you may feel cheated on having missed out on the end of your pregnancy. Another common reaction is to feel that your baby isn't really yours – while she's in the SCBU it may seem as though she belongs to the medical staff. Try to remind yourself that this is your child, and that soon she will be home where she belongs. Be as involved as possible in discussions about her condition and in her care, and try to look forward to the day when she'll be truly yours, and you can take her home.

Helping to care for your baby

All special care baby units welcome parents and actively encourage them to help with feeding, washing, and nappy changing. There may be rooms where you can stay overnight from time to time, and many units provide space for a day or two before your baby is discharged so that you can get used to the normal care routine of a small baby – this is particularly important if you had a multiple birth.

Making contact

Just because your baby is in an incubator doesn't mean you can't touch, kiss, and cuddle her. This sort of contact is vitally important because it actually helps your baby to develop and become strong. If it's a closed incubator, you can reach into her through hand-holes to play and fondle, and you should talk and sing to her as much as you can so that she hears your voice. Open special care cots enable you to stroke and fondle directly. All this will keep her contented and help her to thrive – love is an essential vitamin for premature babies. If it's practical, give your baby as much skin to skin contact as you can. When you hold your baby to your skin, her body temperature rises if she is cold, and then falls once she has warmed up. A successful experiment has also revealed that babies who are born prematurely thrive if they are nursed continuously between their mother's breasts – ask if you can try it. Skin to skin contact is essential for your baby, but it's essential for you, too, in fostering the bonding process. It will especially help you if you're nervous; you may feel this way because your baby is so small and you're finding it difficult to relate to her because she's in a special care unit.

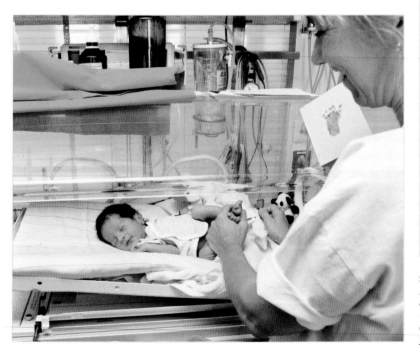

Coping with the technology

Many parents are worried by special care technology. Share your feelings with the staff in the unit and ask if it's possible to see the ward psychologist together. It also helps to understand what the equipment does:

- An incubator provides a warm, humid environment for the baby.

- A ventilator takes over the baby's breathing, getting air into and out of the lungs.

- A humidifier ensures air in the ventilator is warm and moist before it goes into the lungs.

- The apnoea alarm alerts the staff if a baby stops breathing.

- The saturation monitor and blood gas analyser measure levels of oxygen and carbon dioxide in the baby's blood.

- The blood pressure gauge measures a baby's blood pressure.

- A perspex head box may be used to provide extra oxygen when the baby is breathing on her own.

- The glucose monitor records the baby's glucose levels.

- The ECG (electro-cardiogram) monitor measures heart rate.

- The bilirubinometer measures the risk of jaundice.

- A phototherapy lamp treats jaundice with ultraviolet light. A shield protects the baby's eyes.

- A heat shield keeps the baby warm in an open cot.

Spending time with your baby
It's important to spend as much time as possible in the special care baby unit with your baby. It will help to demystify the technology and allow you to bond with your baby.

You and your body

Postnatal check

Your family doctor or hospital obstetrician will examine you about six weeks after the birth. Your baby will also be checked at about this time, and it may happen at the same appointment (see p. 155). This check will make sure that your body has fully returned to its pre-pregnant state. Your doctor will examine your uterus, heart, and blood pressure, your breasts, and any scarring if you had stitches. This is an ideal time to discuss contraception or anything that concerns you. At the checkup your doctor may:

■ Test your blood pressure.

■ Check your heart rate.

■ Check your weight.

■ Examine your abdomen to make sure the uterus has contracted down.

■ Look at your breasts and nipples.

■ Do an internal examination to assess the size and position of your uterus and the state of your vaginal muscles.

■ Check on the site of perineal stitches. Tell your doctor if it's still sore, especially during sex.

■ Carefully check your scar and abdomen if you had a Caesarean.

■ Give you advice about contraception. During the internal examination an IUD can be inserted or a cap fitted.

It takes a woman's body more than nine months to recover completely from pregnancy and childbirth. For the first week or so, you'll be weak and unable to walk any distance or carry anything heavy. Even if you feel well, try not to overdo it, or you'll prolong your recovery period.

Getting back to normal

The medical term for the immediate period of recovery after the birth of your baby is the puerperium. It's defined as the first four weeks, but most women are physically back to normal well before that, even if their emotional adjustment takes much longer. However, you may well be concerned about what is happening to your body during the first week or two after the birth, when changes are rapid but often accompanied by a certain amount of discomfort. When this is your first experience of childbirth, it's important to realize that vaginal discharge, painfully engorged breasts, and unexpected abdominal cramps are quite normal!

How your body recovers

WHERE	WHAT YOU CAN DO TO HELP
Cervix and vagina	Because both were stretched during delivery, they will take at least 7–10 days to regain their former elasticity and close up. Doing your pelvic floor exercises (see p. 38) will help your vagina to tighten again. Start immediately after the birth.
Placental site (lochis)	As the placental site heals, it may bleed for up to six weeks. This discharge (lochia) has three colour phases: red (4–5 days), pink to brown (6–8 days), yellow to white (7–10 days). If you over-exert yourself, you may start to bleed, making the lochia red and copious again, so let your doctor know and rest with your feet up.
Uterus	Immediately after the birth, your uterus shrinks down to the size it was at about the fourth month of pregnancy. By about the tenth day it can no longer be felt in your abdomen – your midwife will check daily to make sure that it is shrinking normally. It takes about six weeks to revert to its normal pre-pregnant size.
Ovulation	If you're not breastfeeding, you may begin to ovulate within 6–14 weeks of the birth; menstruation will follow in anything between 8 and 16 weeks. Breastfeeding hormones can suppress menstruation so you may not have a period for months, but don't rely on breastfeeding as a contraceptive. Use contraception as soon as you want to start penetrative sex again (see p. 137).

Postnatal discomforts

DISCOMFORT	HOW TO RELIEVE IT
Coping with stitches	Discomfort from stitches can last up to a couple of weeks. Don't stand for long periods and have daily baths to prevent infection. Dry stitches with a hairdryer rather than a towel. Keep a bottle of witch hazel in the fridge and apply cold on a sterile pad to soothe the stitches. Occasionally stitches may not dissolve and need to be removed by your midwife or doctor.
Stress incontinence	Leaking urine when coughing, sneezing, taking exercise, or even laughing is a common though embarrassing problem for many women after childbirth. It's the result of stretched and weakened perineal muscles, so once again it's important to concentrate on doing your pelvic floor exercises (see p. 38).
Breast engorgement	Three or four days after birth lactation begins; your breasts become engorged with milk, making them uncomfortably large, hard, and tender. Relieve this by expressing, putting your baby to the breast as often as he wants, and having warm baths or laying hot flannels on your breasts. Always wear a supportive nursing bra.
Afterpains	As your uterus shrinks back you may continue to experience quite severe cramps, similar to menstrual pain, especially during breastfeeding. This is due to the action of the hormone oxytocin, which controls the "let down" of milk in your breasts (see p. 78), and also causes the uterine muscles to contract (see p. 49).
Headaches	In a very few cases (less than 1 per cent), some women experience a severe headache after an epidural anaesthetic. It's caused by a minute puncture in the membrane of the spinal column, made when the needle was inserted. If you experience this sort of headache, you'll be advised to lie down flat and drink plenty of fluids, and you'll be given painkillers, such as paracetamol, until the tiny hole has healed and the headache lifts. This usually takes a couple of days.

Postnatal sex

You can have non-penetrative sex whenever you both feel like it after the birth, but you'd be wise to abstain from penetrative sex until after the lochia has stopped (see p. 136). However, neither of you will probably feel like it for a while. Nature has seen to it that most men have a low sex drive for some time after the delivery of their baby, especially if they are present at the birth. Not surprisingly, low libido lasts longer in women who have just had babies. No one who has vaginal bruises, painful stitches, and enlarged, tender breasts finds it easy to feel sexy; your need for rest and recuperation is much more important. If you've had stitches, make sure your partner feels your scar when it's healed – he'll be much more understanding and compassionate about sex after he's felt the extent of it (see p. 46).

After a Caesarean

If you've had a Caesarean delivery you'll be monitored more closely while you're in hospital, and your stay will be longer than after a normal delivery. The doctors will want to be sure that both you and your baby are progressing well. Even so, your stay in hospital is likely only to be about five days.

Stitches
Stitches are usually dissolvable and do not need to be removed.

Time for recovery
It may only be when you get home that you realize how much the Caesarean has affected you. This won't last for long, but you won't feel completely back to normal for at least a month.

Help in the home
You need to avoid exertion while the wound is healing so it's a good idea if your partner can take extra time off work, or if a friend or relation can stay for a while. You won't be able to lift heavy things, and will probably be warned not to drive a car for several weeks.

Your healing scar
At first your scar just needs to be kept dry and well ventilated, and you can bathe once the dressing is removed. If the wound becomes red or inflamed, consult your doctor as there may be a slight infection that can be treated with antibiotics. Your scar will feel less sore gradually, but may itch as the pubic hair grows back. As the scar is on your "bikini line", it's a good idea to wear pants that come up to your waistline to avoid irritation.

Before you exercise

You can start the gentle programme of exercises given here at any time, but avoid vigorous exercise until the lochia has stopped (see p. 64).

Warming up
Athletes and dancers always warm up before exercise or performing, as they know the damage they could do to their bodies without it. It's equally important for you when doing postnatal exercises. Warming up helps relieve tension and warms up muscles and joints so that they don't overstretch when you begin more demanding exercises. It also helps to avoid cramp and stiffness afterwards.

If you've had a Caesarean
You can do pelvic floor exercises straight away, but don't attempt any other exercises until you've had your postnatal check.

Taking care
Don't exercise if you feel exhausted or unwell, and be careful if you've had back trouble. Avoid sit ups or straight leg lifts.

Resuming sport

Even if you were taking part in a regular sporting activity before you were pregnant, you should avoid strenuous aerobic exercise for at least nine months after the birth. Avoid anything that puts a strain on your abdominal muscles, and don't resume working out in the gym until your doctor advises it. Ask a qualified fitness trainer or sports instructor to give you a graded programme, take it very easy, but don't expect to be back to your previous level of fitness or stamina for at least a year.

Looking after your body

Pregnancy and childbirth aren't illnesses, and your body is designed to recover naturally. However, this doesn't mean it couldn't do with a little help. Gone are the days when women were literally "confined" for several weeks, but you'll need to conserve your energy during the first two or three weeks to help the healing process and to enable you to get breastfeeding successfully established (see p. 78). The fat laid down in your body during pregnancy specifically to provide the calories for breastfeeding will take a few weeks to be used up, but many women are surprised by how quickly they regain their pre-pregnancy shape and weight when they breastfeed.

Postnatal exercises

Losing weight isn't the same as regaining muscle tone; you'll need to exercise the muscles in your abdomen and perineum to bring them back to normal. But finding the time and energy to do postnatal exercises may seem an impossible dream to you immediately after the birth. While you're in the postnatal ward you may be visited by a physiotherapist within a day of the birth. She will explain exactly what has happened to your body and will show you the best way to start exercising. Your abdominal muscles will have stretched and parted to accommodate your growing baby; this muscle tone can be regained if you find ten minutes a day to do the simple exercises given here. Make sure you warm up properly first (see left).

Getting started

Start gently – your muscles and ligaments are still soft from the action of progesterone – and don't forget your pelvic floor muscles (see p. 38); just because you can't see them doesn't mean they aren't important.

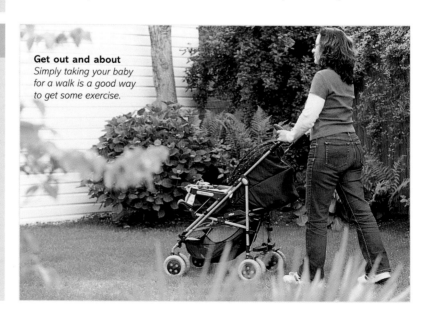

Get out and about
Simply taking your baby for a walk is a good way to get some exercise.

How to exercise

Little and often is best; start with one or two repetitions of each, every day, then progress to ten. Remember to exhale on the effort, and inhale as you relax. Always stop if any exercise hurts.

Cat arching

1 *Kneel on all fours with knees and hands slightly apart. Make sure your back, head, and neck are straight.*

2 *Tighten your buttocks and slowly arch your back upwards. Keep your arms straight, but don't lock your elbows. This exercise is wonderful for relieving lower backache.*

Stomach toner

1 *Lie on the floor, with knees bent and arms straight by your sides. Pull in your tummy muscles and press the small of your back down. Hold for four seconds, then relax.*

2 *Keeping your feet flat, tilt your pelvis up and lift your head off the pillow as far as you can. Don't try to sit up, it's enough just to lift your head and perhaps your shoulders.*

Curl ups (after two weeks)

1 *Try this more advanced abdominal exercise at least two weeks after the birth. Lie down with legs bent as before. Try to reach your knees by sliding your hands up your thighs.*

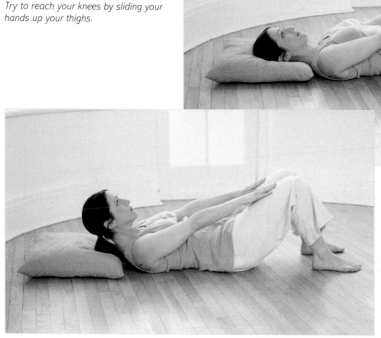

2 *With your hands as close to your knees as possible, as you exhale, pull in your tummy muscles and lift your head for a count of four, then relax.*

Leg lifts

1 *Strengthen your thighs and abdominal muscles with these simple lifts. Lie on your side comfortably, supporting your head with one hand, and balancing your body by resting the other hand in front of you. Make sure your legs are in line with your hip and shoulder.*

2 *Keeping your knee and foot facing to the front, lift your whole leg straight upwards to shoulder height, hold for a count of two and then lower. Do this a few times, then turn over and repeat with the other leg.*

Side bends

*Stand with your feet apart
and arms by your sides.
Slowly bend sideways at
the waist, stretching your
leg outwards at the same
time. Return to upright, and
repeat on the other side.*

Caring for
your baby

The excitement of the birth is over and now you're back home. But as new parents the chances are you'll feel daunted by the sheer work involved in the day-to-day care of your baby. There are practical details to think about, such as making sure you've got all the equipment and clothes you need, what nappies to use, and how to keep your baby clean. And then there are the more serious questions like how to get breastfeeding established, how to pacify your crying baby, and how to cope with broken nights. As time passes, you'll get to know your baby and her needs will become easier to predict and to cater for. It will still be hard work, but if you share the joys and burdens equally you'll find the pleasure of watching your baby grow and develop makes it all worthwhile.

The first weeks

Mother

Your baby's first few months of life would be tiring for you even if you hadn't been through the rigours of labour and birth. Spoil yourself and look after your own needs.

How to be kind to yourself

■ Rest with your baby. Use the time when your baby is asleep to catch up on your own sleep. If he has his longest unbroken sleep in the morning, take advantage of it, or rest in the afternoon when he does.

■ Share with your partner. If things are getting on top of you, he needs to know, for your sake and for your baby's. Encourage him to look after the baby when he's at home; don't be over-protective and try to do everything yourself.

■ Ask for help. If you're feeling isolated, don't soldier on alone. Early offers of help may tail off because friends and family don't want to impose, but they will be glad to be asked.

■ Get out and about (see p. 134). Being tied to the house can make you depressed, so try to get out as much as possible. It's helpful if you have friends locally who are also at home with young babies. You'll probably have met like-minded parents at antenatal classes. Having other new parents around you means you can share the good times as well as the worries, and, as your baby grows, he'll have a ready-made circle of friends to play with.

After all the months of preparation and the excitement of the birth, you're back home and at last you're a family. Now you can get down to the serious business of learning how to care for your child as he grows and develops from a small, vulnerable baby to a social, communicative one-year-old. It's immensely rewarding, but there's a lot to do and it's a full-time commitment from the start.

Finding a pattern

When you become a new parent, perhaps the most difficult thing to adjust to is the fluidity and unpredictability of your new lifestyle. Most people's lives have very distinct patterns, based on doing roughly the same things at roughly the same times, and they feel discomforted if this structure dissolves. Alternatively, you might be used to doing what you want exactly when you want to do it. But trying to impose this sort of orderliness on a young baby is the equivalent of spitting into the wind. If you can both relax and follow your baby's lead, a pattern of some sort will eventually emerge.

Following your baby's lead

Ignore anyone who tells you that you shouldn't pick up your crying baby because "he's only exercising his lungs" or "he'll cry himself back to sleep in a minute" – very young babies shouldn't have to wait. If a baby learns that he has to scream for ten minutes to receive attention, he is laying down a pattern of behaviour that you will not appreciate in the future. So-called "good" babies are either those who are contented because all their needs are met promptly, or those who have been taught by experience that their needs won't be met at once and have become apathetic. You cannot "spoil" a young baby except by imposing a regime that is governed by the clock – and by placing your needs before his. This is what will lead to him becoming discontented and hard to pacify. Helping him to separate his needs from others' needs will come much later on in his development.

Changing your priorities

If you're both following your baby's lead, you'll have to learn to be as relaxed as possible about things like meal times and housework, even if you normally have a set routine and are house-proud. It's much more important for both of you to concentrate on becoming skilled and confident in the practical care of your baby. Initially, there may seem to be a lot to learn and you'll feel clumsy and nervous (everybody does), but you'll soon find that it becomes second nature, and you'll gradually develop a routine that allows you time to fit in household chores at some point in your day.

If you feel low

If either or both of you feels disillusioned or dissatisfied with what you imagined you would be experiencing at this time, you're not necessarily depressed, you're probably just out of sorts. This is natural – you're both tired. If the baby is fractious, a mother may feel that somehow it is her fault and she may also be suffering from the "baby blues" (see p. 132), while a new father may feel inadequate if he's unable to help as much as he'd like, because he's at work. Don't worry, you'll both soon begin to adjust to the new situation, but if negative feelings persist, talk to your doctor or health visitor. They'll help you to realize that lots of people feel the same way, but will also be able to tell if you're suffering from the signs of actual postnatal depression, which is easy to treat if recognized early on (see p. 133).

Reassure each other

If you both start out in the knowledge that these first few months can seem like hard work, you'll be able to reassure each other that you're coping extremely well. If you accept the validity of each other's feelings, and hold on to the fact that any difficulties are temporary, you'll discover that parenthood really is as pleasurable as you expected.

Father

The first few weeks with your baby are important in helping you get used to your new role as a father.

How you can help

■ Support your partner. She will be very tired to start with as a result of going through labour and birth, and from the physical and emotional responsibility of breastfeeding. Provide her with the time and space to meet your baby's nutritional needs, and reassure her constantly that she's doing a difficult job well. Your support can make all the difference.

■ Find time to help. If you're back at work, relish the opportunity to do as much as you can for your partner and your baby when you're at home.

■ Give your baby love. Babies need as much love as they can get, and there's no difference between the love of a father and a mother. If your baby is being breastfed, then obviously he'll need his mother when he's hungry, but at all other times he'll benefit just as much from your closeness and attention. This closeness from you will mean that your baby learns to be secure with both of you, which will help him to settle and take the pressure off your partner.

■ Build a relationship with your baby from the start. Your own feelings as a parent will be strengthened if you spend as much time as possible with him. Being an equal partner in your baby's care will be rewarding and beneficial to you and to your family.

Coping with the night shift

WHAT TO DO	HOW IT HELPS
Prepare yourselves for broken nights	Many babies continue to wake once or twice during the night well beyond 12 months of age. If you're both prepared for this, you'll find it much easier to adjust.
Share the burden	Taking turns to get up is important. You may have followed the traditional pattern of father going to work, while mother stays at home, but remember, looking after a baby is also a full-time job.
Change your sleep pattern	Broken nights are not necessarily sleepless nights. By developing a new sleep pattern, you'll find that you're able to wake, attend to your baby, and then go back to sleep immediately.
Keep your baby close	If your baby's cot is by the side of your bed, you don't have to disturb yourselves too much when he wakes for a feed. Put him back in his cot when you're ready to go back to sleep (see p. 102).
Stay together	Sleeping separately could undermine your relationship as a couple and with your baby. Only sleep in separate rooms as a last resort – for example, because of illness or extreme fatigue.
Avoid sleep deprivation	Long-term sleep deprivation can have serious consequences, so it's better that you both lose some sleep than for one parent alone to take all the burden and become completely exhausted.

Equipment

Safety measures

You'll need to have a major overhaul of general safety equipment throughout your home. Before the birth install smoke alarms, if you don't have them already, and before your baby becomes mobile check you have the following:

■ Covers for all electric sockets.

■ Corner protectors for furniture.

■ Locks and catches for video and DVD players, doors, cupboards and drawers (especially in the kitchen), and the refrigerator.

■ A cooker guard.

■ Retractable flex for electrical goods, such as the kettle, iron, and toaster.

■ A stair gate at the top and bottom of stairs and across the kitchen door or opening.

Providing for your new baby is exciting and rewarding, and you naturally want the best. However, as you set out to plan the nursery, do bear in mind that at first your new arrival will need very little in the way of essentials.

The basics

Manufacturers of nursery "hardware" have recognized that couples expecting their first child are among the biggest spenders around, but you don't need to break the bank to provide for your newborn baby if you stick to the basics shown here.

Baby bath and changing mat
For use in the first 3–4 months, a flat-based bath comes with a stand or can be rested on a firm surface; others fit over the big bath. A changing mat is a comfortable and practical way to avoid mess when nappy changing and at bath time.

High chair
This type of high chair allows your baby to sit at the table with the rest of the family. The seat and foot plate can be adjusted as your baby grows older.

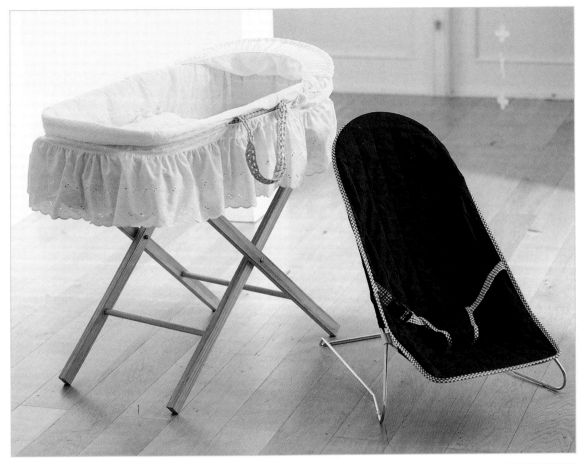

Moses basket and baby chair

A Moses basket is simple and lightweight for a newborn. You could even make linings and trimmings yourself – use cotton fabric. A rigid or bouncing baby chair with back support is useful for young babies before they can sit. Always place the chair on the floor.

Full-size cot

When your baby outgrows her Moses basket, you'll need a cot. Choose one with two mattress positions and a drop-side to protect your back when lifting her.

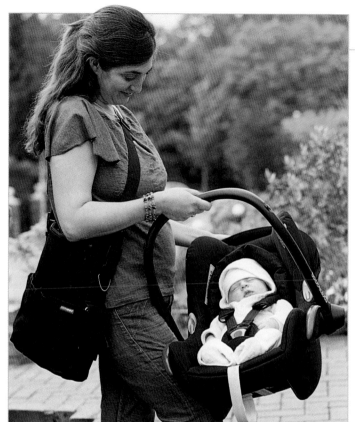

Out and about

Your baby won't be walking until he's at least a year old, and even then he'll need transporting in a buggy or car seat for safety. It's worth looking ahead to future needs when you're thinking about buying any of these larger, more expensive items.

Infant car seat
All babies under 10 kg (22 lb) should be put in a rear-facing seat in the car. These seats can be used in the front or rear seat of the car, but your baby is safest in the rear seat. Rear-facing seats provide better protection for a young baby's head, neck, and spine. Don't use a rear-facing car seat in the front seat of your car if your car has airbags.

Pram and buggy
A pram/buggy combination is ideal. Check ease of folding, and that the height of the handle doesn't make you stoop. This carrycot can be used for babies up to six months or until your baby can sit up by himself. The cot can then be replaced with a seat to make a buggy, which can face towards you or forwards.

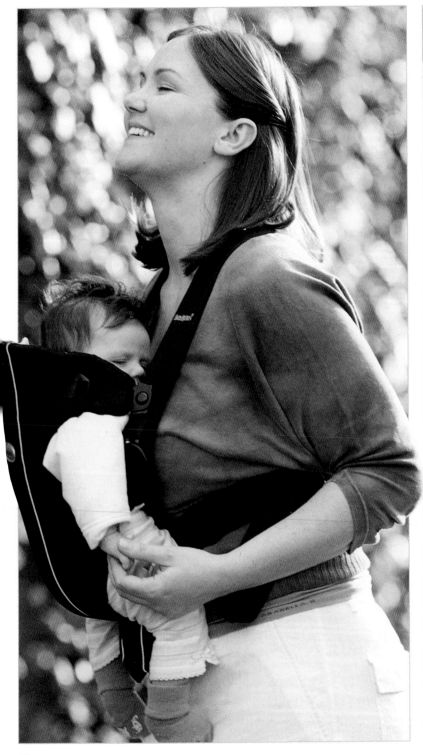

Sling
There are several types of carrying sling suitable for young babies; try them on to see which is most comfortable A backpack may be more comfortable once your baby can sit up.

Buying secondhand

If there's a secondhand baby shop in your area, it's well worth a visit. You can also try shopping at charity shops and car boot sales. However, you should check all equipment carefully, and avoid certain items (see below).

Good secondhand buys
- Clothes, especially newborn baby clothes and outer wear.

- Bedclothes (except duvets), but always wash before use.

- Moses basket, but you may want to buy a new mattress.

- Plastic or wood toys only, but check carefully for cracks or splinters. Avoid anything that has metal or moving parts; even soft toys or dolls may contain hidden metal parts.

- Large plastic items, such as sterilizing equipment.

Possible secondhand buys
- Pram or buggy, but check brakes, folding mechanism, and all of the accessories.

- Cot, but check drop-side mechanism is safe and you may also want to buy a new matress.

- Travel cot. Always check the folding mechanism and carrying case. Buy a new mattress if necessary.

- High chair. Check that all screws are really secure and check crevices for food remains.

- Safety items, such as baby monitors or stair gates, but check that they work properly.

Bad secondhand buy
- Never buy a secondhand car seat, as the seat may have been weakened in an accident.

Breastfeeding

Advantages of breastfeeding

Here are some of the many advantages of breastfeeding.

- Baby and mother bond closely.

- Milk is readily available, sterile, and is the correct temperature.

- Easy for your baby to digest.

- A perfect balance of protein, carbohydrate, fat, salt, and other minerals, vitamins, and iron.

- Protects against infection.

- May protect against allergies.

- Breastfed babies have fewer nappy rashes and their stools are softer and inoffensive.

- Helps burn off fat laid down in a mother's body during pregnancy.

YOU WILL NEED

2–3 nursing bras

Breast pads
disposable or reusable

Breast milk is the most suitable food for your baby, providing all her nutritional needs during her first six months. As a father, you can be involved by supporting your partner.

Getting started

Some people have no difficulty with breastfeeding; but for many others it doesn't go smoothly in the beginning. Don't feel demoralized: follow the step-by-step guide on page 80 and discuss any problems with your midwife, health visitor, or breastfeeding counsellor, who will be happy to give advice at any time. Don't give up without consulting one of them first. Remember, your baby is learning too, so you have to be patient.

Ensuring a good milk supply

When your baby feeds, the milk she drinks first – the foremilk – is thin, watery, and thirst-quenching; the hindmilk that follows is richer in fat and protein, so your baby gets all her nutritional needs at one feed. To ensure that you provide a good milk supply, make sure you are eating a good diet and drinking lots of fluids, especially in hot weather when your baby will be thirsty too. Feed on demand, when your baby is hungry; your body will automatically produce enough. If your baby feeds slowly in the first few days, you may have to express milk (see p. 83) in order for more to be produced. If she feeds often, you will keep pace, no matter how small your breasts are; breast size is irrelevant to the amount of milk you make. However, it is important to rest between feeds, so that your metabolism can catch up. Many women find the mid-evening feed the most difficult as the milk supply is often lower because you are tired, and your baby may be fretful at this time of day. Try resting in the afternoon, preparing an evening meal earlier in the day, or better still, leaving the cooking to your partner.

The "let-down" reflex
When a baby suckles, nerves in the areola stimulate the hypothalamus (●) which stimulates the pituitary gland (■) in the brain to secrete oxytocin, which causes the breast to release ("let down") milk.

Frequency of feeds

Be prepared to feed often – your baby could feed ten or 11 times in 24 hours for the first few weeks. Feeding will take over your life to start with, but you'll find that your baby is contented, goes to sleep easily, and by the time she's six to eight weeks, she'll be feeding more efficiently, and less often. Don't try to impose a rigid routine – your baby will get upset and the stress will affect your ability to feed. During the first few weeks, use alternate breasts for feeds. This helps to balance the milk supply and avoids either breast becoming sore. Many babies find one side easier than the other; if this happens with your baby, put her to the less favoured breast first.

Successful breastfeeding

To establish successful breastfeeding, it's important to understand how your baby sucks. "Sucking" is really the wrong word; in fact she "smacks" the nipple between her tongue and the roof of her mouth. To do this properly she has to latch on properly (see p. 80) with her gums firmly gripping the areola (this stimulates the let-down of milk – see left) and the nipple so far into her mouth that the milk is then squeezed right into her throat for her to swallow.

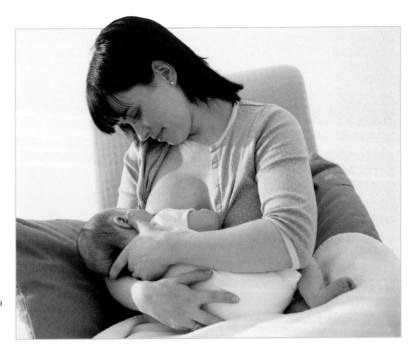

Sitting in a chair
Sit with both feet firmly on the ground. Support your back and arms with pillows and place a pillow on your lap to raise and support your baby if necessary.

Breastfeeding positions

It's important to be in a comfortable position before you start feeding as you're likely to be there for some time. Whether sitting or lying, make sure your baby's whole body is angled towards you; in this position she's more likely to latch on first time.

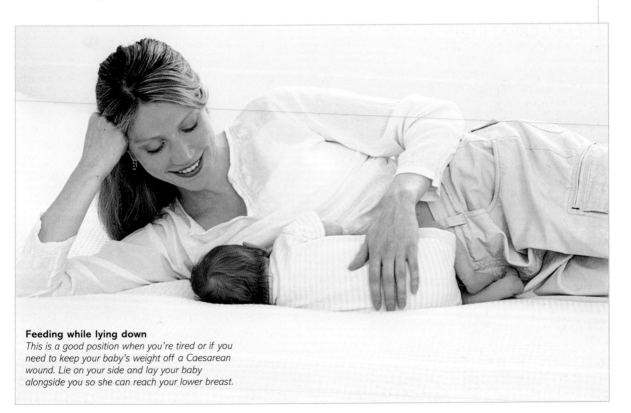

Feeding while lying down
This is a good position when you're tired or if you need to keep your baby's weight off a Caesarean wound. Lie on your side and lay your baby alongside you so she can reach your lower breast.

Latching on

1 *Support your baby along the length of his back and use your hand and fingers to support the back of his neck to bring him up to your breast. Line up your nipple with your baby's nose. As soon as he smells your milk, he'll open his mouth. While your baby is very young, you can gently stroke his cheek; when you do this, he'll turn towards your breast as a reflex action.*

2 *Your baby should "latch on" to your nipple at once. If not, support your breast with your hand and guide him on to it so that he has a mouthful of nipple.*

Baby's gums should encircle the areola

3 *Releasing – a breastfeeding baby creates a strong vacuum on the breast, so when he has finished, you may need to release his grip on the nipple by gently easing your little finger into the corner of his mouth. Never pull your nipple away from your baby; this is a sure way to make it sore and sore nipples (see below) may deter you from breastfeeding.*

Mother

Your breasts need special care when you start breastfeeding. Buy at least two maternity bras – the best you can afford. Take great care of your breasts and nipples. Bathe them every day with water – don't use soap because it defats the skin and encourages sore or cracked nipples. If you can, leave your nipples open to the air for a time when you've finished feeding.

Being determined

Few women breastfeed without encountering problems at least once, and sometimes several times. So while you shouldn't necessarily expect to find it difficult, neither should you be surprised if you seem to have a run of problems. The important thing to bear in mind is that most breastfeeding difficulties can be put right – provided you have support and the commitment and confidence to continue.

Sore nipples

Painful nipples are the most common reason for women giving up breastfeeding. However, there are ways to avoid them. Make sure your baby is correctly positioned and properly latched on and never pull your baby off the nipple (see above). Keep your nipples dry with disposable or cotton washable breast pads or clean cotton hankies. Don't use tissues as they will fall apart. Let the nipples dry naturally at the end of each feed whenever possible. If they become cracked, ointment, such as

Vaseline may be helpful. If your nipples become very sore, feed your baby before he is desperate as he will be calmer and treat you more gently. Try to get the milk flowing before the feed starts by expressing a little first.

Blocked ducts and mastitis

A red, tender patch on your breast may be a sign of a blocked milk duct. You may even feel feverish. Take immediate action by feeding as frequently as possible, or express milk, particularly from the affected side. Massage any lumps gently as your baby feeds. See your doctor if there's no improvement within 24 hours, as you may need a mild antibiotic to clear any infection.

Feeding away from home
One of the advantages of breastfeeding is that it's possible to feed at anytime and anywhere while you are out and about.

Concerns about breastfeeding

YOUR CONCERN	WHAT YOU CAN DO
How long on each breast	Your baby takes 80 per cent of the feed in the first five minutes, five minutes more and he's sucked out the creamy after-milk, so as a rough guide, expect him to spend about ten minutes feeding per breast. Breastfed babies are rarely underfed though they may only feed for a short time, but do not restrict feeds at each breast. If your baby is feeding happily, allow him to take his time.
Slow feeding	Many babies take a few days to get the hang of latching on and may be slow to feed. If this becomes a problem, seek advice. A baby who sucks for a long time isn't necessarily feeding. He may just love sucking. If your baby tends to fall asleep at the breast, let him take all he wants from one side, then offer the other breast first next time.
Baby's weight gain	Don't weigh your baby before and after feeding. Weight gain in breastfed babies should always be calculated over a two-to-three week period, as weight is often gained unevenly. The very rare instances of underfeeding usually occur because the baby isn't properly latched on.
If you're ill	Common infections, such as colds needn't interrupt breastfeeding. Stay in bed and let your partner bring your baby to you just to feed. You could also express milk so your partner can feed your baby instead. If you need medication of any sort make sure your doctor knows you are breastfeeding as some medicines are not recommended for breastfeeding mothers. If you go to hospital, breastfeeding is usually still possible if you take your baby in with you.
Breastfeeding in public	Breastfeeding is the most convenient way to feed your baby, and you should be able to breastfeed anytime, anywhere. It's possible to feed discreetly if you use a nursing bra that undoes easily in front with one hand, and a big shawl or cardigan to screen yourself. A baggy T-shirt or sweatshirt also works – you can tuck your baby up underneath it.

Breastfeeding twins

It's slightly more difficult to establish breastfeeding for twins and it's not easy to feed both babies when you're away from home. But all the usual advantages apply, especially protection against infection – very important to twins because prematurity is more common than with single babies.

What if it's twins?

Don't be put off by people who say you can't breastfeed twins. Lots of mothers prove otherwise and, like all babies, twins benefit enormously from breast milk. Human breasts are quite capable of nourishing two babies, each of whom has the same need to bond with her parents, and you can feed them at the same time once breastfeeding is established.

Get advice Confidence is a crucial factor in breastfeeding twins. Try to talk to other mothers who've done it successfully – there are support groups to help you (see p. 187).

Feeding together To feed your babies at the same time, lay them on their backs, one under each arm with their heads forward, supported on pillows.

One at a time to start with Concentrate on latching on with one baby at a time at first. Feeding singly may be easier in the early days, and gives you a chance to get to know each baby individually. However, this does take much longer than feeding together.

There's plenty of milk Breastfeeding is always controlled by demand, so your breasts will produce as much milk as your babies need. If one feeds more readily than the other, put the slower baby to the breast first; the stronger baby will stimulate more milk.

Look after yourself Eat heartily, have lots to drink, and rest whenever you can. Although twins' practical needs are the same, there are two of them to look after, and you'll tire easily. Make sure you get as much help as you can.

Feeding together
Once breastfeeding is established you can try breastfeeding your babies together.

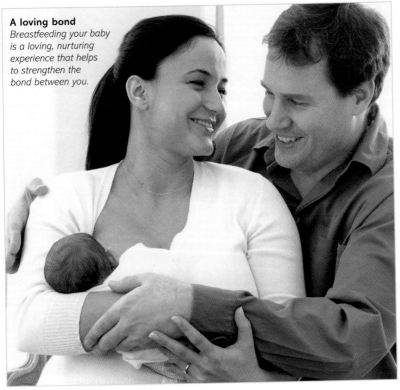

A loving bond
Breastfeeding your baby is a loving, nurturing experience that helps to strengthen the bond between you.

Father

Your support is essential.

What you can do to help

■ Be gently encouraging.

■ Don't leave your partner to feed the baby alone unless she asks you to – she could feel isolated and you'll feel neglected.

■ Your partner may like to express milk that you can give in a bottle at night. Undo your shirt and hold your baby against your skin to mimic breastfeeding.

■ Be aware that your partner's breasts may be tense, sore, and very sensitive for the first few weeks of breastfeeding.

Expressing milk

When you're breastfeeding you can express milk so that your partner can feed your baby; it also helps to relieve overfull breasts in the first days. If your baby is in a special care baby unit (see p. 62), you can express milk to feed her. Few women find it easy to express milk, so don't be disheartened – it's a knack that takes a bit of learning. If you "leak" milk while feeding, place a breast shell against the other breast, and keep the milk in a sterile container.

Using a breast pump

You can express milk more quickly using a pump, which applies a rhythmical suction to the breast. The hand pump works by fitting the funnel of the pump over your areola to form an airtight seal. You then operate the lever or plunger to express the milk. Electric pumps are more expensive but are quicker and easier to use. They also imitate the baby's sucking cycle more closely. An electric pump is best if you need to express often – for example, if you're going back to work before weaning.

Expressing milk by hand

1 *Massage your breasts with flat hands, beginning at your ribs and working towards your areola, gradually going over the whole breast.*

2 *Then roll your fingers and thumb together below and above your areola so that you press on the wider milk ducts behind the nipple.*

3 *Collect the milk in a sterile bowl, transfer it to a sterile container, and keep it in the refrigerator for a few hours. Freeze it for longer storage.*

Hand pump

Electric pump

Bottle-feeding

Sterilizing and preparing bottles

Hygiene and making up feeds correctly are important if you are bottle-feeding to avoid health problems with your baby. To ensure your baby thrives and to avoid infection:

- Buy equipment well in advance and practise cleaning and sterilizing bottles.

- Always wash your hands thoroughly before handling bottles and feeding your baby.

- Always follow the manufacturer's instructions carefully when sterilizing bottles.

- Bottles should be fully immersed in sterilizing fluid and left for at least two hours or according to the manufacturer's instructions.

- With 6–7 feeds in 24 hours for the first few weeks, change the sterilizing fluid twice a day. Later you can reduce this to once a day.

- Make up batches of six bottles at a time and store them in the refrigerator. When all but two bottles have been used, make up some more.

- Never add extra scoops of formula or sugar.

- When a feed is over, pour away leftover milk, clean and rinse the bottle, cover it and place to one side until you are ready to sterilize it.

- Never give a baby leftover milk from a bottle because it may be contaminated. Always use or make up a fresh bottle and keep a couple of cartons of ready-made formula for emergencies.

I'm not going to pretend that bottle-feeding is as good for your baby as breastfeeding, but I don't want you to feel guilty, either. If you're undecided, look back to the sections on breastfeeding so that you're aware of its positive advantages. Bottle-feeding does, however, mean that both of you can share all of your baby's care equally.

Feeding your baby

Either of you can bottle-feed your baby, but bottle-feeding really allows a father to come into his own. When you are giving your baby a bottle, you can mimic the closeness of breastfeeding by cradling him close in the crook of your arm. Hold him so his face is 20–25 cm (8–10 in) away from yours, in a position where he can make eye contact with you (see p. 61). If possible, open your shirt and hold him against your bare skin.

Giving your baby a bottle

Before you start, check also that the flow from the teat is neither too fast nor too slow – before giving the bottle, tip it up to make sure the teat produces a flow of several drops a second. Your baby may break naturally for a burp halfway through the feed, but it isn't necessary to force him to burp by rubbing his back; if he's still hungry he'll just get upset. If he seems comfortable, let him feed without a break until he's had enough.

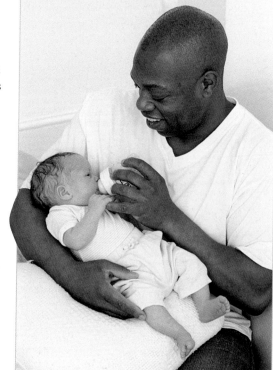

Bottle-feeding your baby
Cradle your baby close enough to keep eye contact throughout, and talk to him while you feed. If necessary, put a pillow on your lap to raise him. He'll soon learn to associate the pleasure of feeding with the sight of your face.

Making up a feed

YOU WILL NEED

Steam or chemical sterilizing unit

Hot, boiled water

Powdered formula
with measuring scoop

Straight-backed knife
for levelling powdered formula

6–8 bottles, teats, and covers

1 *Fill the scoop provided and level off the formula with the back of a knife. Do not pack the formula down.*

2 *Check you have the right amount of boiled water in the bottle and add the formula a scoop at a time.*

3 *Check you've added the right amount of formula. Never add extra scoops of milk, it could be dangerous for your baby. Put the cap on the feeding bottle.*

4 *Shake the bottle well. Allow to cool and store in the refrigerator until you want to use it. Never keep bottles of formula for more than 24 hours.*

5 *When you are ready to feed, take the bottle from the refrigerator and warm the milk by placing it in a bowl of hot water. You can also cool hot milk by placing it in cold water.*

Keeping bottles clean

Scrupulous hygiene is essential if you are bottle-feeding. Milk can be a rich breeding ground for the bacteria that cause diseases such as gastroenteritis, so sterilize bottles, teats and all other equipment used for feeding until your baby is six months old. Clean bottles and teats thoroughly as described below before sterilizing. Once your baby is over 12 months you can wash the equipment in a dishwasher.

■ Scrub bottles and teats with a bottle brush and hot, soapy water to remove all traces of milk, then rinse well in cold water.

■ Wash the teats thoroughly, paying attention to the inside rim and making sure that the holes are also clear. Then rinse in cold water.

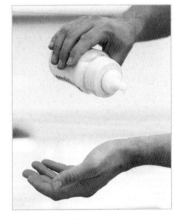

Testing the milk
Always check that the milk is not too hot or too cold before offering it to your baby by shaking a few drops on to your wrist. The milk should be blood temperature, which means it should feel neither hot nor cold against your skin.

Nappies

Nappy rash

Nappy rash is preventable if you always change your baby's nappy promptly, particularly after she's had a bowel movement; bacteria in faeces breaks down the urine to release ammonia which can irritate and ulcerate the skin. Always keep your baby's skin clean and well aired. Use barrier cream only as a preventive measure. If your baby does become sore, leave her nappy off whenever possible and let her kick on her changing mat. Apply nappy cream at every change. Check with your doctor if the rash persists for more than two to three days.

You'll have to use nappies for at least two and a half years, until your baby gains full bladder and bowel control, so it's worth familiarizing yourself with the most efficient way to change your baby. Give some thought, too, to which type of nappy best suits your circumstances – there's certainly plenty of choice nowadays.

Which nappies to use

There's a wide variety of disposable nappies available and you may be bewildered by the choice. If you want to use reusable nappies, there are several more modern alternatives to the traditional terry towelling square that requires safety pins. All types have their advantages and disadvantages. Unless you use a nappy laundry service, reusable nappies are a lot more trouble as they have to be washed and dried, while disposable nappies are more expensive, even taking into account the hidden costs of washing and drying reusables. There's been discussion about the adverse impact on the environment of disposable nappies both in their manufacture and disposal; reusable nappies are undoubtedly more ecologically sound in the long run.

Nappies, liners, and fasteners

Here is a selection of nappies. Provided your baby is changed as often as necessary she will be happy in whatever style you choose.

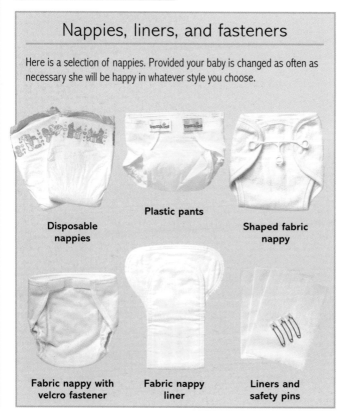

Disposable nappies

Plastic pants

Shaped fabric nappy

Fabric nappy with velcro fastener

Fabric nappy liner

Liners and safety pins

Fabric nappies

Traditional terry towelling squares are bulky, and can be uncomfortable for your baby when she's mobile. Modern reusables are usually shaped, and many types have strong velcro fastenings or you could use pinless fasteners, so you don't have to worry about using safety pins. If you're using these, it's a good idea to also use disposable or reusable liners (see box left) to avoid heavy soiling with faeces.

Nappies for boys or girls

The most important consideration when choosing nappies is to make sure they accommodate your baby boy and are comfortable for your baby girl. Some manufacturers of disposables have taken the differences between the sexes into account: boys tend to wet the front of nappies so boys' disposables have extra padding in the front. Girls tend to wet the back of nappies more, and this is also accounted for in the design of girls' disposables.

Cleaning your baby

Your baby will need cleaning and changing whenever her nappy is soiled or wet. The number of changes will vary from baby to baby.

Cleaning girls

Always clean your baby's vulva and anus from front to back to avoid spreading bacteria from the anus to your baby's vagina. Don't clean inside the labia; just rinse away faeces gently with damp cotton wool.

1 Lift your baby's legs by holding her feet or ankles. Use cotton wool or baby wipes to clean the labia on the outside only.

2 Use a clean piece of cotton wool or baby wipe to clean the vulva, wiping from front to back.

Cleaning boys

Cover a boy's penis with a tissue as you take off his nappy in case he passes urine. Clean around the penis and scrotum with damp cotton wool. Don't try to pull back the foreskin as this remains fixed until your son is much older.

1 Lift his legs by holding both ankles as shown. Clean around genital area with lotion. Use a different piece of cotton wool each time you wipe.

2 Make sure all soiling is removed. Work from the leg creases in towards the penis.

YOU WILL NEED

Changing mat

Tissues

Nappy

Bowl of warm water or baby lotion

Cotton wool or baby wipes

Barrier cream

Bin with lid or nappy sacks

Changing your baby's nappy

Always change your baby on a firm flat surface, covered with a changing mat or towel. Protect your back by using a changing table of the correct height, or kneel beside the bed. Never leave your baby alone on the changing mat if it's on a surface above floor level. Even a newborn baby can wriggle off a mat, particularly if he's upset or angry. Collect together all the equipment you need before you start. Dispose of faeces in the toilet if possible; but don't flush disposable nappies or nappy liners down the toilet. Dispose of dirty nappies in nappy sacks, preferably placing them in a covered bin.

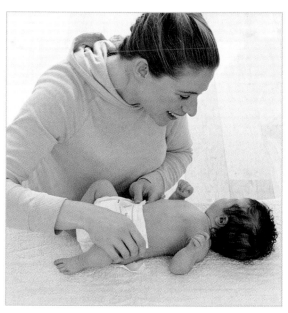

1 Remove the soiled nappy and clean carefully as shown on page 87. Make sure all creases are clean and dry if you used water to clean. Slide the clean nappy under your baby, lifting her buttocks gently into position.

2 Using both hands, bring the front of the nappy up between your baby's legs, as high as it will go. Tuck in the corners securely around her waist, ready for fastening.

3 Holding the nappy in place with one hand, fix the adhesive tabs firmly on to the front flap of the nappy.

Talk to your baby
Use nappy changing time as a chance to chat to your baby and enjoy her company – unless it's in the middle of the night. She's much less likely to get upset if her attention is fixed on you.

Keeping your baby clean

Bathing tips

To bath your baby as quickly and as safely as possible:

■ Wash or bath her in a room that is warm and draught free; it doesn't have to be the bathroom. Use a bucket to carry the water and to fill and empty the bath.

■ If you use a sponge and face cloth, make sure they are reserved strictly for your baby's use and wash them frequently.

■ Never poke about inside your baby's ears with a cotton bud as you could easily damage her delicate eardrum. Only remove ear wax that is visible at the opening.

YOU WILL NEED

Cotton wool
for face, eyes, and nappy area

Cooled, boiled water
for washing the eyes

Bowl of warm water
for washing face and body

Soft towel
for wrapping and drying

Nappy changing equipment
(see p. 86)

Clean clothes

Very young babies don't get dirty, so they don't need frequent bathing – but bath time provides a perfect opportunity for cuddling and playing that infants come to relish. It also gives fathers a chance to spend time with their babies. Later, bath time will be part of your baby's bedtime routine, a signal that it's time to wind down.

While your baby is young

Many parents are understandably nervous of bathing their newborn baby while she's still tiny and seems so vulnerable. It is, however, worth remembering that a baby is quite resilient provided she's handled gently but firmly, so try to be as confident as possible. You'll be shown the safest and easiest methods for bathing your baby a few days after the birth by a midwife at the hospital or when she visits you at home. As with all aspects of caring for your baby, bathing her will soon become second nature once you've given yourselves time to get used to it. The first few times, your baby may get quite distressed when she's being bathed, so don't feel you have to bath her every day. Thorough cleansing using the "topping and tailing" method outlined below is quite sufficient.

Topping and tailing

"Topping and tailing" means cleaning your baby thoroughly by washing her face, hands, and nappy area, without undressing her completely. You can do this most days as part of your baby's nappy changing and dressing routine and then just give her a bath every two or three days. This will save you time and is less distressing for your baby.

1 Undress your baby on a changing mat or towel. Leave her vest on or wrap her in a towel. Gently wipe her face, ears, and neck folds with cotton wool moistened with warm water. Pat her dry, making sure that you have dried thoroughly between her neck folds.

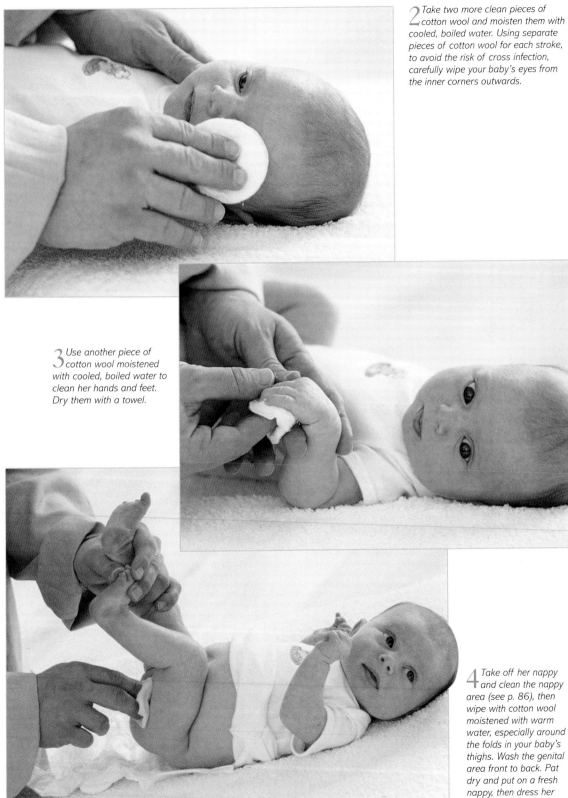

2 Take two more clean pieces of cotton wool and moisten them with cooled, boiled water. Using separate pieces of cotton wool for each stroke, to avoid the risk of cross infection, carefully wipe your baby's eyes from the inner corners outwards.

3 Use another piece of cotton wool moistened with cooled, boiled water to clean her hands and feet. Dry them with a towel.

4 Take off her nappy and clean the nappy area (see p. 86), then wipe with cotton wool moistened with warm water, especially around the folds in your baby's thighs. Wash the genital area front to back. Pat dry and put on a fresh nappy, then dress her in clean clothes.

Bathing your baby

Choose a bath time that suits you and your baby; it doesn't always have to be in the evening, especially if your baby tends to be fretful at that time of day. However, if you're working parents, bathing your baby in the evening is often a good way for you to spend time with him; you can even have a bath with him when he's older (see p. 95) to make it more fun! Make sure you've got all of the items you need within easy reach.

YOU WILL NEED

Baby bath

Two towels

Baby bath solution

Cotton wool
for face, eyes, and nappy area

Cooled, boiled water
for washing the eyes

Nappy changing equipment

Clean clothes

1 Fill the bath 5–8 cm (2–3 in) deep, putting cold in first. Test the temperature with your elbow or wrist; it should only feel warm.

2 Undress your baby down to his vest and wash his face and neck. Wrap him firmly in a towel, then, holding him under your arm and supporting his head over the bath, gently wash and rinse his hair with water from the bath. Pat his hair dry with a towel.

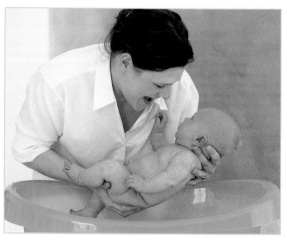

3 Leave a dry towel ready for after the bath. Unwrap the first towel, remove the nappy, and lift your baby into the bath, supporting his head and shoulders firmly with one hand, and his bottom and legs with your other hand.

4 Holding your baby in the bath and supporting his head with one arm, gently wash his body with your free hand, and encourage him to kick and splash in the water.

5 To get your baby out of the bath, raise his head and shoulders with one hand and slide your free hand under his bottom as before, then lift him on to the dry towel. Wrap him up immediately so he doesn't get cold. Pat him dry all over, paying particular attention to the folds of his neck, bottom, thighs, and under his arms, then put on his nappy and dress him.

Bathing an older baby

When you use the big bath, bear in mind that your baby could drown in just an inch of water (see p. 123). Take the following precautions to avoid accidents:

■ Have all equipment on the floor beside the bath and change your baby there. It's safer than carrying a wet slippery baby to a chair.

■ Put a non-slip mat in the bath.

■ Kneel on the floor to support your baby, and to prevent straining your back.

■ Never leave your baby alone in the bath, even if she can sit up.

YOU WILL NEED

Non-slip bath mat

Sponge or flannel

Baby bath solution and shampoo

Face shield
to protect her eyes from shampoo

Towel

Nappy and clean clothes

Once your baby is three to four months old and has good head control, you could start using the big bath. Once she has got used to it, she will appreciate the extra room to play in the water. The same principles apply – keep your baby warm before and after the bath, don't over-fill the bath and check that the water isn't too hot.

Using the big bath

Making the transition from the baby bath to the big bath can cause some babies distress, while others love it. It's a good idea to begin by putting the baby bath into the big bath the first few times so that the change is gradual and less frightening. Once your baby has got used to it and can sit up in the bath by herself, she'll begin to look forward to it as part of her routine, and enjoy bath-time games and play (see opposite). You'll find bath time can become a riotous affair with lots of shouts and splashing, but the problems may come when you want to get her out! It's advisable to make bath time a part of your baby's overall bedtime routine (see p. 103) so that it acts as a clear signal to her that the day is over.

The big bath
Kneel or sit beside the bath so that you're at the right level to hold and support your baby easily.

Giving your baby a towel bath

Cleaning your baby by towel bathing her is a halfway house between topping and tailing (see p. 90) and a proper bath. It's a useful method if your baby isn't feeling well or if she gets distressed when she's having a bath. It's also much quicker and more convenient for you, for those times when she needs a thorough wash, but you're short of time.

Top half first
■ Collect the same equipment as for topping and tailing (see p. 90).
■ Undress her to her nappy and wrap her lower half in a towel. Wash her face, neck, and upper body and pat dry.

Lower half
■ Put a clean vest on your baby. Remove the nappy, wash her legs and feet, followed by her nappy area.
■ Dry your baby thoroughly, then put on a clean nappy and clothes.

Making bath time fun

Older babies really enjoy bath time and it's an excellent time to catch up on your baby's developing personality and skills if you aren't able to be with her during the day. Bath time is a wonderful opportunity for creative play and you can use it to help stimulate her development in a variety of ways. Babies love the freedom to sit in the warm water and you'll find that your baby will be endlessly fascinated by filling things, pouring, and splashing water. This really is learning through play – your baby is finding out about the properties of water and other liquids. Help her to do this by:

■ Using simple household items like plastic cups and jugs or spoons and sieves to show your baby what holds water and what doesn't, and how water can be poured and stirred.

■ Introducing floating toys such as boats or traditional bath ducks that your baby will enjoy handling.

■ Having fun with your baby by taking her into the bath with you; have a lovely skin to skin soak together. Keep the water at an even temperature with a slow trickle from the tap – you should be lying with your head at the opposite end from the taps.

Hairwashing

Even though your baby may love her bath, hairwashing may continue to be a problem if she hates having water poured on to her head or over her face, especially if it goes in her eyes. Don't worry; this is very common. Take your time in getting your baby used to water on her head and face; make a game of it by dripping tiny amounts over her head from time to time. Until she's more confident, you can simply sponge her hair clean or wipe it with a face cloth.

Some babies love having water on their faces and don't even mind it in their eyes. If your baby likes water, you can use the bath shower attachment or a cup to rinse her hair and make a game of it. But even the mildest baby shampoo will sting your baby's eyes a little, so it's advisable to use a face shield to keep the soap and water out of her eyes until she's old enough to keep them shut or to hold her head back for you. Dry her hair with a towel and brush it with a soft brush.

Trouble-free hairwashing
Use a simple face shield to keep water and shampoo away from your baby's face and eyes. Pour water gently so there's no danger of it splashing back.

Father

Your baby will grow to love bath time, particularly if it is her special time with you. Encourage this bonding by handling her with confidence; the more often you do it, the less nervous she (and you) will be. Giving a bath is a positive way of contributing to your baby's care, and she'll know you're an equal partner in her life with her mother.

Make the most of bath time

■ When you have a bath with your baby, lay her on your chest half in and half out of the water. Smile and talk to her all the time as you clean her.

■ Splash water gently over her body carefully, avoiding her face. This way your baby will learn to enjoy, and be unafraid of, water.

■ Allow plenty of time; a bath is not much fun for either of you if you have to rush. Remember, sharing a bath with your baby is also a good and enjoyable way for you to wind down after a stressful day at work.

Dressing your baby

Choosing clothes

Look for clothes that are simple to put on and take off, and quick to wash and dry:

■ Choose roomy garments, with loose elastic at the cuffs.

■ Snap fasteners are better than buttons. Avoid ribbons as they may be difficult to undo.

■ Avoid pure wool, which may irritate skin. Choose non-irritating fabrics, such as cotton.

■ Only get machine-washable, colour-fast clothing.

■ Always look for labels that indicate clothes are inflammable.

■ Clothes can safely be bought secondhand, but check for inflammability, shrinkage, and the condition of fastenings.

■ Nightdresses are quick to put on and allow easy access to the nappy.

■ Buy adequate protective clothing to avoid sun damage (see p. 118).

YOU WILL NEED

BASICS FOR A NEW BABY

6–8 vests or body suits

6–8 stretch suits

2–3 cardigans

2–3 pairs of socks

Protective clothing and sunhat for sun protection

1 blanket or shawl

USEFUL EXTRAS

2 pairs of scratch mittens

2 nightdresses

All-in-one pram suit

Babies grow out of clothes very quickly in the early months so don't spend a lot of money on first-size babywear. Many of the presents you will be given for your baby will be tiny outfits that will only fit your child for the first few weeks, so you should concentrate on buying a few practical, simple items for the first four months.

How to dress and undress your baby

Many parents are nervous of dressing their very young baby, particularly when it involves handling his "wobbly" head with its soft fontanelle (see p. 55). Always lay him down on his back on a changing mat or towel to dress and undress him; it's safer and you'll both feel more secure. Although your baby doesn't know day from night, nightdresses may be easier to use when he's tiny. By the time he's three or four months old, he will have developed some head control, and you can safely dress and undress him on your lap, if you haven't had the confidence to do so previously.

Putting on your baby's vest

Vests are probably the most awkward items of clothing to put on a tiny baby, because they have to be put on over his head, which is the biggest yet least manageable part of his body. Most vests are now designed with wide, "envelope" necks or shoulder fastenings to make it easier for you to slide the vest over his head.

1 Lay your baby on a flat, firm surface on his back. Stretch the neck opening of the vest or body suit as wide open as you can with both hands.

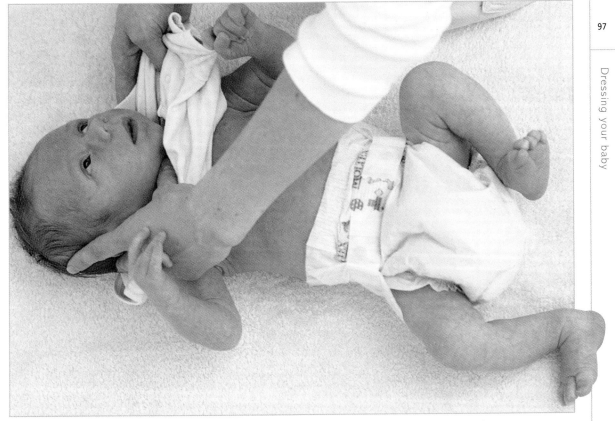

2 Slide the vest over your baby's head, gently lifting his head up to bring it over to the back of his neck.

3 Widen each sleeve or armhole with your fingers and bring your baby's arms through, fist first, one at a time. Draw the vest down over his body.

Practical clothes for older babies

Once your baby is sitting up, and especially when she becomes mobile, clothes have to be robust and comfortable, as well as machine-washable. Look for:

■ Bigger sizes, especially with outdoor clothes, so movement isn't restricted and she doesn't grow out of them too quickly.

■ Clothes that have easy access to the nappy area, such as dungarees or all-in-one suits with snap fasteners, or tights.

■ Lightweight clothing to protect your baby's skin from the sun. Use a wide-brimmed sunhat and shirts with sleeves and collars.

■ Soft boots or socks with non-slip soles for when she starts to pull herself up to stand.

Putting on a stretch suit

Stretch suits are very practical and economical items of clothing for you to buy for your baby. They're particularly useful at first because they allow freedom of movement, easy access to the nappy area, keep your baby warm but not too hot, and they are simple to put on even the tiniest baby. They are ideal for all-day use for the first three to four months and can also be used as sleep wear when your baby is older. To put on a stretch suit, follow the steps illustrated here; to take it off, reverse all the steps, beginning by undoing all the fastenings.

1 *Undo all the fastenings of the stretch suit and lay it on a flat surface. Then, lay your baby on top of the suit so that her neck lines up with the neck of the suit.*

2 *Put your baby's legs into the legs of the suit feet first, one at a time. Fasten the suit under the nappy area so that she can't kick her way out again.*

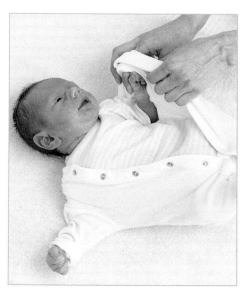

3 *To put her arms in, roll back one arm of the stretch suit, holding it open with one hand. Then guide your baby's arm, fist first, into the arm of the suit and roll the sleeve down into place. Repeat with the other arm and do up the rest of the fastenings.*

Dressing older babies
*Once your baby can sit up, you'll find
she's a lot easier to dress. But she may
also wriggle and protest when you want
to put on her clothes, so hold her firmly
while you dress her. You could make a
game of it to keep her occupied.*

When your baby sleeps

Mother

If you find you're trying to get your baby to sleep as much as possible, ask yourself why.

Does your baby need to sleep?
Trying to get your baby to sleep when he doesn't need to is pointless. He's longing for your company, so talk and play with him instead; put him in a baby chair so that he can watch what you're doing. Research has shown that even young babies are very receptive to interaction with their parents, and with increased stimulation overall, your baby is much more likely to sleep more soundly and for longer.

You need rest too
You may become overwrought if you're suffering from lack of sleep. Being over-tired builds resentment, makes you irritable and liable to get things out of proportion. If you're exhausted, express breast milk (see p. 83) so your partner can do the night-time feeds for a couple of days so that you can get some rest.

YOU WILL NEED

FOR THE FIRST THREE MONTHS:

4 small cellular cot blankets
as cotton is better than wool

6 flat cotton top sheets

6 fitted cotton mattress sheets

Spare mattress (optional)

Portable Moses basket, cradle, or carrycot (see p. 75)

Young babies spend up to 14 hours of any 24-hour period asleep. Unfortunately, this doesn't often coincide with their parents' sleeping pattern, because it takes a few months for babies to learn the difference between night and day.

How babies sleep

The way babies fall asleep differs from adults; adults can crash suddenly, whereas babies sleep lightly for about 20 minutes, then go through a transitional stage before reaching deep sleep. Nothing will wake them, until they've had enough sleep. This means that babies who are simply "put down" will not necessarily go to sleep peacefully. You may need to nurse your baby to sleep for quite a while, so try to be patient, particularly at night, when you're longing to go back to bed yourself.

Where should a baby sleep?

Where a baby sleeps isn't important to him to start with. He won't automatically fall asleep when put into a darkened bedroom; light doesn't bother him at all. He's much more likely to be disturbed by being too hot or too cold. Your baby will be happiest going to sleep hearing your voices and the household noises that he is used to in the background so let him sleep in a Moses basket or carrycot in whichever room you happen to be.

Using a baby monitor

If you leave your baby in another room, set up a baby monitor so that you can hear him as soon as he wakes. He may feel disturbed by the silence when you leave the room, and this could make him more fretful; leave the door open so he can hear you moving around – unless you have a cat that may climb into the cot. Avoid going back into the room once your baby is asleep; your smell could wake him, so resist the temptation to check him too frequently.

Use a Moses basket
While your baby is small, put him to bed in a Moses basket or carrycot. You can then keep him in the room where you are most of the time, while he sleeps.

Putting your baby to bed
Lay your baby down to sleep on his back, supporting his head and body with both hands. Make sure you don't let him become too hot (see p. 102).

Encouraging longer sleeps at night

A young baby needs food at regular intervals, so he'll wake for a feed when his body tells him to. The way to encourage your baby to sleep for a stretch (four, then rising to five or six, hours) during the night is to make sure he's taken in sufficient calories to last

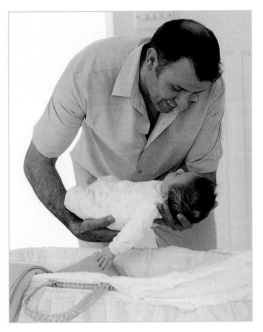

that long. This means feeding him whenever he shows he's hungry during the day. As he steadily gains weight, he can go longer between feeds and by about six weeks he could be sleeping for at least one period of about six hours – hopefully during the night. When he wakes for a night feed make as little fuss as possible – feed him in bed; if he needs changing, do it quickly in a dim light. Don't make this a time for chatting and games and he'll learn that waking at night doesn't bring any special privileges.

Rescue package for a sleepless baby

Night after night of broken sleep is wearing for parents, and a young baby who perhaps only "catnaps" during the day makes it hard to catch up. Use this checklist of strategies to reduce unnecessary fatigue.

Be aware of background noise Don't shield your baby from the sounds of your home. They won't disturb his sleep; in fact some babies are soothed by the rhythmic noise of household appliances!

Keep him close to you At night, put your baby's cot next to your bed so that you can take him into your bed to feed him. Then put him back in his cot afterwards with minimum disturbance.

Play music Babies respond well to soothing music (classical is best). Keep certain pieces for when your baby shows signs of tiredness.

Carry him in a sling Rhythmic movement can hasten sleep, but your baby may wake up when you stop moving. Carry him around in a sling when you're in the house, whenever possible. As well as being relaxed by the constant movement, your baby will be comforted by your body and your smell if he is this close to you.

Give him plenty of fresh air Fresh air is said to tire babies out. In fact, it's probably the stimulation they receive from the sounds and sights outside, or simply the movement of trees or branches, that makes them sleepy.

Father

Understanding the way your baby's sleep patterns work will help you to tune into his and your partner's needs.

Being realistic
Your new baby will probably sleep less than you think. He spends 50–80 per cent of the time in light sleep, when he wakes very easily. His sleep cycle – light, deep, light – is shorter than an adult's sleep cycle, so he's vulnerable to waking each time he passes from one sleep state to another. He's programmed to wake up for all kinds of reasons – when he's wet, hot, cold, unwell – because his survival depends on it. It's good to know that light sleep is likely to make your baby more intelligent because the brain remains active and it enhances brain development.

Having a sleep routine
Your baby has to be deeply asleep before he'll settle so try a tranquillizing sleep routine – gentle rocking, quiet songs, and talking. He's deeply asleep when his eyelids don't twitch and his limbs feel limp. Lay him down and gently pat his shoulder at about 60 beats a minute for a few minutes.

Getting home late
If your baby is asleep when you get home from work, ask your partner if your baby can nap in the afternoon so that he's awake later. Be patient if this isn't possible. Try getting up earlier and spending time with your baby before work.

Safe sleeping

The way babies are put to bed has an effect on Sudden Infant Death Syndrome or what's commonly known as "cot death". The number of babies dying has halved due to better awareness about this:

■ Stop smoking – and NEVER let anyone smoke in the same room as your baby. Don't let anyone smoke in your home at all.

■ Always lay your baby on her back to sleep so that her breathing is unimpeded and she can lose heat from her front, face, and head.

■ Don't let your baby get too hot, as she isn't very efficient at controlling her temperature. If the air temperature feels hot to you, it's very hot for her.

■ Don't increase the amount of bedding when your baby is unwell.

■ Never over-wrap your baby. Cover her with a cotton sheet and cellular blankets according to the room temperature (see right).

■ Lay your baby in the "feet-to-foot" position at the end of the cot so that she can't wriggle down under the blankets and get too hot (see below).

Feet to foot
Lay your baby with her feet touching the foot of the cot, even if it means her head is halfway down the mattress.

Wakeful babies

Most babies develop a routine of sleeping for perhaps two hours in the morning and again in the afternoon, but there are always exceptions. While wakeful babies can be trying, they reward you in the end as they're usually very bright and affectionate, so don't be downhearted. Your baby is wakeful because she loves you and craves your friendship; she doesn't mean to starve you of sleep, she just wants to learn and be sociable. Every minute spent awake with you, she'll be forging new links with the world and developing many skills. Think about this, too, when she's awake during the day; if she isn't tired, why should she sleep? From her point of view, it's much better for her to stay with you, so don't be surprised if she cries when you leave her.

What you can try

■ Keep her temperature even; touch her skin to check that she isn't too cold or hot, add or remove blankets if necessary (see below). Check the room temperature; a temperature of about 18°C (65°F) is comfortable.
■ Change her nappy if it's wet or soiled and soothe the nappy area with a bland nappy cream (zinc oxide), if necessary.
■ Use a rocking cradle or push her rhythmically in her pram.
■ Play her a tape of the human heartbeat, the sound she heard in the womb.
■ Play her music you listened to during pregnancy, or an old-fashioned musical box with a simple repetitive melody can be really effective.
■ Play her a tape of you and your partner quietly talking.
■ Put the cot on alternate sides of the bed each night so that you can take it in turns to see to her. Talk to her and rock her; you don't need to pick her up.
■ If she's obviously reluctant to sleep, get her up and put her in her baby chair where she can see you.
■ Hang a mobile over her cot so she's got something interesting to watch when she wakes up. A mobile that plays music is ideal.
■ Fix a "baby gym", with different noises and textures, across her cot or attach it to the bars so she can reach for it when she's bored.

What bedding to use

TEMPERATURE	WHAT TO USE
14°C (57°F)	A sheet and four blankets or more
16°C (60°F)	A sheet and three blankets
18°C (65°F)	A sheet and two blankets
20°C (68°F)	A sheet and one blanket
24°C (75°F)	A sheet only

Blankets and bedding

Use enough bedding to keep her comfortably warm (see left). When your baby is under 12 months, don't give her a pillow, and don't use quilts, duvets, or baby nests because they also prevent loss of heat.

Sleep and your older baby

As your baby grows, her sleep pattern will gradually change; she'll begin to stay awake and alert for longer periods during the day, even after feeds. When she's being stimulated with play and talk from you, she'll start needing longer periods of sleep to recharge her energy levels. The trick is to persuade her that these longer sleep periods should be at night, to align with your own.

Establishing a bedtime routine

Your baby may well get upset at bedtime – she could be anxious about being separated from you (see p. 162), or she may simply want to continue playing, so establishing a bedtime routine is essential to build her confidence and to help her learn that there is a time when playtime has to stop. Set up your own routine at a time to suit all of you – for example, if you're working you may want it to be a little later – but try not to vary the routine, whatever time you do it. A suggested routine might be as follows:
- Give her the final meal of the day – preferably not her main meal (see p. 113).
- Give her a bath without too much romping, and change her into her nightclothes.
- Spend a quiet time in your baby's room; sing gentle songs, or read a story (depending on her age and stage of development).
- Give her the last breastfeed (unless your baby still wakes at night).
- Lay her in her cot, with any comforter or security object she has become attached to, turn the dimmer switch down low, then sit quietly with her for a minute or two.
- Go out of the room quietly, saying good night, and leaving the door open.

The bedtime routine
Allow time for quiet play with your baby, with books and toys. Remove hard objects when you lay her down.

YOU WILL NEED

FOR 3–12 MONTHS:

4 cellular cot blankets

6 flat cotton top sheets

6 fitted cotton bottom sheets

Full-size cot (see p. 74)

NURSERY EXTRAS:

Dimmer switch
for the nursery light

Baby monitor

Cot toys (see below)

CD or tape of soothing music

Daytime naps for your older baby

As babies grow older they sleep less and less, but up to 12 months your baby may still nap in the day. Up to the age of three many toddlers still rest during the day:

- To help your baby relax and drop off, put her in her favourite place, which may not be her room. Make sure she has any special comforter or security object with her. Play calming music, let her have toys and books, and keep her within earshot so she can hear you bustling about. If she calls out to you, it's probably only for reassurance, so calmly call back.

- If she doesn't want to sleep, that's okay; just make it a quiet time when she can sit in her cot and play. But never let her cry for longer than a few minutes without going to her. If she's unhappy, that defeats the purpose of the nap.

- If your baby falls asleep in the car, or her pram, never wake her suddenly. Like you, she'll need time to adjust. Never leave her asleep alone in the car or in her pram outside a shop.

When your baby cries

What makes a newborn cry

The circumstances of your baby's birth may affect the amount that he cries. It helps if you understand the possible underlying causes of a fretful baby's behaviour. Try not to become impatient with him as it will be out of his control. He'll begin to settle as he gets older. Your baby may cry more:

■ If you had a general anaesthetic.

■ If you had a forceps delivery.

■ If he was born after a long labour, after which babies tend to sleep in short bursts.

■ If he is a boy. Boys may cry more than girls in new situations. Try not to make the mistake of some parents of boys who have been known to attend to them less, in the mistaken belief that it will "toughen them up".

All young babies cry at some time during the day. Whether it's a subdued grizzle or a full-throated roar, a baby's cries are his only means of communicating his needs. Having said that, there is no doubt that a persistently fretful baby can be a strain for parents, so it's worth thinking about the underlying causes. Look upon crying as conversation rather than an irritant designed to upset you.

Responding to your baby's cries

Research shows that babies do better if you respond promptly when they cry. It's a mistake to think of a baby as "good" if he doesn't cry much and one who does as "naughty", because a baby's cries have nothing to do with good or bad behaviour. Responding to your baby's cries is a crucial part of bonding – your attitude to your baby in the first few weeks forms the blueprint for your future relationship with him, and for all his future relationships. He'll learn kindness and sympathy from you, which is why you should always answer his cry, whatever anyone else tells you. A loved baby will be secure and when the time comes he will be able to take separations in his stride if he's learned that you will answer his needs. A baby who's left to cry is more likely to grow up clingy and attention-seeking because he's learned that he has to work harder to make you respond to him.

Why you should respond promptly

■ Your baby is longing to communicate with you, but his repertoire is limited to start with. Crying is the only way he can convey his feelings so don't just ignore him.
■ Your baby will develop good communication skills and outgoing, friendly behaviour.
■ It will make him secure and self-confident.
■ It will not "spoil" your baby or teach him "bad habits"; you can't spoil a baby this way, only love him.

What happens if you don't respond

■ Not responding to your baby's cries is a form of rejection, and your baby will soon sense this.
■ If you don't respond, he will cry for longer, continuing until he gets the attention he needs.
■ He will be driven to create a pattern of frequent crying.

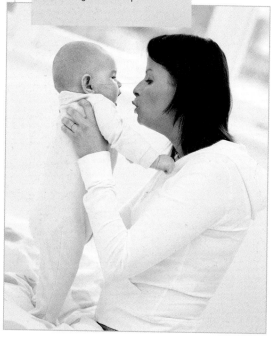

Giving your baby attention
All babies thrive on the company of their parents, and will cry because they miss the comfort of your presence. Try to give your baby as much contact as you can.

Persistent crying

Some young babies have prolonged bouts of crying, which typically occur in the late afternoon and evening, and can last for anything between two and four hours. Babies often begin this pattern of persistent crying at about three weeks of age, and will usually have grown out of it by about three months. This pattern of crying has become known as "colic", because as the baby becomes increasingly upset and difficult to soothe, he may often pull his legs up and arch his back as if experiencing abdominal pain. In fact it's probably misleading to give it any special name, because there doesn't seem to be any known cause for this pattern.

Getting through it

A baby who is persistently fretful may cry readily at other times, not just in the evening. However, the evening pattern of crying can be a particular strain for parents, especially if one or both of you has been working during the day. It may be that your baby senses and reacts to your tiredness at this time. Although this crying pattern may only last three months, this period can seem never-ending to new parents who have to deal with their baby's distress day after day. Trying some of the suggestions for soothing your baby given below and overleaf should help you through this difficult time.

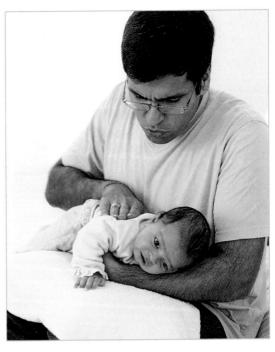

Soothing "colic"
If your baby cries persistently, you may find that laying him across your lap makes him more comfortable. Support his head and then gently massage his back and legs.

What to do when your baby cries

PROBLEM	DESCRIPTION	WHAT YOU SHOULD DO
Hunger	If your baby has been asleep for two or three hours and begins to cry insistently, he is probably ready for a feed.	Give him a feed. If he cries afterwards, he may not have had enough so offer more. If it's very hot, offer him a drink of water.
Discomfort	A cold, wet, or soiled nappy could be uncomfortable enough to cause your baby to cry. Your baby may also be too hot or too cold.	Check and change his nappy if necessary. Treat nappy rash (see p. 86). Check bedding and air temperature (see p. 102).
Insecurity	A jerky movement, bright light, or sudden noise can startle a young baby. Many babies are also upset by being undressed and bathed.	Cuddle your baby to promote security. Handle your baby as gently and firmly as possible when dressing or bathing.
Fatigue	Your baby will cry when he is tired, and may become quite upset when over-tired, which can make it doubly difficult to soothe him.	Create a soothing bedtime ritual (see p. 103) of rocking or stroking when you lay him in his cot, or push him in his pram.
Boredom	As your baby grows, he is more aware of people and cries because he wants company.	Cuddle him; at 4–6 weeks, sit him in a baby chair where he can see and hear you.
Pain	Your baby may have earache, abdominal pain, or persistent nappy rash.	Contact your doctor if he's hard to soothe, off his feed, or appears unwell (see p. 120).

Soothing your crying baby

Use a dummy

Encourage your baby to find his thumb or use a dummy or pacifier. There is no stigma attached to a baby sucking a dummy, but make sure it is sterilized and never sweeten it with honey or juice. However, it may only be a temporary relief so it's probably better to look for the underlying cause of the crying, keeping the dummy as a last resort.

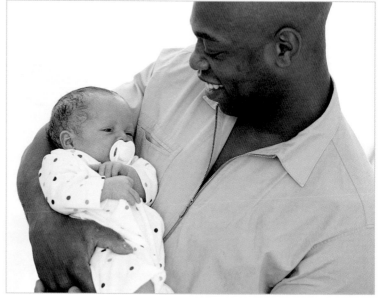

Hold upright

Bring your baby up against your shoulder and gently rub her back. (Put a cloth on your shoulder to protect your clothes from any regurgitated milk.) Walk around, gently singing or talking to your baby.

Carry your baby in a sling

Put your baby in a sling and carry him around with you. Your baby will love being close to you and will enjoy the movement as you walk around.

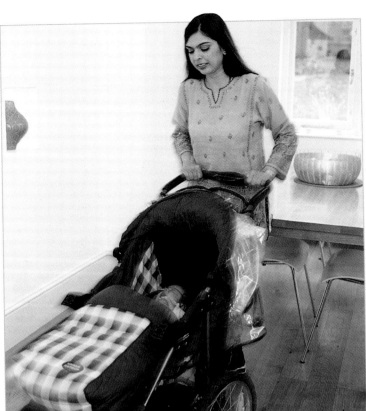

Comfort with movement

Most babies are soothed by regular movement: it was what they were used to in the womb. Put your baby in a rocking cradle (make sure it conforms to safety standards) or in her pram and gently rock her backwards and forwards while you sit and watch television or eat a meal.

Lay your baby on your chest

Lie on the bed or sofa, well supported by cushions. Lay your baby on your chest and gently rub her back. It will relax both of you, but never fall asleep with your baby like this because of the increased risk of cot death.

Accepting help from others

Sometimes a crying baby can make parents who are already tired from broken nights feel quite desperate: this is the time to seek help. Don't ever feel that you are failing as parents if you accept assistance; countless other parents will have felt as frustrated and exhausted as you because their babies have cried a lot and have been difficult to soothe. Jump at the chance if your baby's grandparents or other friends or relations offer to look after your baby for a while so you can get out on your own for a couple of hours' break, or enjoy some unbroken sleep. If they don't offer any help, don't be afraid to ask them. There's no need to feel guilty – they will be glad to have the chance to relieve you and it will help you to get things back into perspective. It's a great help, too, to talk to health or baby care professionals, who are there to support you.

Comforting your older baby

As your baby grows and becomes more aware of her surroundings, her pattern of crying will change because it's not the only way she can communicate with you now. Her reasons for crying will also be easier for you to both predict and interpret. You'll begin to distinguish between frustration, hunger, pain, or loneliness. Even when your baby is beginning to become more mobile and independent, the best way to comfort her if she's unhappy is with your company, hugs, and cuddles.

Comforters

Towards their first birthday, many babies will have become attached to a particular comforter – a favourite soft toy, a cloth, or blanket – that probably helps them sleep and that may be grabbed when they're feeling a bit insecure and upset. Other babies become attached to a dummy or suck their thumbs (see p. 106). This is perfectly normal and there's no point in distressing your baby by removing a comforter on the grounds that it is a "bad habit"; it isn't. As your baby's confidence and independence develop after her first birthday, she'll gradually become less dependent on her comforter, although it may take a year or so. It's a good idea to have some spares in case the main one needs a wash.

Teething and crying

Your baby's teeth will normally start to come through from about six months (see p. 154), so she'll dribble a lot and her gums will occasionally be sore. Your baby may become rather grizzly when she's teething and it's usually quite obvious if she's uncomfortable; she'll want to chew a lot and may have a hot, red area on her cheek. However, it isn't a good idea always to blame persistent crying on "teething", when in fact your baby may be bored (see right), or even unwell (see p. 120).

Helpful grandparents
Grandparents know that you need a break and they enjoy developing their own relationship with the baby.

Troubleshooting

There are lots of reasons why an older baby may cry.

She's bored
Your baby may cry from boredom if left alone, unable to hear your voice and with nothing to look at or play with. You are her favourite playmate so keep her where she can see you and you can talk to her, and don't leave her for long periods alone in her cot if she's crying. Some babies do play happily in their cots for a while after waking, so leave toys and books within reach.

She's frustrated
As your baby grows, her desire to do things outstrips her ability to do them and so she gets frustrated and often starts to cry as a result. She may also cry if you don't let her have something she wants. Change her toys frequently – her attention span is still short. Find time to play with her (see p. 174).

She's frightened
At about six months your baby will cry when she's separated from you and she'll be nervous of other people, even when she knows them well. Right from the start, get her used to seeing you leave the room and come back in again. This way she'll gradually learn that she can trust you always to return to her. Make sure she meets lots of other people before she reaches this stage and learns that even if you leave her with someone else for a while, that you always come back.

She's ill or has hurt herself
If your baby hurts herself, you'll know at once from her cry, but it may be more difficult to tell when she's ill. See pages 120–123 for what you should do if your baby is ill or has an accident.

Touch and massage

Massage tips

Babies love massage as much as you do. It's a good way to calm an unsettled baby because it feels nice to him. It's also an expression of love and your baby knows it, and has the added advantage of relaxing you too. Always prepare yourself carefully for massage:

■ Make sure the room is really warm. Lay your baby on a soft blanket or towel.

■ Play his favourite music or a recording of a heartbeat. Talk in a low, gentle voice or sing a song quietly.

■ Although massaging your baby's skin directly is best, many younger babies don't like being undressed. If your baby is one of these, dress him in a cotton vest or similar garment, through which you can easily feel his body.

■ Work around his body, massaging both sides with slow even strokes. Keep your face close to your baby's and look into his eyes as you massage him. This is very powerful for both of you.

Being touched is an essential part of the bonding process that helps young creatures to thrive. Premature babies gain more weight on lambswool blankets than cotton ones because it feels as if they're being stroked when they move and they feel contented.

The importance of touch

Your baby is born sociable and he craves physical affection. This is best communicated through touch, cuddles, being gently held, kissed, and nuzzled. It's important, therefore, that you're both completely free with your physical affection from the start. Your baby longs to be close to you and to be carried, and he will cry less and be more easily comforted if you carry him. Remember also that being carried in a sling close to your body feels like being cuddled to a baby (see p. 106), and allows you to do other things at the same time. Small babies are much stronger than you think so be firm, but avoid sudden jerky movements – your baby may think he's falling and he'll be startled rather than comforted. As your baby gets older you can be more robust with him; he'll enjoy tickling and rolling about on the floor with you, but don't overdo it if he becomes at all distressed, and don't blame him if he pulls your hair or scratches you – under a year old he won't know that it hurts.

Massage

▽ **Neck and shoulders**
Using fingers and thumbs, gently massage your baby's neck from her ears to her shoulders and from her chin to her chest. Then stroke her shoulders from her neck outwards.

△ **Chest and abdomen**
Gently stroke down your baby's chest following the line of her ribs. You can use one hand and then the other in a continuous stroking movement, but don't press too hard. Massage her abdomen in a circular motion with one hand, working outwards from the navel. Talk and sing softly to her all the time.

△ **Arms**
Lay your baby on her back. Stroke down each arm using your fingertips, first from wrist to elbow, then from elbow to shoulder. Gently squeeze all along her arm, starting from the top.

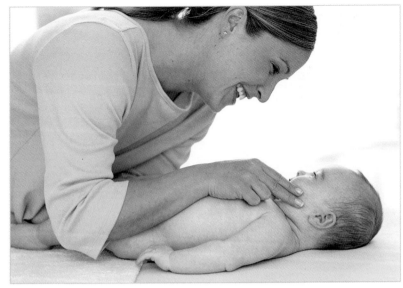

Physical affection

As children grow up, they need the reassuring and loving embrace of caring parents more, not less as some parents may think. They should be encouraged to express their emotions – boys just as much as girls. Indeed, a child's ability to achieve some kind of emotional stability is more or less determined before the age of 12 months – a sobering thought, but nonetheless true.

Emotional feedback

A child learns to master his emotions by getting sympathetic feedback from adults that mirrors the emotions he's feeling. If your baby holds out a hurt hand, what helps most – as any parent knows – is lots of sympathy, "kissing better", and cuddles. A child doesn't grow out of the need for physical affection because these positive signs of parents' care are necessary for emotional growth. If you deprive a child of physical affection, you deprive him of an essential "growth vitamin".

Your baby needs you both

This applies equally to both parents, and continues throughout babyhood, childhood, and, in some cases, into adolescence. Nothing should be allowed to discourage loving parents – both mothers and fathers – from doing what their child needs them to do.

△ **Head**
Using both hands, lightly massage the crown of your baby's head using a circular motion, then stroke down the sides of her face. With your fingertips, massage her forehead and cheeks, working from the centre outwards. This is particularly calming for a fretful baby.

▷ **Feet and toes**
Rub your baby's ankles and feet, stroking from heel to toe, and then concentrate on each toe individually. Your baby may kick her legs and curl her toes while you're doing this. If she's less than three months old show her her toes – it will help her to realize they're part of herself (see p. 159).

(see p. 159)

◁ **Back**
Once you've massaged your baby on her front, gently turn her over on to her tummy and massage her back. Using both hands, run your palms down her back from under her arms to her buttocks, pressing gently against her spine with your thumbs. Talk to her all the time, as she can't see your face.

▷ **Legs**
Massage your baby's legs one at a time. Place your free hand on her tummy, then gently squeeze her leg from the thigh down to the ankle.

Weaning

Trouble-free weaning

Knowing what food to give and when to give it, will help you to introduce it with confidence.

What age to start
Don't start weaning until at least six months; before that, a baby's digestion can't cope.

What to offer
Offer a simple, semi-liquid food once a day. Only introduce one taste at a time. Start with a non-wheat cereal mixed with her normal milk, as it's closest to what she's used to, then gradually offer pureed fruit or vegetables. Only introduce food at a second meal when she happily takes the first. Milk is still her main food for at least the first three months.

How much to give
Start with a teaspoonful a day for a week, as her digestive system needs time to adapt, then go on to two, before giving solids at another meal as well. Use the suggested weaning schedule (see opposite) as a guide. Once she's used to solids, she may prefer them first, then her milk feed.

YOU WILL NEED

TO START WEANING:

2–3 fabric plastic-backed bibs

2–3 feeding spoons and a beaker

FOR THE OLDER BABY:

2–3 moulded plastic bibs

2 non-spill plastic bowls

Two-handled training beaker

Weaning may seem like a huge step. There are so many questions: when to start, what to give, how much to give, but it needn't feel so daunting if you try to think positively and see it as encouraging your baby's independence rather than as an obstacle.

Introducing solids
Weaning is rarely a problem from the baby's point of view, but some babies take longer than others to get used to having solid food as well as their normal milk feeds. It really doesn't matter – until six months, milk is enough for many babies' complete nutritional needs. However, after that time they will need the extra calories, vitamins, and minerals in solid food, as there won't be enough for them in milk alone (look at the weaning chart opposite for a suggested pattern of feeding).

When you introduce her first solids, choose a feed when you know she's usually alert and awake – for instance, at midday, halfway through her milk feed. Sit your baby on your lap or in her baby chair and offer tiny amounts at first on the tip of a sterilized plastic spoon. Don't force it into her mouth; brush her upper lip with the spoon and let her suck it off. She might splutter and dribble a bit the first few times, but keep trying.

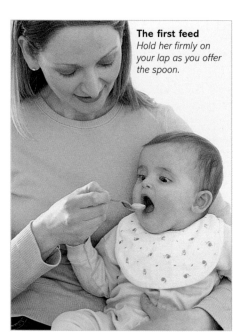

The first feed
Hold her firmly on your lap as you offer the spoon.

Extra fluid
Remember milk is a food, it isn't a drink, and so from the moment mixed feeding is introduced, your baby will also need another fluid to drink from a bottle or cup. Cooled boiled water is best. Start with 15 ml (½ fl oz) of fluids between feeds, increasing gradually according to your baby's needs.

Trouble-free meal times
Just as it was important not to get hung up about how much milk your baby drank when you were establishing breastfeeding, try not to worry now about how much she is eating, or indeed about how much is going on the floor! It's going to be messy – until the age of five or six all children

Weaning schedule from six months

FEEDS	WEEK 1	WEEK 3	WEEK 6
1st feed	Milk feed	Milk feed	Milk feed
2nd feed	Half milk feed 1 tsp cereal Finish milk feed	Half milk feed 1–2 tsps cereal Finish milk feed	3–4 tsps cereal Milk feed
3rd feed	Milk feed	Half milk feed 1–2 tsps pureed fruit or veg Finish milk feed	2–3 tsps pureed chicken and veg 2–3 tsps pureed fruit Water
4th feed	Milk feed	Milk feed	2–3 tsps pureed fruit or veg Milk feed
5th feed	Milk feed	Milk feed	Milk feed

are messy eaters – so be philosophical and clear up afterwards. As long as meal times are happy and relaxed, don't worry and don't allow them to become battlefields. You can't win – your baby simply refuses to eat (you can't force her) and the battle is lost. She's cute enough to learn that food is a weapon she can use to manipulate you, so don't join in the struggle.

Enough to eat?

Even if you think your baby isn't taking enough food, she is. Don't make the mistake of forcing adult standards on her. Think of a balanced diet in terms of what you offer your baby over a period of time, such as a week, and make sure it has variety; accept that there's bound to be a certain amount of waste. Don't worry about fads either; she's eating what her body needs.

Starting self-feeding

Self-feeding is an important step to your baby's independence, so be patient with her:

■ Use shaped plastic bibs that catch spilled food, and put a plastic sheet under the high chair.

■ Give your baby her own spoon and offer food that is of a stiff consistency, such as mashed potato or other pureed vegetables, in a non-spill bowl. Never mind that she gets very little at first, she'll have a lot of fun. Have a spare spoon handy so that you can feed her, if needed.

■ Even if she finds a spoon difficult, she'll love feeding herself with finger foods (see p. 117). Finger foods can also keep her busy if the meal isn't quite ready.

■ Above all be flexible; if one food doesn't suit, try another – no single food is essential.

■ Introduce a trainer cup with a spout for drinks as soon as your baby can manage it. Some breastfed babies never accept a bottle and go straight to a cup for water. Others prefer a bottle for water and may take time to get used to a cup.

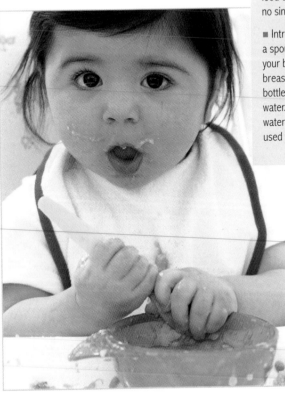

Relaxed self-feeding
While your baby feeds herself, have your own spoon to feed her at the same time.

Best food for your baby

Foods to give

Vary your baby's diet so that he learns to like different tastes and textures. Include:

■ Fruit and vegetables: wash them thoroughly in cold running water, and peel potatoes, carrots, apples and peaches to avoid the risk of pesticide residues. Aim to give some vitamin C at each meal, whether as fruit, vegetables, or juice, as it helps your baby's body to absorb iron.

■ Milk: from seven months use full-fat cow's milk in cooking. From one year, give as a drink.

■ Meat and fish: try to offer at least one serving every day of lean meat or boneless fish.

■ Protein in the form of low fibre foods such as cheese or tofu, if your baby has a vegetarian diet.

Foods to avoid

Don't worry too much, but do take some sensible precautions:

■ Don't give foods containing wheat flour or gluten before your baby is seven months old as he may find them difficult to digest.

■ Don't add sugar or salt – sugar encourages bad habits and bad teeth; salt is too much for your young baby's kidneys to cope with.

■ Avoid giving your baby soft-boiled eggs until he is about one year old.

■ Very high-fibre breakfast cereals have little place in your baby's diet as they are too difficult to digest.

■ Avoid unpasteurized cheese until your baby is at least two.

To grow and develop well, babies need as varied a diet as possible; research shows that babies who are offered a wide menu to choose from invariably choose a healthy diet and accept varied tastes. On the other hand, if they're only given fast foods and sweet things, they'll inevitably want chips and ketchup with everything.

What your baby needs

To provide for your baby's healthy nutrition, he needs complex carbohydrates from such things as sugar-free cereal, wholemeal bread, potatoes and other vegetables, rice and pasta; protein from lean white meat, fish, and pulses such as beans, and, after he's about seven to nine months, eggs and cheese; and the vitamins and minerals contained in fresh fruit and vegetables. He needs some fat, but he should be able to get enough for his nutritional needs from the other foods you give him, especially milk. Avoid the "empty" calories of sweet foods like biscuits and sugary cereal: look at the food pyramid below to see the proportions of each type of food your baby needs for healthy growth and development.

Joining family meals

As soon as your baby is sitting in his high chair he can join you at the table for meals. The sooner you can include your baby in this, the sooner

The food pyramid
Once your baby is used to a variety of tastes, you can plan his diet to include a combination of foods from each group. The "pyramid" of foods shown illustrates the rough proportions of each type that you should try to give to your baby.

Give least of fats, oils, and sugars.

Give a little more of proteins: meat, fish, eggs, cheese, and pulses.

Give your baby fresh fruit and vegetables as part of his daily diet.

Give most of complex carbohydrates: bread, rice, pasta, porridge oats, potatoes (not fried or roast).

your baby will learn by example what is and isn't acceptable behaviour at the table. Some suggested menus for varied, healthy meals are given in the chart below. Remember, a baby's stomach can't hold very much and he'll need to eat more often than an adult. Don't insist he finishes his meals and give him snacks between meals if he needs them.

Suggested menus for an older baby

TIME	DAY 1	DAY 2	DAY 3
Breakfast	Rice cakes Chopped hard-boiled egg Milk	Mashed banana Wholemeal toast fingers Milk	Cottage cheese or yogurt Wholemeal toast Milk
Lunch	Vegetable or chicken casserole Stewed apple Diluted fruit juice	Mashed potato and cheese Pear slices Diluted fruit juice	Strained lentils and mixed vegetables Banana and yogurt Diluted fruit juice
Snack	Toast fingers Peeled peach slices Milk	Rice cakes Peeled apple pieces Milk	Rusks Peeled seedless grapes Milk
Supper	Cauliflower cheese Semolina and fruit puree Diluted fruit juice	Pasta with sauce Yogurt and fruit puree Diluted fruit juice	Tuna, mashed potato, courgettes Rice pudding Diluted fruit juice

Food hygiene

Bacterial infections picked up from badly prepared food can be dangerous for babies and children so be careful with hygiene.

■ Always wash your hands thoroughly before handling any food and after you've handled raw meat.

■ Store raw meat away from other foods in the refrigerator and keep fish in the coldest part.

■ Clean the spout holes of your baby's feeding cup regularly.

■ Always throw away leftover baby food. To avoid waste, prepare very small amounts and freeze in individual containers.

■ Don't reheat cooked baby food unless you're able to bring it to the boil, and cook it thoroughly for at least five minutes to kill bacteria.

■ If you're using a microwave, follow the manufacturer's instructions exactly for times. Stir the food thoroughly to ensure the heat is evenly distributed.

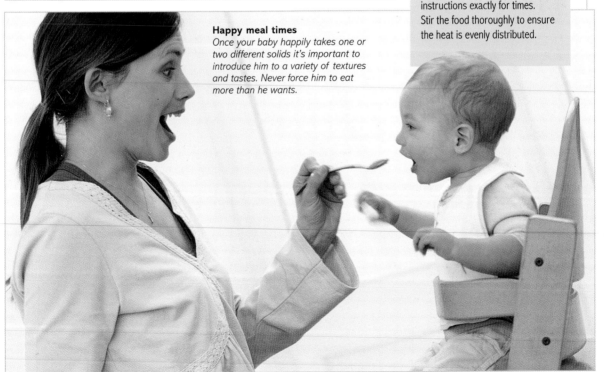

Happy meal times
Once your baby happily takes one or two different solids it's important to introduce him to a variety of textures and tastes. Never force him to eat more than he wants.

Finger foods

If your baby has difficulty using a spoon, she'll enjoy having some finger foods, which are easier to handle. Don't give her very small things that she might choke on and never leave her alone with finger foods.

Make meal times fun

It's frustrating to find that good food is being thrown on the floor or wiped over the high chair, but remember that your baby will eat if she's hungry. If she starts to throw food about, she's probably bored with eating because she's had enough so she's moving on to experiment with the textures instead. Try tempting your older baby to try new tastes with fun food such as the example given here, and she'll learn to see meal times as enjoyable occasions.

Fun foods
Encourage your baby to eat by making her meals look fun and attractive. Make her vegetables into a friendly face, for example.

Finger foods

Once your baby is more than seven or eight months and has been weaned onto solid foods, she'll want to try feeding herself so give her easy-to-hold finger foods. Try:

■ Any fresh fruit that's easy to hold, such as a banana or peach: remember to peel and remove pips.

■ Vegetables, particularly carrots, cut into a shape that's easy to grasp. Don't cut them too small.

■ Pieces of dry, sugar-free cereal.

■ Wholemeal bread or rusks (without grains), toast fingers, bread sticks, or rice cakes.

■ Cooked pasta shapes.

Teething foods
When your baby is teething she'll like to chew and suck to soothe her gums. Any piece of raw vegetable or fruit that's large enough to hold easily and can be sucked or chewed makes a good teething food.

Out and about

There are lots of activities on offer for new parents and their babies:

■ Coffee mornings and parent-and-toddler groups (see p. 138).

■ Music groups for babies.

■ Swimming – ask if your local pool has parent-and-baby sessions.

■ Baby movement classes may be run at leisure centres.

■ Baby massage classes, probably run by a natural health centre or local yoga teacher.

Sun protection

Babies have very little skin pigment so they have much less protection from the sun's ultraviolet rays than adults. Direct sunlight can cause skin damage and skin cancer later in life.

■ Use factor 25 sunscreen/sunblock as well as the natural protection of shade and clothes. Apply the sunscreen to his face, neck, ears, back of hands and feet – not all over his body – 20 minutes before going out.

■ In very hot weather, avoid the sun between 11am and 3pm.

■ Dress him in a wide-brimmed hat and protective clothing.

■ Be aware that your baby is still at risk on cloudy days.

■ Make sure the pram or buggy has a protective hood or umbrella to shade your baby.

Try to get out and about with your baby as soon as you feel up to it. It's good for both of you – it helps get him used to travel, new places, and people, while giving you a change of scene and keeping you in touch with the world outside your home.

First outings

The first few outings that involve more than pushing the pram around to the local shops may seem daunting, and you'll probably be a bit nervous and unsure about how your baby will react. Keep calm and try to relax – your baby will pick up on any anxieties you have. You'll soon become a family of seasoned travellers. The easiest time to be out and about with your baby is while he's small and portable. Make the most of it because when he's toddling and needing constant supervision, the

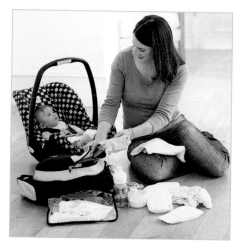

Your travel bag
You'll need a bag large enough for everything you need for your baby. Include factor 25 sunscreen/sunblock to protect your baby against sun damage (see box left).

range of outings will become more limited for a while. Don't be too ambitious on your first outings – go to the park, or for coffee at a friend's house. Make sure you're confident about being away from home with your baby before you go further afield. Travel at off-peak times when there's less congestion, especially if you're travelling by bus or train.

Going shopping

There's no need to leave your baby at home when you go shopping as most supermarkets and department stores now provide facilities to help parents with babies (see chart opposite) and some even have creche facilities. Shopping malls can be more difficult if they are on more than one level, but most have lifts as well as escalators. When you are in the supermarket:

■ Always use a supermarket trolley that is appropriate to your baby's size and weight and strap him into the seat with a harness. Be aware that he may try to grab items off the shelves.

■ Shopping tends to make children hungry and therefore fretful. Avoid this by taking a snack and drink with you. These will provide refreshment for your baby and also keep him occupied.

Shopping with your baby

FACILITY	WHAT TO LOOK FOR
Parking spaces	Some stores have dedicated parent and baby parking spaces close to the entrance.
Wider checkouts	Good supermarkets have at least two wider than average checkouts to accommodate prams.
Special discounts	Some stores offer discounts for parents with a baby under 12 months.
Baby care	Supervised creches are available at some stores, as long as you're there to be called if necessary.
Changing and feeding	Many stores have a baby changing area in their toilets, and some have a room where you can breastfeed – but if you're happy just to sit out of the way to feed your baby, don't feel you have to do it in private. Just ask an assistant.

Public transport tips

Planning ahead is the secret to trouble-free travel by public transport:

■ If you're travelling alone, make sure you can manage everything yourself.

■ Allow plenty of time to reach the station or airport to avoid the extra stress of worrying about missing a train or aeroplane.

■ On an aeroplane, feed your baby on takeoff and landing as sucking reduces the risk of earache caused by changing air pressure.

■ If you're flying long-haul, try to book a seat with a bassinet so that your baby can sleep in mid-flight.

■ A portable car seat is invaluable, though for air travel you may have to pay for an extra seat on busy flights if you want to use one just for your baby.

Travelling by car

Rear-facing car seats (see p. 76) make travelling by car with a young baby relatively trouble-free, but your car seat must be correctly fitted. Car seats can be put in the front or back seats, but don't use a rear-facing seat in the front passenger seat if you have an air bag. Correct fitting is equally important when your baby graduates to a fixed seat in the back. Keep a few nappies, wipes, and nappy sacks in the car for emergencies. The sun can be a problem for babies, so use a detachable blind on your car window to provide shade.

Using a backpack
A backpack is more convenient for an older baby than a buggy if you like to do a lot of walking.

Holidays

If you're going away with a very young baby, you may feel more comfortable not going abroad in case you need medical help. Having said this, small babies – especially breastfed ones – often travel abroad very well, but it's sensible to take out adequate medical insurance. Whatever the age of your baby, when you're away you should:

■ Check how far you'll be from a doctor's surgery, medical centre, or hospital.

■ Make sure the cot in your holiday accommodation conforms with safety standards – the tour operator, travel agent, or Tourist Information Office should be able to reassure you on this. Alternatively, take your own travel cot – modern designs are safe and compact.

■ Always make sure your baby is protected from the sun (see box opposite): use adequate sunscreen, dress your baby in protective clothing, and keep him in the shade.

Caring for your sick baby

Medication

The doctor may prescribe a medicine, such as liquid paracetamol or an antibiotic, for your baby's high temperature or infection. Give her the medicine in her mouth using a sterile dropper or medicine spoon. Always give the dosage recommended by the doctor or instructed on the bottle.

Taking your baby's temperature

A raised temperature usually means your baby is fighting off an infection. Take her temperature with a digital thermometer. Hold it firmly under her bare armpit for three minutes. Bear in mind that the temperature in the armpit is about 0.6°C (1°F) less than actual body temperature. You can also use a temperature strip, although these are less accurate. Don't use a thermometer in your child's mouth until she's at least seven years old.

Checking the temperature
Place the thermometer under your baby's bare armpit and hold her arm across her chest to keep it in place.

If you suspect that your baby isn't well, don't hesitate to get medical advice. You're the best judge of when your baby is unwell because you know and understand her moods and personality.

Nursing your baby

When babies are ill they are often grizzly and fretful, probably waking more frequently at night and needing constant attention and cuddles. However, a very ill baby will become listless and unresponsive. If your baby has a cold, it might make feeding difficult as she won't be able to breathe properly through her nose. Be patient and let her come up for air when feeding, but if this becomes a real problem ask your doctor or pharmacist for nose drops.

Recognizing a fever

The best way to recognize a fever is to lay your hand on your baby's brow. If her skin is hot, red, and clammy she has a fever. When the temperature is very high, she may also shiver.

Lowering temperature

If your baby has a very high fever, you should lower it to prevent overheating. Remove all her clothing, but don't let her get too cold. If she's over three months, you may also give her liquid paracetamol (see above left).

Preventing dehydration

Dehydration in babies under 12 months can be dangerous, and steps must be taken to replace lost fluids, sugar, and salt. Signs of dehydration in babies are general listlessness and a sunken fontanelle (the soft area of skin on the top of the skull). Your baby may also wet her nappy less frequently. When your baby has a temperature, or when the weather is hot,

Cooling baby
Undress your baby if she has a fever, but check she's not getting too cold.

make sure she doesn't become dehydrated by offering the breast more frequently or giving her cooled boiled water in a bottle or on a sterile spoon.

If your baby suffers from vomiting and diarrhoea for more than 24 hours, always consult your doctor. If you are bottle-feeding, try giving half-strength milk and encourage your baby to drink water with or without rehydration salts (available from your doctor or pharmacist). If your baby has been weaned, stick to a bland diet. Babies who are breast fed should continue with their normal milk feeds. If you're breastfeeding, give rehydration fluid in a bottle, if possible, before the feed. If your baby won't take a bottle, you will need to breastfeed more often to maintain fluid intake.

Mild diarrhoea can sometimes occur when you introduce new types of solid food (see p. 112) – if you suspect this is happening, stop giving your baby that particular food and then try again after a couple of weeks.

Recognizing an illness

AILMENT	WHEN TO CALL THE DOCTOR
High or low temperature	■ If your baby's temperature rises above 38°C (100°F) and she's obviously ill, or if it rises above 39.4°C (103°F), and she doesn't seem ill. ■ When your baby's temperature goes up and down. ■ If your baby is unusually quiet and limp and her skin is cold, though her hands and feet are pink (see p. 123).
Breathing difficulties	■ If your baby's breathing becomes difficult. ■ The rate of breathing speeds up and you notice her ribs being drawn sharply in with each breath.
Loss of appetite	■ If your baby is under six months and refuses to feed either at the breast or from a bottle. ■ If your older baby refuses food when he is normally a good eater.
Vomiting	■ If your baby is burping up whole feeds or the vomiting is violent, prolonged, or excessive, it can cause rapid dehydration and medical help should be sought straight away. However, all babies regurgitate a little milk from time to time after feeds.
Diarrhoea	■ If the stools are watery, possibly greenish in colour, foul smelling, and are abnormally frequent. ■ If diarrhoea is accompanied by a raised temperature, you should always consult a doctor.
Rashes	■ If you notice an unusual rash it can be a sign of infection, especially if it's accompanied by a raised temperature, or it might be an allergic reaction. Your baby's doctor will want to examine the rash. ■ One type of rash caused by meningitis is very serious and should be treated as an emergency (see above right).

Meningitis

This is an inflammation of the membranes that cover the brain, resulting from an infection. Viral meningitis is relatively mild; bacterial meningitis is life-threatening and requires immediate action. The main symptoms can develop over a matter of hours.

Symptoms
In a baby under 12 months the main symptoms are general irritability, a slightly tense and bulging fontanelle (see p. 60), fever, and a rash consisting of flat, pink, or purple spots that don't disappear when you press them. There may also be listlessness, vomiting, loss of appetite, and pain in the eyes from light.

What to do
Press a glass to her skin to see if the rash remains visible through it. If you think she has meningitis, get her to a hospital immediately.

Febrile seizures

These can happen when children have a rapid increase in temperature due to infection. This causes the brain cells to discharge impulses to muscles, which contract jerkily. Although frightening to see, they are fairly common and rarely serious. The risk of epilepsy is very small.

Symptoms
Loss of consciousness and uncontrollable twitching of limbs. There may also be frothing at the mouth and the eyes may roll back.

What to do
Clear a space and remove her clothing to lower her temperature (see opposite). Call a doctor.

Emergency first aid

First-aid materials

Keep a box of first-aid materials in your home. Make sure that any carers, such as babysitters, know where it's kept. It should include the following:

- Adhesive plasters.
- Sterile dressings – don't open these until you need to use them.
- Bandages.
- Cotton wool.
- Scissors and tweezers.
- Adhesive tape or safety pins.

The following isn't a substitute for proper first-aid training, but it's a good idea to familiarize yourself with the information here so that you know what to do in an emergency. Always keep as calm as possible.

Checking to see if your baby is unconscious

Tap or flick the bottom of his foot. Try calling his name to see if there's any response – never shake a baby. If there is no reaction, check to see if he is breathing before you call an ambulance.

If your baby is unconscious

Check whether or not he is breathing. Place a hand on the baby's forehead and tilt his head back gently to open the airway to the lungs. Remove anything obvious from his mouth, but don't put your finger in his mouth to look for anything. Place a fingertip on his chin and lift it gently. Put your ear near his mouth and look along his chest. Look for any movement and listen and feel for breathing – for up to ten seconds only.

If he is breathing

Keep the airway open *If he is breathing, cradle him in your arms, with his head lower than his body, and take him to the phone with you while you call an ambulance. If possible, ask someone else to phone for you.*

If he is not breathing

Rescue breathing *If he's not breathing start rescue breathing. Make sure that the airway is still open. Breathe in, then place your mouth over the baby's mouth and nose and blow steadily into his lungs until the chest rises (called an effective breath). Repeat. If the chest does not rise,*
- *Adjust the baby's head.*
- *Re-check the baby's mouth to see if there is anything obvious blocking the airway.*
- *Check that the seal is airtight.*
- *Try again, but don't try more than five times and stop if you succeed in delivering two effective breaths.*
- *Check for signs of circulation. Look for signs of breathing, coughing, or movement for no more than ten seconds.*
- *If there is circulation, continue giving rescue breaths for about a minute (15 breaths), then call an ambulance. Continue with rescue breaths until the ambulance arrives.*

How to resuscitate

Cardiopulmonary resuscitation *If there is no sign of circulation, begin cardiopulmonary resuscitation – a combination of rescue breaths and chest compressions.*
- *Hold the baby's head with one hand.*
- *Put the index finger of your other hand in the centre of the nipple line on the lower part of the breastbone and place your forefinger beside it.*
- *Press down sharply to a depth of 2 cm (1 in) five times.*
- *Give one rescue breath.*
- *Alternate five compressions and one rescue breath until help arrives, the baby moves, or you are too tired to continue.*

Emergency first aid for accidents

INJURY	WHAT HAPPENS	BEFORE YOU GET MEDICAL HELP
Severe bleeding	If your child has an accident that causes severe bleeding, you must act quickly to stop the bleeding before seeking help.	Press firmly on the wound and raise the injured part. Keep it higher than the baby's heart. Cover the wound with a sterile dressing and bandage the dressing in place.
Head injury	If your baby bumps his head he may become concussed, which usually leads to a brief loss of consciousness.	Make your baby comfortable and treat any bleeding (see above). Take him to a doctor, even if he appears to be fully recovered.
Electric shock	Your baby may get an electric shock if he plays with electrical sockets or flex. This can cause his breathing and heart to stop and cause burns to his body.	Immediately switch off the current at the mains. Stand on dry insulating material, such as a telephone directory, and push the source away from the baby with a broom.
Drowning	Just 2.5 cm (1 in) of water is enough to drown a baby if he falls forward. Never leave him in a bath alone, even if he can sit unaided.	Carry him with his head lower than his chest. If he is unconscious, begin resuscitation immediately (see opposite).
Bites	Bites can range from minor insect stings to animal bites and the treatment will differ accordingly.	Wash an insect bite thoroughly and cover it with a plaster. For an animal bite, follow the procedure for severe bleeding (see above).
Burns and scalds	If your baby is burned or scalded, you need to act quickly to cool the burn and remove any clothing from the affected area before it begins to swell.	Cool the burn with cold water for ten minutes. Remove restrictive clothing from the area and cover the burn with clean material. Don't apply anything to the burn.

Choking baby

If your baby is choking on something he may turn blue and make strange noises because he is trying to cry. Don't turn him upside down or shake him. Try to clear any blockage in his throat as soon as possible with the procedure below.

Clearing a blockage

Take the following action *before calling an ambulance:*
- *Lay the baby face down along your forearm and keeping your hand flat, give him five sharp slaps between his shoulders (see left).*
- *If the blockage is not cleared, turn his face up along your forearm and, supporting his head, place two fingers on the lower part of the breastbone. Press down and forward along the breastbone. Check the baby's mouth. Do this up to five times, checking the mouth each time.*
- *If the blockage is still not clear, repeat the back slaps and chest thrusts three times, then call an ambulance.*
- *If the baby becomes unconscious at any stage, start treatment for unconsciousness at once (opposite).*

Hypothermia

Hypothermia occurs when the body temperature falls below 35°C (95°F). The temperature-regulating mechanism in babies is immature, so they can lose body heat rapidly in a cold place.

The symptoms
He will look misleadingly healthy because his skin will have a pink glow, but it will feel cold. He may refuse to feed, be limp, and quiet.

What to do
Call a doctor. Warm him gradually. Take him into a warm room and wrap him in blankets. Put a hat on him and hold him close to your body so that he benefits from your warmth.

Your special baby

Early signs

Although the rate of normal development is enormously varied (see p. 147), it may become apparent that your baby's development is delayed. Don't leap to conclusions, but as parents, you're likely to be the first to recognize some of the signs.

Hand awareness
A baby becomes aware of her hands at about eight weeks (see p. 158). At 12–16 weeks this interest wanes, but may last up to 20 weeks in a baby whose development is delayed.

Grasp reflex
From birth to about six weeks, a baby wraps her fingers tightly around anything placed in her palm, then the reflex fades as she begins to gain control of her hand movements. This reflex lasts longer in a developmentally delayed baby.

Exploration with the mouth
At about four months, a baby puts everything in her mouth. Most stop at one, but a developmentally slow child will go on longer.

"Casting"
From 8–16 months, all babies go through the stage of "casting" – dropping things to see where they fall . This lasts longer in a baby whose development is delayed.

Dribbling
Most babies achieve mouth control at 12 months; slow babies dribble for much longer.

Chewing
Most babies develop the ability to chew, even without teeth, by about seven months. A developmentally delayed baby will take longer.

Fortunately, few parents ever have to learn that their baby has a problem. This doesn't make it any easier for those parents who have to face the fact that their baby has a condition that is going to affect, and perhaps dominate, her life, and theirs too.

Diagnosis

Your baby will be examined by the midwife at birth and by a paediatrician before you leave the hospital (see p. 61). They may find something that requires further investigation at this point. If not, you may be the first to spot that something isn't quite right (see left). Talk to your family doctor who should refer your baby for an expert assessment – insist that this happens if you're concerned. Among the first things to exclude are impaired hearing or vision; these should be tested at your baby's developmental checks (see p. 153).

Coming to terms with the news

Whenever you find out about your baby's disability, you'll need time to adjust to the shock and pain. Every new parent has expectations and hopes for their child, and it's as though all of these are dashed in the space of a few minutes. In many ways, it is like a bereavement; you need to mourn for the baby you thought you were expecting, the perfect, able-bodied child you longed for, and come to terms with the special baby you have. In time, of course, this child will be your perfect child, and you'll feel ashamed that you ever thought her second-best, but in the early days, it's almost impossible not to feel a sense of loss.

Talk to others

Many of the congenital conditions that affect children and babies are extremely rare, but it will help you enormously if you can find other parents to talk to who have a child with exactly the same problem as your own. Your doctor, health centre, or local Social Services department can help put you in touch with specialist organizations. These may have self-help groups that include other parents who are in the same or a similar position to you (see p. 187).

Physical problems that can be corrected

With advances in neonatal paediatric surgery, many of the physical problems babies are born with can be corrected, even in the first months. This is a worrying time because it's distressing to see your baby having to undergo a series of operations. It can also be a strain emotionally (and financially), particularly if the hospital treating your baby is a long way from your home, but it helps to know that there is every chance that your baby will be able to grow up to be a normal healthy child.

Recognizing developmental problems

A baby with a developmental problem is going to reach her milestones (see p. 146) at a slower than average rate, and in some cases may not reach them at all. You may notice quite early on that your baby is behind from various signs, such as unusual quietness, lack of alertness, no interest in her surroundings, floppiness (lack of muscle tone), docility, and sleeping for long periods. Sometimes a baby who's been termed "good" turns out to be a baby with a problem, because this kind of baby cries rarely, makes little noise, and doesn't interact well with her environment.

Later signs

As your baby grows older, at around seven or eight months you may notice that her attention span is very short and she'll spend time moving quickly from one toy to another instead of examining one slowly and carefully as most babies do. Later still, she may be over-active and have difficulty in concentrating on a single activity. She may also be reserved and unresponsive to people, even when she knows them very well.

Avoid comparisons

Comparing one baby with another is never a good idea, but if you have a baby with delayed development it's doubly important to see your baby for herself, rather than against the standard of other people's children. With perseverance, the support of specialists, and encouragement from you, your baby will reach some of her milestones (see p. 146) eventually, and the reward of seeing her do so will give you huge satisfaction.

Other people's attitudes

Most people don't have direct experience of a disability, and have little idea of how to react to a disabled person or child. Indeed, this may have been your own position until recently. Almost inevitably there will be those who will say the wrong thing, make a crass comment or remark without thinking. You'll just have to remind yourself that their insensitivity comes from ignorance and embarrassment and they probably don't mean to be offensive. Try not to let this get you down; be open about your baby's disability so that it doesn't become a taboo subject.

Giving a lead

What you'll find is that many of your family and friends will take their lead from you in learning how to relate to your child. Make it clear that although her disability may be permanent, she is in no way inferior to anyone else and has the same right to love, understanding, and support as any child. You'll need courage, but you'll discover, like many other parents of disabled children, that you've got an inner strength that you never thought you would have. If you can be positive and hopeful about your child, and show by example how much you value her individuality and personality, other people will learn to do the same.

How you can help

If and when your baby is diagnosed with developmental delay, disability, or learning difficulty, you'll be given specialist advice on how to stimulate her both physically and intellectually. Here are some ideas:

■ Stimulate your child from birth. Do this visually – make sure she can see your face close up as much as possible and hang a picture of a face down the side of the cot. Stimulate her aurally by playing music or a heartbeat, by talking and singing. Use touch with different textures, such as lambskin, cotton, rubber, or plastic.

■ Talk and sing to your baby in pronounced rhythms and rhymes, such as "Jack and Jill".

■ Read and talk aloud to her as much as you can.

■ Make her aware of her body with gentle clapping games and baby massage (see p. 110).

■ Find toys that are educational and enjoyable and show her how to play with them (see p. 146).

■ Introduce her to as many people as possible.

■ Give her lots of love and make her feel secure. Praise her often.

■ Give her lots of cuddles and kisses; make sure others do, too.

■ Never scold or punish her slowness.

■ Encourage her to be independent – help her to try to do things, even if it's hard.

■ Be patient when she's frustrated. Life will be a bit more difficult for her, especially when she realizes that she can't do things that others her age can.

Adapting to
parenthood

As well as mastering the practical care of your newborn baby, you need to think about your lifestyle and your relationship so that you're able to get the most out of being parents and a family. Your baby will undoubtedly be your main priority and it's easy to let him soak up all your emotional and physical energy. But to maximize the many joys of parenthood, it's worth ensuring that you have time for each other and time for yourself. You are, after all, still individuals and still in a loving relationship and it would be wrong to think that your baby could fulfil all your needs. How easily you adjust will depend on your individual circumstances: having a good and equal relationship with each other already and an adequate support network can make the transition to parenthood that much easier. If you have difficulty in adjusting at first, don't worry – things will get easier. Parenthood is full of ups and downs, but if you work together to get the balance right, hopefully it will turn out to be all that you wanted it to be.

Helping each other

Mother

If you're at home with your baby while your partner is at work, you may begin to feel that you know your baby better than he does. Or, you may feel that you don't get enough help from him. Think about how your attitudes may affect your partner.

Supporting your partner
■ Try to avoid thinking that your partner isn't as "good" as you are at caring for your baby. By encouraging him to get involved with your baby's care and to share the work load, you'll all benefit.

■ If your partner is tired after work, be patient. Let him unwind, then encourage him to spend time with your baby as a way of relaxing, not as a chore. Bathing the baby is often both a good way for him to look after the baby and to relax (see p. 95).

■ Tell him about your day. If it's been difficult, don't bottle it up, but, equally, try not to convey it accusingly as if it's his fault.

Building your self-esteem
■ Be proud of your achievements. As the main carer, take pride in the upbringing of your baby.

■ Keep in touch with work colleagues so that you're up-to-date with career developments and gossip! That way it will be less of a shock when you return.

■ Try to have some time away from your baby, on your own and with your partner (see p. 134).

New parenthood is a joyful but testing role, when both of you are faced with a new set of priorities and when expectations come up against hard realities. So spare a thought for each other's needs, as well as those of your baby.

The initial impact of the baby

As first-time parents you may seriously underestimate the amount of work and disruption caring for a baby entails and the extent to which this affects your relationship. Many couples are shocked to find that rather than bringing them closer together, their baby can bring to light differences that drive them apart. This is normal and very much part of your growth into parenthood, when you begin to lay the foundations of your new parental relationship with your baby and with each other.

Different patterns of bonding

While two-thirds of mothers bond with their babies almost immediately or within a few days, many fathers admit that intense paternal feelings take much longer to develop. Many mothers are overwhelmed by the depth of their feelings for their baby. Unfortunately, some fathers view this as an obsession, to which they are not sympathetic, and they resent

Sharing the care
Your baby needs the protection and love of both his parents. Sharing his daily care will help you and your partner to really understand each other's needs and feelings.

Defusing areas of conflict

WHAT TO DO	HOW IT HELPS
Discuss who does what	You probably both have views about what roles men and women should play; this can be a powerful hidden agenda. Discuss how you feel and be prepared to have your views challenged.
Talk about your expectations	Disappointed expectations may produce disillusionment so it's best to give and take in those areas where your views diverge, even though you won't escape hard choices.
Listen to each other	Try to talk openly about your feelings and think about how to express them. Do this in a way that avoids accusation, sarcasm, or belittling your partner. Give "I" rather than "you" messages.
Resolve conflict immediately	Resolve conflict by determining the cause and coming to a mutually agreed solution. A common area of conflict is when you have differing views on the division of labour (see below).
Put your family first	Self-denial isn't a very popular concept these days, but if you're to turn your trio into a family you'll each need to forego some individual pleasures in the interest of building that family.
Learn to cope with stress	Reactions to stress differ from person to person. Try to evolve together a pattern of "stress management" for difficult periods, to minimize any possible damage to your relationship.

Father

If you're at work and your partner is at home with the baby, try to see her point of view. At work, you'll have the challenges and friendships of working life to stimulate you, while your partner may be missing these if she's stopped work to look after the baby, and she may be finding the change difficult.

Supporting your partner

■ Telephone her at different times of the day – several times a week. If you're near enough, go home for lunch every now and then.

■ Let her know what time you're going to be home and stick to it. She'll need a break in the evenings and this is valuable time for you to spend with your baby.

■ Share the ups and the downs. If you've had a rotten day at work, talk to her about it, but listen to her and be sympathetic if she's also had a bad day.

■ Make sure she has time out to relax away from the baby and to see her friends (see p. 134).

Becoming more involved

■ Even if your partner is at home with the baby most of the time, remember that your role in caring for your baby is vital and will be very rewarding for you.

■ Find out what happened during the day and what milestones your baby may have reached – then spend time with your baby so that you can experience them too.

■ Try to use your weekends and days off to have extended time with your baby.

being excluded from their partner's affection and attention. A man whose partner breastfeeds, often feels excused from nurturing as a consequence, driving a wedge between himself and his baby. Fathers who are involved in their baby's daily care, will strengthen their paternal bond in the early weeks and close the gap between how fathers and mothers feel differently about their baby.

Division of labour

By far the biggest bone of contention between new parents is how they should share caring for the baby and the work load that goes with it. Many fathers do their fair share, but others help with the fun tasks, such as bath-time and bedtime stories, but are less enthusiastic about changing nappies, washing clothes, and getting up in the middle of the night. This attitude is inappropriate – parenting should be a partnership. Find ways of sharing the drudgery and the delights of caring for your baby. Look positively at her development and how you can stimulate and enjoy it together (see p. 146). You and your partner should think of parenthood as one of the most demanding jobs you can have, and reinforce each other's equal responsibility to succeed in this new role.

Learning to cope

Minimizing stress

Most family arguments happen at stressful times. Early in the morning when you're only half awake, it's easy to feel clumsy and irritable. If you're in full-time work, you may bring stress home with you, making it more difficult to cope with the demands at home. It's at times like these that you both need to work together to help each other; taking out your stresses on each other or on your baby will probably only make things worse:

■ Try to find ways of relaxing with each other and by yourselves (see p. 134).

■ Try to be honest about how you're feeling to help prevent any misunderstandings.

■ Don't try to do too many things at once – you'll only get frustrated and over tired.

■ Try not to bring work home with you – physically or mentally.

Negative feelings

Having negative thoughts towards your baby because he's kept you up all night or because he's crying is normal. There's no point in refusing to accept how you feel; it doesn't make you wicked. It's abnormal, however, to use violence as a way of expressing yourself; if your temper is really being pushed to the limit, talk to someone or take time away before you do something you'll regret.

Caring for a baby tests all parents. Getting through the difficult times is part of being a parent; you'll learn from every occasion and be a better parent and partner for having come through it.

Why anger is normal

If your baby cries for long periods or sleeps only for brief intervals, you're bound to feel concerned and worried. If this worry is then compounded by a feeling of impotence, it often expresses itself as anger. You may sometimes be seized by acute feelings of helplessness, guilt, and inadequacy when nothing you do seems to pacify your baby. At such times it's difficult not to feel victimized and the worry can often quickly escalate to resentment and then anger. You may also feel angry that nothing you do seems to work, and resentful that you're left with little time or energy for your own needs. These are very natural feelings.

Breaking the circle of negativity

The knowledge that your tension and frustration can be communicated to your baby will only increase your anxiety, which will in turn make the baby feel more insecure. It's very easy to become locked into a vicious circle of negativity. Your baby will express this in the only way he knows, by crying, and his crying will further unnerve you. This circle must be broken.

Talk to someone Telephone someone you can confide in; just getting your feelings out in the open will help to put everything into perspective. Talking to other parents in the same situation is often useful – you'll realize that how you feel is very normal. You should also talk to your partner, but remember he or she may also be feeling exasperated; try to talk to each other when you're able to go out without the baby or when the baby is asleep. If none of the above is possible, speak to your health visitor or doctor.

A change of scene If you're alone with your baby during the day, get out of the house. The change of scene will help to relax you and being driven in a car, wheeled in a pram, or walked in a sling can often soothe a baby. In the short term, if you feel yourself being engulfed by anger, leave the room or put the baby in another room until you feel calmer. When your baby is older, make sure you have adequate time away (see p. 134).

If your baby is difficult to love

Just like both of you, your baby has his own personality. He may be happy and smiling all the time, or he may be reserved and seemingly unsociable. He may be independent and not very affectionate, or clingy and easily upset. Remember, your baby doesn't choose to behave in a certain way to spite you – it's just how he's made. As with all relationships, you need to keep the communication channels open with your baby. You have to get to know what makes him tick and accept that you're not going to have an easy relationship with him all the time.

Maintaining affection

Some babies don't like to be handled or cuddled very much; others go through phases of being unsociable. If a baby doesn't want attention, he will tend to stiffen his body and cry when you hold him. Most babies will become more sociable with time, but if you're particularly worried, seek advice from your health visitor. Try to do the following:

■ Accept that babies are sometimes just difficult and don't blame yourself.
■ Don't thrust unwelcome attention on him – it may make matters worse.
■ If your baby is more affectionate with your partner, be grateful! Don't take this personally; babies often go through periods when they prefer or cling to one partner and this will pass with time.
■ Remember, your baby will respond to you so make sure you're smiling and being affectionate towards him.

When your baby misses you

If you have invested time in your baby and bonded closely, you'll have created a feeling of rightness when you're together that is shattering when you're apart. An upheaval, such as returning to work, the preferred parent being away for a while, or the introduction of a childminder may make your baby unsettled. This is most likely to reveal itself in him being fretful, fussy, needing more cuddles than usual, and a change in his eating and sleeping patterns. If your baby appears to be very unhappy, reassess the situation; for example, it could be that he's unhappy with his childminder. To help your baby when you're away from home:

■ Telephone frequently.
■ Ask your partner or childminder to talk about you to your baby.
■ Leave an item of your clothing for your baby to hold and some photos of yourself.
■ Tape yourself singing and talking to your baby.

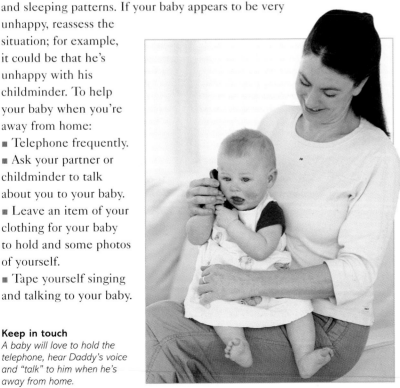

Keep in touch
A baby will love to hold the telephone, hear Daddy's voice and "talk" to him when he's away from home.

A fretful baby

Most parents experience a period when their baby is consistently fretful and demanding for no apparent reason. The inability to communicate what's wrong can be very frustrating for both of you and your baby.

Why he may be fretful
■ He may not be receiving as much stimulation as he needs. Babies who can sit up and who would like to explore their surroundings, but who can't yet crawl can become frustrated.

■ If your baby is teething, he may be experiencing discomfort or even pain (see p. 154).

■ If you're particularly stressed, your baby may be picking up your heightened tension.

Getting through it
■ Remember, your baby's behaviour is normal. Much of your frustration stems from his inability to communicate. This is natural and not a failing in him or you.

■ It doesn't mean that you're inadequate if your baby is going through a bad patch. Most parents experience difficult periods.

■ Try to accept your feelings rather than get angry with yourself and you'll find it easier to keep an overall positive attitude.

■ Try to keep things in perspective by sharing any negative feelings with each other or a friend.

■ There are particular ways that a crying baby can be comforted. Try some of the suggestions outlined on pages 104–107.

Feeling low

Helping each other

In the days after the birth, when "baby blues" may be rife, you'll both need to support each other. Just sharing the day-to-day care of your baby and listening and being there for each other will help.

What fathers can do

■ Encourage your partner to talk about the things that are getting her down. Give her lots of attention and affection.

■ Boost her self-esteem. She may feel unattractive and dislike her body – tell her how much you love her often and that she's beautiful.

■ Take her shopping for clothes. Be patient and compliment her. Don't push her to lose weight.

■ Encourage her to join a mother-and-baby support group and make it easy for her to go.

■ Encourage people to visit if that's what she wants, but, if not, help to maintain her privacy.

What mothers can do

■ If you've got the blues, try your best not to take out your tensions on your partner. Try to express how you're feeling. If you need a cuddle, tell your partner.

■ Remember that your partner also has some big adjustments to make and may be finding it difficult too.

■ Make sure your partner has time with the baby. It will create problems if he feels left out.

■ Try to limit the number of visitors. Your partner may feel excluded if your house is crowded with female friends and family.

The "baby blues" usually last a few days, but in some mothers they go on for months due to postnatal depression. A partner needs to know the difference between the "blues" and depression so that he can help and knows when to seek medical advice.

Baby blues

The "baby blues" are mood swings caused by hormonal changes. In all likelihood this period of feeling low one minute and euphoric the next won't last beyond the first week, but you'll still need a lot of support to get through it. Maybe the "baby blues" are a natural sign to those around you that you need time and space to come to terms with being a mother. That's certainly how a concerned partner, relative, or friend should deal with it; although you'll find that because your hormones are all over the place, you'll also cry when someone's nice to you!

Why you get the blues

Your hormones, progesterone and oestrogen, will have been high during pregnancy. After you have had your baby, these hormone levels drop and your body may find it difficult to adjust. This can have a marked effect on your emotions. With this, exhaustion from the labour, and lack of sleep, it's not at all surprising that you may not be feeling on top of the world.

What you can do

■ Give yourself time. Accept that you'll feel like this for a short time and that what you're going through is incredibly common.
■ Accept offers of help and don't try to do everything yourself.
■ Try to talk about your feelings and have a good cry if it helps.
■ Tell your partner you need a lot of love and affection, but remember this is a time of upheaval and change for him, too.

When fathers get the blues

Most fathers feel an anticlimax after the birth. There are so many changes and if your partner is feeling low, you'll be called on to be a tower of strength, which can be a huge strain. Try to think of the first few months as a period of rapid change that is testing for both of you; when you come through it, you'll be closer than you were before. If you get really unhappy, talk things over with your health visitor, doctor, or a close friend.

Postnatal depression (PND)

If symptoms that started out as the common "baby blues" don't go away and, in fact, start to become worse, you could be suffering from postnatal depression. This is a temporary and treatable condition that varies from woman to woman. It can develop slowly and not become obvious until several weeks after the baby's birth, but if it's diagnosed and addressed early enough, there's a good chance of a fast cure. Health visitors are trained to recognize the symptoms and treatment ranges from something as simple as talking to a friend, health visitor, or doctor about how you feel, to taking medication, such as anti-depressants, for more severe cases.

Why postnatal depression happens

There are many reasons why postnatal depression occurs. It depends on you as a person, your personal circumstances, and the way your baby behaves. Research shows that the following risk factors may make you more susceptible to postnatal depression:

■ If you enjoyed a senior position at work or high-flying career before the birth, it can be difficult to adjust to the status change.
■ If you already have difficulties in your relationship, the baby may make them worse; this in itself may lead to disillusionment and low self-esteem.
■ If you had an unexpected difficult birth experience (see p. 50), you could easily feel demoralized and feel that you've failed in some way.
■ If you've had depression in the past.
■ A very demanding, sleepless baby can trigger postnatal depression from sheer exhaustion.
■ If you have particularly difficult living conditions and no support network, this can make postnatal depression worse.
■ If you've bottled up your emotions and not sought help early on.

Seeking help

Many women are too embarrassed to admit how they feel, fearing that it will appear that they've somehow failed. Talking about how you feel is the most important thing you can do. Once you accept that you're not "mad" and that there are things you can do to help yourself, you are one step on the road to recovery. Once you seek help you'll be guided to:

■ Understand how you feel and learn to express this.
■ Learn to prioritize, devote more time to yourself and find ways to relax.
■ Visit the health visitor more regularly and seek support.
■ Begin taking medication if your postnatal depression is very extreme.

What fathers can do

You may feel helpless because you don't understand postnatal depression. Remember, it's temporary and treatable, so try to be patient. You can be a huge help if you make an effort to understand and do the following:

■ Talk and listen to your partner. Never tell her to pull herself together – she can't. Don't assume she'll snap out of it – she won't.
■ Mother the mother – encourage her to rest and eat and drink properly.
■ Encourage her to be with the baby as much as she wants so that she can take things slowly and gradually work out how the baby will fit in.
■ Make sure she's not alone too much as she'll fear isolation.
■ Go to see the doctor first for advice as your partner may refuse to accept that she's ill. The doctor may arrange to visit her informally at home.

PND signs to look out for

Signs and symptoms may include:

■ Anxiety – in particular, a mother may worry about her baby and refuse to be parted from her.

■ Irrational fears, for example about being left alone.

■ Loss of appetite.

■ Insomnia.

■ Fatigue.

■ Lack of concern with appearance.

■ Making mountains out of molehills.

■ Withdrawal from social contact.

■ Feeling negative and inadequate.

■ Growing feelings of despondency and helplessness.

Postnatal psychosis

Postnatal, or puerperal, psychosis, is the rarest and most serious form of postnatal depression. It affects about one in 1,000 women, usually in the first three months after the birth. Urgent medical help is needed. Symptoms include:

■ Sleeping all day.

■ Crying for long periods.

■ Being tense and anxious.

■ Being manically jolly and behaving oddly.

■ Being paranoid and hallucinating.

■ Thinking about harming herself and the baby.

Time out

Mother

You need time out, but so does your partner. He needs his own time with the baby, time alone with you, and a chance to relax away from work and home.

How to help your partner

■ Encourage him to have an occasional night out with friends or time to continue a hobby, even if he's been out at work all day. It's good for anyone who works to relax this way, as long as it doesn't take over his life to the exclusion of you and your baby.

■ Make the most of your time at home with your partner. He may feel left out, so make the effort to make him feel special, particularly when the baby is asleep.

How your baby gains

Spending short periods away from your baby can make you a better parent, so don't feel guilty:

■ You'll appreciate your baby more when you see him again.

■ A break will help you feel relaxed and rested, which will mean you'll be able to cope better.

■ It's good for him to get used to you going out (he'll soon learn that you always come back). He'll begin to gain confidence and develop his social skills by having to relate to others.

Being a new parent is undoubtedly a tiring and time-consuming experience, but you need to have time out for you and your partner – individually and together. Making time for yourself is not a luxury, it's a necessity. You'll need to be well organized, but it'll be good for your relationship and good for your baby.

Make time for yourself

■ If you're the primary carer, incorporated into your daily timetable should be at least half an hour devoted entirely to yourself, when you can have a soak in the bath, read a magazine, or just have a friend to visit.

■ When your baby is asleep, take the opportunity to rest; if you're feeling tired, having a catnap is more important than cleaning the house. Don't be hard on yourself – it's okay to sleep in the middle of the day, especially if you're having to get up during the night.

■ Time away doesn't only mean half an hour away from your baby when he's asleep; it means time away from the home environment. If you arrange to see a friend, suggest that you visit her or meet her somewhere. If you're at home you're more likely to become involved with your baby.

■ Arrange a "baby swap" with other parents: they look after your baby alongside their own on a particular day or evening, and then you do the same for them. Ask friends and relatives to help out, if they live nearby.

■ Find out if the local leisure centre or gym has a creche – and use it!

Be flexible with your daily routine

You can roughly plan your day, but don't be too regimented and inflexible. The needs of a young baby change all the time and if your baby wakes up unexpectedly you may not be able to have the half an hour you wanted. Try to be relaxed about it and take a break later in the day.

Accept help from others

It will be much easier to make time for yourself if you learn to accept offers of help. Don't be stoic and don't feel you're somehow a failure because you let someone else look after your baby. Just say yes, gracefully, and then do your own thing – you deserve it. It's very normal to feel strange about leaving your baby to begin with, but this will pass with time once you've learned to trust your helpers. Your baby will also benefit in many ways by not only being with you all the time (see left).

Spending time together as a couple

An important part of keeping the communication channels open with your partner is to find time when you can be alone together. Doing this is possible, but may require planning. It will seem odd to book a time to see your partner, but if you try to be spontaneous about it, you'll always find an excuse or decide that your baby is more important. Sometimes it may only be possible to spend time together in the house, but try to find times when someone else can look after your baby so that you both have the opportunity to go out and have uninterrupted time as a couple.

At home
■ Try to continue any rituals you had before your baby was born, such as having a drink together in the evening, sharing a bath, or just doing the crossword. Try not to talk about your baby all the time.
■ Cuddle up together for half an hour on the sofa; this precious time together will help you to keep some semblance of normality and act as a reminder that you're still a couple, as well as being parents.

Going out
■ Don't turn down invitations and, if possible, try not to take your baby with you all the time (although it may be easier to do so in the first six to eight weeks). Find a reliable babysitter and, if you're breastfeeding, express milk (see p. 83) so that you don't have to cut your evening short.
■ When your baby is a bit older, find people you can rely on – such as grandparents – to look after him for a longer period of time so that you can take the opportunity to have a weekend away together.
■ Continue hobbies you enjoyed together before the baby was born, such as playing sports (see p. 66). If you can't find a babysitter, go swimming as this is something you can all enjoy together (see p. 139).

Grandparents
Your baby's grandparents can loom large in your life both positively and negatively. If they respect your privacy, and your right to bring up your children your way, grandparents are unquestionably the best friends, helpers, and supporters you and your baby will have.

Making the most of their help
Grandparents are the people most likely to encourage you to have time off, not least because they'll want to spend some time with their grandchild. Make the most of this. Let them be a part of your baby's life and have their own relationship with him – the bond between grandparents and grandchild can be priceless for your child and for them. It is, however, important to get the balance right, not least because you don't want to fall out with the people who are your best helpers:
■ Don't let bossy parents or parents-in-law take over, pop around every five minutes, or turn up uninvited. If they live nearby, try to get into a routine that suits everyone; for example, choose a particular day of the week for them to look after your baby.
■ Be clear from the outset about how you want to bring up your baby to prevent any misunderstandings later on. Make sure that when grandparents look after your baby they do things the way you like them done, and not the way they think best.

Father
Sharing the care of your baby will help you understand how your partner feels and how important it is for her to have some time off.

How to help your partner
■ Take your baby out shopping or just out for a walk at weekends to give your partner some space.

■ Be fair to your partner – if she has stayed in with the baby while you've been out with friends, offer to do the same for her.

■ Share the cooking, even if you've been at work. Treat yourselves to a takeaway occasionally.

Babysitters

Use a babysitter who has experience with babies and young children, and preferably one who is recommended by friends. Don't use someone under 16 years old in case a problem arises that he or she may be too inexperienced to handle. When you go out the babysitter will need:

■ Telephone numbers for you and a relative or neighbour.

■ The location of the first-aid kit (see p. 122) and an explanation of how to use the baby monitor.

■ An idea of your baby's routine and what to do if he wakes up.

■ Feeding equipment and details of what your baby should be fed.

■ Nappy changing equipment and a change of clothes.

Sex and parenthood

Mother

Given your new responsibilities and possible physical discomforts (see below right), having sex is unlikely to be a high priority.

Your body image
You may feel unattractive if you have stretch marks and feel bloated, but your partner is probably less bothered about these things than you think. However, you do have to start liking yourself again before you can enjoy sex. Consider exercising (see p. 66); if nothing else, you'll feel better about yourself. If you're breastfeeding, you may be uncomfortable about your partner touching your breasts. Tell him – he may share your feelings.

Your baby
You're likely to be completely preoccupied with your baby and having sex may be the last thing you want to think about. This is normal, but once you decide to resume sex try to put the baby to the back of your mind.

Your partner
Don't put up with uncomfortable or painful sex because you feel dutiful. Your main priority is your baby and, although your partner needs to feel loved, you can show that in other ways. Remember, although you're preoccupied and fulfilled by your baby, your partner may not be to the same extent. Talk about this and how it affects your feelings about sex.

Your sexual relationship will, for a short time, be one of the many aspects of your partnership that has to adapt. Talk openly to each other about your sexual needs and expectations so this doesn't become a difficult issue.

Your feelings about sex

Don't just have sex because you think it's what your partner wants and don't expect to have sex after a certain time. It's normal to feel sexually different now that you're in the dual contradictory role of being a parent and a lover. You may even feel guilty about wanting or thinking about sex because you feel you should be looking after and thinking about your baby. Don't take sexual rejection personally. Talk to each other and try to understand the reasons for wanting or not wanting to resume intercourse. Sex can only become a problem if you let it, and it should be easily resolved if you keep talking to each other about how you feel.

How sex can help Looking after a baby can cause tensions and problems. Having intercourse at the right time, when you're both ready for it, may be just what you need to reaffirm your desire and affection for each other.

Physical considerations

You can generally resume sex when you both feel ready (unless you have been advised to wait for any reason), but there may be physical problems that will deter you from resuming sex in the first weeks after the birth.

Vaginal discomfort It's normal to feel too sore and tender to resume penetrative sex. The vagina will be bruised, making sex painful even if the childbirth was free of intervention. If you had an episiotomy (see p. 46), you may not be able to tolerate anything rubbing against the site for many months. Also, the glands that normally lubricate the vagina will not function effectively because of hormonal changes, so it's advisable to use a lubricating cream, which is available from your pharmacist.

Lochia (see p. 64) Don't resume penetrative sex until this discharge has stopped, which may not be for up to six weeks.

Breastfeeding Your breasts may leak milk during intercourse, especially when you orgasm, which can be a shock unless you're both prepared for it.

Tiredness Given the choice between having sex or sleeping, most new parents would choose the latter. Until you have more of a routine, and have found ways to have time to yourselves, it's difficult to resume a normal sex life. Try to be understanding if either one of you is too tired for sex.

Libido It appears that the sex drive in both new parents is much lower than normal and it returns slowly over a matter of months.

Caesarean Although you won't have any vaginal discomfort, a Caesarean is major abdominal surgery. You're likely to feel very tender for around six weeks and should wait to resume sex until you're fully recovered.

Contraception

The last thing you're likely to want when you're looking after a newborn baby is to find that you're immediately going to be parents all over again! The midwife or family planning adviser will ask you about contraception before you're discharged from hospital and you will also be asked about this at your six-week check (see p. 64). You can become pregnant if your periods have not started and you can be fertile as early as three weeks after the birth of your baby.

Breastfeeding Breastfeeding does reduce fertility, but you have to be feeding very regularly (at least every four hours and for some women, more often) to prevent ovulation. Breastfeeding is not a contraceptive.

Methods of contraception

TYPE	ADVICE
Pill	Those containing oestrogen are not prescribed for women who are breastfeeding because they reduce milk production.
Mini-pill	These only contain progestogen, which does not inhibit milk production, but they may worsen any postnatal depression (see p. 132) by inhibiting the natural production of progesterone. The mini-pill must be taken at the same time each day.
Condom (male and female)	These should be used with a contraceptive gel for comfort and security. A female condom may cause discomfort if you're bruised and sore after childbirth.
IUD (inter-uterine device) and diaphragm	Your cervix may have enlarged and won't return to its normal size for 2–3 months. If you used an IUD or diaphragm before you were pregnant, you'll need a new one. Some doctors will fit this at the 6-week check (see p. 64), although others prefer to wait a bit longer.

Having sex

Without it being an automatic prelude to sex, you should both feel that you can engage in physical contact whenever you feel like it. It's important that you continue to enjoy sex and find what is right for both of you – talk about your preferences and be open to trying new things.

Foreplay It's good to build up your sex drive through foreplay – touch and caress, massage each other with aromatic oils or take a bath together.

Non-penetrative sex For the first few times, maybe quite soon after the birth, try bringing each other to orgasm through gentle manual and oral sex. Consider being experimental; for example, you could try using some sex toys, such as a vibrator.

Comfortable positions Once you feel confident enough to try penetrative sex, experiment with different positions to find the ones that put least pressure on the sore areas. Stop at any time if the mother feels discomfort.

Father

It's quite natural to have a low sex drive (see below) for a short time after your baby is born. It's often a good thing because it allows you to concentrate on your baby. Many men, though, do want to resume sexual activity sooner than their partners.

Reasons for a low sex drive
- Being too tired and preoccupied with the baby.
- Having witnessed the birth.
- Sharing a bedroom with your baby.
- Feeling that your partner's body (especially her breasts) belongs to the baby and finding it difficult to think of her sexually.
- Being frightened of physically hurting your partner.

Understanding your partner
- Start being closer and more affectionate gradually and you'll soon begin to see your partner as your lover again.
- Don't expect too much from your partner too soon. Sex will be much less enjoyable for you if she's not ready or comfortable.
- Your partner may find it difficult to relax during sex as she will be listening for your baby's cry. Be understanding and try to find time when you can be alone without your baby (see p. 134).
- If your partner cuddles you or you're just being affectionate with each other, don't assume you will have sex. This will only upset her, disappoint you, and probably cause an argument.

Your new world

Playgroups and creches

Playgroups and creches range from informal arrangements between several parents to professionally organized sessions, where a trained supervisor offers a wide variety of play-based activities:

■ The playgroup gives you a chance to meet other parents, and your baby an opportunity to make friends with other children and adults.

■ A child of two and a half can be left at a playgroup for a couple of hours, but many also have a mother-and-baby group where parents can go with their babies. You must stay with your baby, though, as the playgroup won't have the resources to look after her.

■ Many shopping centres, leisure centres, and supermarkets have creches where babies and children can be left for a couple of hours. You must, however, stay in the vicinity in case you're needed.

Being a parent becomes a huge part of how you see yourself and how others see you. Your priorities change and this takes some getting used to. Caring for your baby is easier and more fun if you meet other parents and use the facilities available to you.

Other parents and children

Being a parent will extend your range of friends to include those who have children. As well as counteracting the demoralizing effect of mid-morning and early-afternoon isolation that can be the curse of solitary childcare, making friends with other parents benefits you in many ways:

■ You mix with other people who are equally focused on being a parent.
■ It's a good way to introduce your baby to relationships outside the family, which helps to develop her social skills.
■ Parenting is a learning process – you'll be breaking new ground every day and be able to exchange tips with the friends you've made.
■ You'll have people who understand the difficulties you're going through because they're going through them too.

How to meet people

A good way to make friends who have children is to stay in touch with some of the parents you met while pregnant, particularly if you live in a rural area where there may be fewer activities. If you have a spring or summer baby, you'll probably meet people in the park or playground.

If your baby is born in the winter, find out about activities from your health visitor or local library.

When parenthood is not enough

It used to be thought that being at home with a baby was a satisfying way for a woman to spend her most creative and active years; the same would rarely be thought of a man. But

Meeting people
Forming friendships with other parents and their babies can be hugely beneficial to you and your baby.

nowadays many women would be far from fulfilled by simply being a parent. Some who've tried to do it, because they believe that it's the best start they could give their child, have found the experience quite limiting, especially when they don't have the support of the extended family.

Learning to adapt

In a society where the worth and freedom of the individual, the opportunity for self-development, and an obligation to be oneself are constantly cited as legitimate goals, it's not surprising that most people are ill-prepared for the narrowing of horizons that comes with caring for a baby. You and your partner simply won't have as much of yourselves left over as before and this doesn't sit easily with the kind of ambitions bred by modern society.

Finding fulfilment Women who want to take an active part in the wider world, and have been educated and trained to do so, can hardly be expected to substitute an intimate relationship with the washing machine for the stimulation and satisfaction they derived from their work. The thousand joys of nurturing babies and children don't, for some women, wholly compensate for the loss of a fulfilling life outside the home because the joys are not the same. You can't make up for a lack of vitamin A by taking large doses of vitamin B. It goes without saying that full-time parenthood is a worthwhile career for a person who is happy in it, but anyone who hankers for more out of life than pure domesticity need never feel ashamed. Just because you have interests beyond day-to-day childcare doesn't mean you don't love your baby and it will not harm her.

Avoiding isolation Many people decide to become parents with the view that it will be a temporary – never total – denial of their needs and ambitions. This is why it's important – and, ultimately, in the baby's best interest – that you don't feel trapped by your parenting role. What most of us understand as isolation is the absence of other people and for those who spend their days caring for children, this means other adults. However much you love your baby, it's important to have the stimulation of adult interaction, which is why you need to get out and meet people.

Working from home

To make the transition to being a parent easier and less of a shock to the system, some women try to keep some of their old self by working from home. The information technology revolution has made this possible for more women than ever before, but it's not as easy as it sounds, especially if it's attempted too early on:

■ You must have a routine with your baby in order to do justice to your work and to make sure you don't end up working in the evenings.

■ It's important to make sure you're not just dividing your time between work and your baby; you need time for yourself and with your partner.

■ It's likely that you'll still need to organize some form of proper childcare (see p. 172) and this could mean that you miss out on precious time with your baby in her early months.

Activities at home

You'll be at home for some of the time, so getting together with other parents to host social activities at home is a good idea. It's also a good way for your baby to get used to different people at home. Here are some ideas:

■ Coffee morning: this is a good and cheap activity, giving you the chance to chat as your babies play.

■ Lunch party: provide simple snack food, so that you can eat and baby watch at the same time. Ask friends to bring a contribution (especially for their babies) or just take it in turns to host lunch.

■ Home-selling party: this is a good way to be sociable and earn some money. It involves presenting and taking orders for products, such as household goods or books, and earning commission on what is sold. Before you start, always check that the company you're working for is reputable.

Leisure centres

A good way of getting out is to join a leisure centre. Find one that has creche facilities (see opposite) so that you can take your baby with you – some have a "soft room" where your baby can play safely. Most swimming pools offer parent-and-baby sessions and your baby, equipped with suitable buoyancy aids, will enjoy the water as soon as she can hold her head up confidently (at about four months). Remember, you should avoid high-intensity exercise for the first nine months and while breastfeeding.

Single parents

Accepting help

Most couples struggle to bring up a baby without help, so as a single parent don't think you have to do it all yourself. Having guaranteed time for yourself during the week is good for you and for your baby:

■ Try to build up a small network of people you can depend on.

■ If you have several helpers, spread their time with your baby throughout the week.

■ Ask a relative or friend who's not working to stay once a week so that you get a good night's sleep, especially if you're working.

■ Seek the help of voluntary organizations (see p. 187) if you don't have people you can rely on.

■ Make sure you're getting all your financial benefits and any maintenance payments from the absent parent, if applicable.

■ If you know other single mothers, "baby swap" with them so that you both get a chance for some time to yourselves.

■ Don't be embarrassed or too proud to accept gifts – people would probably have given you these even if you weren't single.

Negative reactions
Some people may judge you and your ability to bring up your baby. Dealing with this can have a positive effect – many single parents become determined to prove that they can raise a happy and contented child. Criticism can also put pressure on you, making you feel that you can't ask for help, but you can, so try to remember this.

Being a single parent and being without a good support network can be physically and emotionally exhausting, but the knowledge that you've done it alone can be hugely rewarding for you and good for your baby.

Single parent by choice?

If you've chosen to be a single mother, you may be more prepared emotionally, practically, and financially for looking after a young baby and look forward to the prospect. If you've split with your partner during the pregnancy or soon after the birth, you may have more difficulties. Coping with the emotional problems of separating from someone while looking after a young baby is bound to have an impact on your ability to cope. In this situation, it's more important for you to ask for and to accept help.

Lone parenting can be positive

Being a single parent is by no means all doom and gloom. You and your baby can benefit in many ways from the special relationship you'll form:
■ Single parents tend to develop a much closer bond with their babies; they don't have to share their love between a partner and a child.
■ Extended family – grandparents, aunts, and uncles – often get more involved when there's only one parent. The baby can greatly benefit from this network of support and love.
■ Looking after a baby alone is a great achievement. You'll strengthen as a person as you watch your baby develop.
■ If you're single because your relationship has broken down, you've made the right decision; it's better for the baby to live with one fairly contented person than two people who are at war.

Balancing your relationship with your baby

I believe in showing boundless affection to babies, but you do need to balance your relationship with your baby – some lone parents may invest all their emotions and energies in their baby and use him as an emotional crutch. You don't have to be a mother and father; being a responsive parent is good enough. Your baby has no notion of lacking a second parent; he's happy with you, so you don't need to over-compensate.

Encouraging independence

You and your baby will have a very close and important one-to-one relationship and no one can take that away from you, but babies need and thrive on exposure to others and should be encouraged to interact with a wide range of people. Introduce him to other adults, and children, so he gets used to being without you now and then. This will make it much easier for you and him if you have to introduce a childminder.

Feeling isolated

All single parents are bound to experience feelings of loneliness and yearn for adult company. When the baby is very young, he won't be the best company as he only sleeps, cries, and feeds; as he gets older and begins to develop skills, you'll want the company of others so that you can share the pleasure and joy of this with someone else.

Having a social life

It's important that you have adult company outside of work as well as time away from your baby and, of course, if you want to build future relationships you have to get out and meet people:

- If it's difficult for you to go out for financial or childcare reasons, invite people to your house for a meal – ask your guests to bring a course.
- Get to know other mothers – they'll probably be glad of the company.
- Ask people if they will babysit – you don't know unless you ask.
- Find hobbies, classes, and events that have creche facilities.
- Find out about local activities so that you can meet other parents.

Sharing your baby's development

As your baby develops new skills (see p. 146), don't be afraid to share your joy with your relatives and friends – if they're close to your baby, they'll love to hear about it. Keep your own record of when each milestone occurs; when there is only one of you it will be more difficult to remember them.

Potential difficulties

DIFFICULTY	HOW TO DEAL WITH IT
Financial	With only one income, you're more likely to struggle financially and be unable to provide your baby with as many toys and clothes as you would like. Make sure you're getting all the benefits to which you're entitled, especially from your ex-partner. Remember that material possessions are not the most important things you can give to your baby.
Tiredness	If you're looking after your baby alone, the physical and emotional strains will be more of a problem. Catnap whenever your baby does. Try to take proper breaks and ask for and accept offers of help.
Concerns about the baby	If your baby becomes ill, you're unlikely to have someone there to reassure you and keep things in perspective. Look at pages 120–123 and consult your doctor as early as possible to minimize your worries.
Childcare	Affording childcare (see p. 172) can be a struggle for single parents. You may find that local council-run nurseries make special provision for babies of single parents. Look into sharing a nanny with another parent. If there is a creche at work, or one could be set up, this would minimize having to transport the baby around.

The single father

There are very few men who are the sole carers of a young baby, but for those that are the pleasures and most of the problems will be the same as those of a single mother. Remember that fathers can do everything that mothers can do except breastfeed.

The benefits
Although being a single father isn't ideal, a single father may benefit in ways that wouldn't have happened had he been sharing the care with his partner. Research has shown that single fathers are more satisfied parents, feel closer to their child, and are more confident and effective than the average father.

The problems
Isolation may be the main problem that occurs for the single father. Like a father who stays at home while his partner works (see p. 176), a single father may find the female-dominated environments that he is faced with difficult and, sadly, there may be those who question his ability to bring up his baby properly.

The absent parent

Try to keep communicating with the absent parent:

- Try to reach an agreement on access arrangements and on how you want to raise your child.

- Ensure that he or she is clear about financial support required. Seek legal advice if necessary.

- Try to spend time together as a family occasionally, and, if appropriate, encourage the other grandparents to see your baby.

The instant family

An "instant family" may be created through adopting a baby or by joining a ready-made family. A new baby brought into either situation can raise issues that aren't present for most new parents.

Questions and concerns

Adopting a baby is a big decision. You're bound to have doubts and fears about this new responsibility.

What if I can't cope?
All new parents have days when they can't cope (see p. 130). As an adoptive parent, you may have the added pressure of feeling that you're responsible for someone else's child and may have had less time to prepare. Don't be afraid to ask for help; use the adoption services as they're there to help.

What kind of child will I raise?
No one can predict the kind of person a child will turn out to be. Each individual is unique, so even biological parents have no idea whether their children will resemble them physically or in terms of personality.

Will I be a good enough parent?
Your motives for wanting to adopt and your suitability will be analysed before you're accepted as adoptive parents. It's natural to question whether you'll be good parents, but I think the most important aspects of being parents have nothing to do with being the birth parents. These are:

■ Your feelings and actions towards your child.

■ Your sensitivity to your child's individual needs.

■ Being consistently loving and accepting.

■ Being fair and firm in setting limits for your child.

Adopting a young baby

If you're fortunate enough to adopt your baby when she's very young, then everything said about bonding in earlier chapters applies to you. Babies come equipped with a strong urge to bond with their parents, or to anyone who gives them loving care, so you'll be off to the same promising start as everyone else. What may be difficult, is that you won't have had the nine-month buildup to the birth and the internal bonding in the same way as a pregnant mother. On the other hand, as an adoptive parent you may have a stronger yearning for a baby than a natural parent. This makes you ideally placed to be a generous and loving parent, so be confident.

Adopting an older baby

If you adopt a baby when she is a few months old, it's really important that you find out as much as possible about the circumstances of her life up to the time when she came to you. This will help you to compensate for any experiences on which she has missed out and for any delay in the developmental stages you would normally expect her to have passed through. Don't, however, worry about her development too much; your baby may not have been affected at all by not being with her natural parents. Even if it has affected her, in the right loving environment your baby will soon be able to catch up.

Bonding with an older baby

Trust is the basis of all good relationships between babies and their parents; if you have adopted an older baby, you may have to work harder to establish this trust than parents who have had their babies with them from birth. An older baby is likely to have been placed with foster parents for the first few months of her life and will have formed a strong attachment to them. Your baby may not immediately react as you had hoped; she has to learn how to respond to and accept your love and affection, and this takes time. Be reassured, however, that if you are relentless in offering your baby love, comfort, and affection, she will eventually learn to trust you and to accept and reciprocate your feelings.

A new baby in the stepfamily

If partners with a stepfamily decide to have a baby of their own, the dynamics of the family will change. While the baby may act as a uniting force within the family, her arrival may equally provoke some of the anxieties and tensions that were present at the formation of the family.

How stepchildren are affected

Your stepchildren's reaction to your baby will depend on how old they are, their relationship with you, and their past experiences. If their parents have split up recently, it may be more difficult; they're again being asked to adjust because of the actions of their parents.

Insecurities The news of the baby may remind the children of a previous breakup, and feelings, such as rejection and fear of losing a parent, may resurface. They may worry about the baby being seen as more precious and more desirable because she is a product of the present (your preferred) relationship, rather than of the past (your rejected) union.

Realization Many children from broken marriages live in hope that their parents will reunite. A new baby is a clear sign of commitment between their parent and stepparent, which often brings the truth home.

Relationship with stepparent If you and your stepchild have already established a good relationship, the arrival of your baby will cause fewer problems. If there are underlying tensions, the new baby may be the catalyst for resentment and anger.

Second time around A man who has a child later in life may change his priorities and be a more devoted father. Older children may resent not getting this attention when they were growing up. It's also common for children to find it distasteful for a parent to start a new family.

How you can help

Once the baby is born, your stepchild may become more accepting. To minimize problems talk to him as early as possible. Ask him to tell you his concerns and reassure him that you still love him and that there's space and time for everyone to enjoy the baby. Encourage him to develop his own relationship with your baby. He may enjoy some responsibility, but don't abuse this – older stepchildren may resent being used as babysitters.

Deciding to have a baby

A couple may decide to bring a new baby into the stepfamily for a variety of reasons. One partner may be childless and want a baby of his or her own. The other partner, who is already a parent, may feel less of a need. Even if they both have children, they may feel that a baby will make them and also the whole family closer.

Planning ahead

■ There may be financial obligations to an ex-partner and children from a previous relationship that can make affording a baby more difficult. Also, be aware that stepchildren living with you may resent having to sacrifice new clothes or going out because of the baby.

■ Do you have room for the baby? If it means that stepchildren will have to move out of, or share, a bedroom discuss this as a family rather than just telling the children it will happen. If you have to move house, will it make it more difficult for visiting stepchildren to stay?

Telling an ex-partner

It's always better for your ex-partner to hear that you're having a baby from you rather than from someone else and they definitely shouldn't be told by the children — some people are shocked at their feelings when they hear the news and worry that their own children will lose out. However, if you have a good relationship with your ex-partner and he or she reacts positively to you having a baby, this could also have an effect on how your children handle the news.

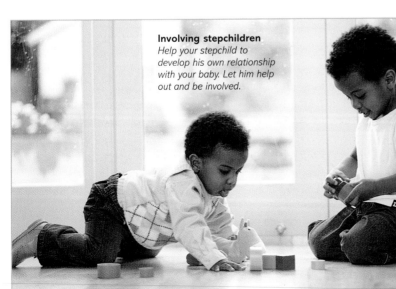

Involving stepchildren
Help your stepchild to develop his own relationship with your baby. Let him help out and be involved.

Your baby's
development

Your baby is developing from day one and it's one of the most fulfilling aspects of parenthood to watch him grow and learn. You'll become fascinated by his skills and amused by how he tries to copy you. In 12 months, he'll change from a tiny helpless newborn into a sturdy and sociable toddler who very much has a mind of his own. Your role as parents is crucial in your baby's development: you are his first teacher and friend and by being aware of the stages of development you can encourage certain skills at certain times. It's important, however, to remember that your baby's physical and mental development is individual to him, so never push him beyond his capabilities. Your baby mainly learns through play: he'll love it if you're his playmate and although you should show him how things work, it's essential to his sense of self and independence that he finds out how to do things for himself. He also learns by watching others, so encourage his social skills; getting to know other people is crucial to his development.

How babies develop

New skills

You'll see clear signs when your baby is close to acquiring a skill – a "milestone". Watch for the signs and only then match your efforts to her development and give her games to help. With correct timing she'll acquire skills at 100 per cent of her potential. If you force her too early or leave it too late, she'll acquire the skill, but not at her full capability. Main milestones are:

■ Smiling at a distance (6 weeks).

■ Discovering her hands and feet (3–4 months).

■ Blowing bubbles – the first sign of real speech (5 months).

■ The ability to transfer an object from one hand to the other (6 months).

■ Knowing her name (6 months).

■ Sitting unsupported (7 months).

■ "Getting" a simple joke like peep-bo (8 months).

■ Wanting to feed herself (9 months).

■ Crawling (9 months).

■ Pointing to an object with her forefinger (10 months).

■ Picking up objects with her finger and thumb (10 months).

■ Swivelling around while sitting to reach a toy (10 months).

■ Putting things into containers and taking them out (11 months).

■ Saying her first word with meaning (11–12 months).

■ Walking unsupported (12–13 months).

One of the most fulfilling aspects of parenthood is watching and sharing in your baby's development. Encourage her to learn new skills, while allowing her to develop at her own pace.

Newborn babies

Your baby starts to develop from the very second she's born and she'll be longing to learn. You'll see evidence of this if you watch an infant just after birth. Every baby enters the world in a state of "quiet alertness" and this state of intense focus on her surroundings can last up to an hour. She's a sponge ready to soak up information about her new environment:
■ She recognizes your voice – and your partner's – immediately. She's heard these voices for months and switches on to them instantly.
■ Your baby is born with her sight at a fixed focus of 20–25 cm (8–10 in); if you hold her at this distance from your face at birth, she can see you clearly and she will smile at you.
■ She has an acute sense of smell and will be able to inhale and register the natural scent (pheromones) from your body.
■ She'll "mouth" in response to you if she can see your face and your lips moving (at a distance of 20–25 cm/8–10 in); she's attempting conversation.

Stimulating your baby

Both of you are your baby's first teachers and playmates. You must feed her with all kinds of stimulation, through play and through the way in which you interact with her, if you want to help her develop to her optimal potential. Your job is to teach her to be imaginative, adventurous, curious, helpful, and generous. There is no limit to the amount of praise and encouragement you should give her as she learns new skills and begins to discover her world.

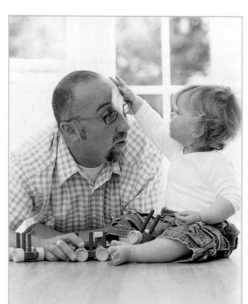

Being a playmate
Show your baby how toys work. This will help him to learn more quickly and he'll enjoy you joining in.

Rules of development

Your baby develops to her own timetable and it's pointless trying to set a different one. Remember the following:

■ No two children develop at the same rate so don't compare your baby to other babies – even if they did walk or talk before her.

■ Development is continuous, although certain skills will be acquired in a spurt while other skills slow down. For example, when a child is mastering walking, she may turn into a sloppy feeder.

■ A baby won't learn to say words with meaning before she's about ten months old and won't speak until much later.

■ Development of the whole body depends on how mature the brain is and whether or not brain, nerve, and muscle connections have grown. Your baby can't learn a skill like walking or talking until all the connections are in place. Bladder control is not possible until 18 months (see p. 181). If you expect her to use the potty any earlier, this is likely to lead to failure and could slow down your baby's progress later.

■ Development proceeds from head to toe (see p. 150) so a baby can't sit until she can control her head and she can't stand until she can sit.

■ Skills gradually become finer; for example, at about five months she "grasps" with her open hand; at eight months she can pick things up with her fingers and, when all the nerves and muscles have connected, she can pick up an object with her index finger and thumb.

■ Be aware that over-stimulation is as bad as under-stimulation; if there is a constant barrage of noise and movement, your baby may become very confused and gain very little in terms of development.

Positive discipline

Teaching your baby right from wrong starts at the very beginning, but it's the way you teach her that will affect her physical and emotional well-being:

■ Praise and reward her good behaviour and ignore bad behaviour, especially if it occurs at meal times.

■ Discipline her through love, praise, and encouragement. Never use anger and smacking – this can have a damaging effect.

■ Set useful tasks to help her understand the discipline of a daily routine – for example, encourage her to feed herself and brush her hair.

■ Hold your finger up and say "no" firmly if she's likely to harm herself, others, or cause damage. She'll understand this from around four months.

Helping your baby to develop happily

WHAT TO DO	HOW IT HELPS YOUR BABY
Set realistic goals	Set appropriate goals for your baby; for example, don't expect her to be able to play properly with toys designed for older babies. If you do this, it will outstrip her skills and she will become unhappy, frustrated, and demoralized. Always concentrate on accomplishments, not deficiencies, and praise your baby with theatrical gestures.
Be a playmate	You are your baby's first playmate as well as her teacher. Make time to play with her whenever you can – even if it means the washing up has to wait another hour! Babies have to be shown how to do things, so get down there and join in – your baby will love it. But don't interrupt when she's engrossed in something; it's hard enough for her to concentrate and see a job through to completion, without being distracted.
Encourage speech	Encourage your baby to talk – even when she's only gurgling. Keep her eyes 20–25 cm (8–10 in) from yours when she makes noises, especially when feeding and talking to her. That's her first experience of feeling valued and a valued baby will grow up to be a child who talks to you about everything – good and bad.
Repeat everything	Repeat and repeat words and actions until you're sick of it. You must tell your baby the same thing over and over again – using the same even tone of voice – and show her how to do things. It will all be worthwhile once she understands and begins to copy.

Boys and girls

Newborn babies

The differences in behaviour and development of boys and girls begin at birth and continue as they grow and develop (see p. 182). In newborn babies, the differences are mainly in the way they use their senses to perceive things and in the kind of things in which they show an interest.

Hearing
Hearing in boys is less acute than in girls, which means they have more difficulty in locating the source of sounds. Girls are more easily calmed by soothing words because of their acute hearing. Whisper close to your baby boy's ear to stimulate his hearing and to help calm him.

Speech
A baby girl uses her voice to get attention earlier and more often than a boy. If a newborn boy hears another baby cry, he'll join in but will stop crying quite quickly, whereas a girl will cry for longer.

Sight
A newborn girl responds enthusiastically to visual things. A boy quickly loses interest in a design or picture and requires much more visual stimulation up to the age of about seven months.

Social skills
Boys are as interested in things as they are in people, while girls show a clear preference for the human face. This female trait continues into later life as an ability to intuitively read facial expression. Encourage your son to develop his social skills by holding him 20–25 cm (8–10 in) from your face so he can see you clearly.

It's a biological fact that there are differences in behaviour and development between boys and girls from birth. Don't enforce stereotypes, but help your baby to develop skills that don't come as naturally, such as language for a boy and spatial skills for a girl.

Differences in brain development
Gender differences stem from the way the brain develops in male and female embryos. For a baby to learn and develop, certain connections have to have taken place between the right and left halves of the brain. Girls grow these connections earlier than boys (many are already in place when girls are born), which enables them to adapt faster to their new environment after birth. Connections form in a boy's brain more slowly and because of this later development, a baby boy will need slightly more help from you to reach his milestones (see p. 146).

Avoiding stereotypes
Stereotypes influence children and, worse, they tend to make people label certain qualities as inferior and superior – the latter usually being attributed to males. When children are taught to think, feel, and act in line with a stereotyped model, it can stunt their personal growth. Individuality should be encouraged, regardless of gender.

Discouraging stereotypes in a girl
■ Encourage physical activities usually associated with boys; these will help your baby's muscle development.
■ Make her feel important through eye contact and by using her name; this helps her to develop a sense of self.
■ Don't always whisper baby talk to her.
■ Don't only provide her with soft toys.
■ Don't only give her dresses and pink clothes to wear.

Spatial skills
Help your daughter to develop spatial skills by encouraging her to play with practical toys.

Gender differences up to age six

WHAT DEVELOPS	GIRLS	BOYS
Natural ability	Girls are better at language skills like talking, reading, and writing and they tend to keep this ability.	Boys are slower to develop language skills, but from a very early age they show superior spatial skills.
Social skills	Girls are more sociable than boys – they're more interested in people and feelings and display this regard for others even in the first 12 months.	Boys are generally more interested in objects than people and feelings. Unlike girls, they tend to look after themselves rather than groups.
Behaviour and personality	Girls cope better with stress and are more conciliatory. They tend to have fewer behavioural problems than boys.	Boys tend to be more aggressive, competitive, and rebellious than girls. They're more likely to develop behavioural problems.
Physical growth	Girls walk earlier than boys. They grow faster and more steadily – they don't tend to have growth spurts. They gain bladder and bowel control earlier.	Boys shoot ahead physically after five years. They develop faster during growth spurts, when many skills tend to emerge over a short time.

Father

Think about your attitudes and the type of activities you're encouraging, as these influence how your child develops and comes to see him or herself.

Influencing your daughter

As a father, you may consciously or unconsciously reinforce your daughter's femininity. Fathers often involve boys in "rough-and-tumble" games, whereas they'll be more gentle with girls. Expose your daughter to all kinds of activities and let her choose – rather than limiting her to traditionally feminine pastimes like ballet and drama introduce other activities like football too. Don't fall into the trap of believing some behaviour is acceptable in boys and not in girls – you diminish your daughter if you do this. Try to be aware that your daughter is very likely to feel devalued if she sees you devaluing her mother.

Influencing your son

Research shows that boys learn how to behave from their fathers. You can encourage your son to develop the more attractive male qualities (such as gentleness and a sense of responsibility) rather than the less desirable ones (such as being aggressive, dominant, and confrontational) simply by the way in which you behave. Your son will watch your actions and will imitate you in every respect. The quality of fathering that he receives from you is the most critical factor in how he views himself as a male.

Discouraging stereotypes in a boy

■ Don't stereotype him into the traditional male role with over-boisterous games, loud talk, loud toys, and by only dressing him in blue clothes.

■ Don't burden him with all that "big boys don't cry" "stiff upper lip" stuff; big boys do cry, and he's only a child!

■ Little boys are naturally very loving – make him proud of that and don't sneer when he shows affection.

■ Stress gentleness from when he's very young.

■ Let him have a doll and soft toy to cuddle.

■ Play down aggression by being gentle, but firm.

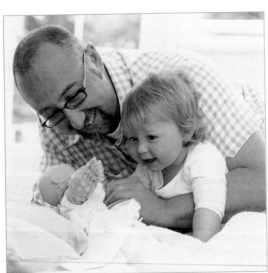

Being a role model
You can positively influence your son by actively joining in with pastimes traditionally associated with females.

How your baby grows

Concerns about weight gain

A baby's growth is an important indicator of health and well-being, but don't become blinkered about weight gain – it isn't the only issue. Any real discrepancies between length and weight should be picked up at your baby's developmental checks (see p. 155), but, if you're concerned, speak to your doctor beforehand.

What if my baby isn't gaining weight?
Some babies remain the same weight for a while and then have a growth spurt. So don't worry if your baby doesn't gain weight over, say, one week or appears to have lost weight. Don't be tempted into switching to bottle-feeding in the hope of improving "slow" weight gain. In fact, if you breastfeed your baby he's likely to grow faster, especially in the first few weeks.

What if my baby is overweight?
Some babies are naturally fatter than others, which may lead to some physical development happening slightly later. If you're concerned that your baby weighs too much for his age, seek medical advice, but don't reduce his intake of food as this could affect growth and development. The aim should be to maintain his weight at the current level until his length catches up. Research does, however, show that the pattern of heart disease and adult obesity can be set very early by being overweight from overfeeding. never press your baby to finish off the last drops of a feed.

Your baby's physical development will be monitored closely at the developmental checks (see p. 155): growth (centile) charts, which show the rate of growth expected for your baby's weight and gestational age at birth, will be used to map his progress. In the first year he will grow faster than at any other time in his life. Physical development starts at the top, which is why his head looks large, and from the inner parts to the extremities, which is why his hands and feet look tiny. Remember, your baby's development is individual to him; don't worry if he appears to be growing faster or slower than other babies. All babies grow at their own rate.

Weight

When a baby is born, the question "How heavy was he?" comes only second in the West to "Is it a boy or a girl?". Although people will place importance on your baby's weight, it is not the only sign of growth and it is important not to use this as the only way to judge his well-being (see left). Your baby's weight will be monitored at the developmental checks (see p. 155); you can also have him weighed at your local baby clinic or doctor's surgery. Babies are normally weighed naked. One feature all babies have in common is chubby arms and legs; this is due to uneven fat distribution and your baby will not lose this until he begins to use his limbs and becomes active.

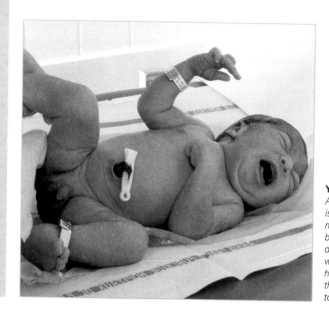

Your newborn
At first, a newborn is floppy and has no head control. As bone and muscle develop, your baby will learn to control his head, which is the first step towards walking.

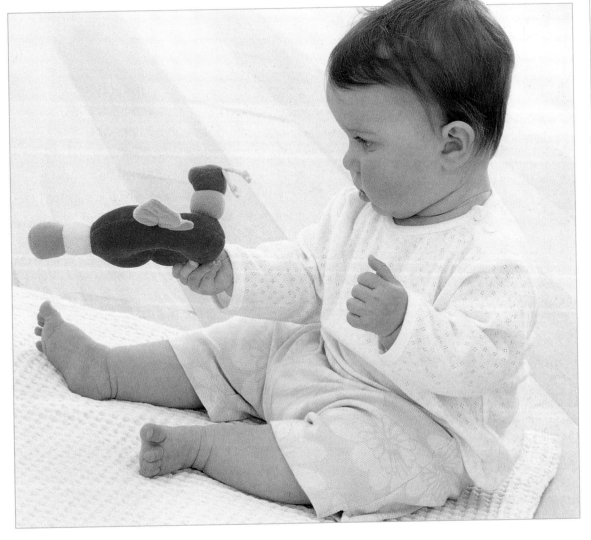

At seven months
Once your baby learns to control her head, she will learn to sit, at first propped up by cushions and later unsupported.

The normal pattern of weight gain

- In the first few days your baby may lose ten per cent of his birth weight.
- By the tenth day he'll have regained his birth weight.
- In the following six months he'll gain weight rapidly, at a rate of about 1 kg (2 lb) each month.
- In the second six months weight gain slows down and he'll put on around 500 g (1 lb) each month.

Length (height)

Your baby's size is partly due to inheritance – if you're both tall, the chances are you'll have a long baby. The biggest increase in length occurs in the first six months, after which growth slows down. If your child appears well and healthy, there's no reason for you to worry about his growth rate; any pronounced disproportion between length and weight will be investigated at the developmental checks (see p. 155).

12 months
At around a year he should be able to stand unsupported and perhaps be ready to take his first steps.

An approximate guide to a baby's growth rate

- A newborn full-term baby is on average 50 cm (20 in) long.
- Her length will increase by 25–30 cm (10–12 in) in the first year.
- On average, boys tend to be taller than girls for the first two years.

Head size

A newborn baby is top-heavy, with a disproportionately large head – this gradually alters over the first four years. Head circumference is monitored at the developmental checks; if the proportions don't even out, it could alert doctors to certain, rare, medical conditions.

How the proportions change

- A newborn baby's head circumference is about 35 cm (14 in), which is disproportionately larger than the rest of her body. By the time she is 12 months old, the size of her chest and head should have evened out.
- When a baby is born, her head makes up one quarter of the length of her body, compared to an adult's head, which makes up around one eighth.

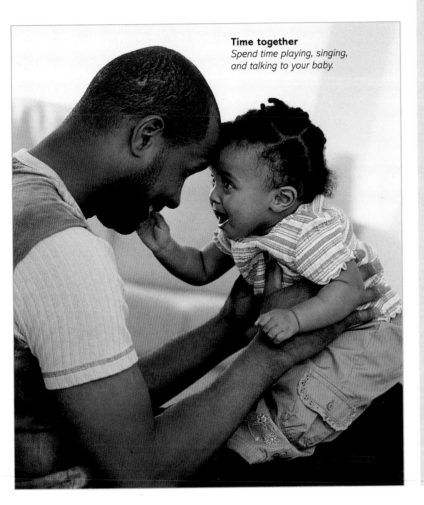

Time together
Spend time playing, singing, and talking to your baby.

How the senses develop

In the first year, your baby will begin to discover her world through her senses.

Vision
Your newborn has limited, but excellent, vision; at a distance of 20–25 cm (8–10 in) she sees clearly, so keep your face at this distance from hers when talking or smiling and she'll respond. At six weeks her eyes focus at any distance and both eyes work together. By three months she has full perception of colours; at six months she can see more detail and by one year her vision is well developed.

Hearing
She recognizes your voice and your partner's from birth, and will turn her head when you speak, so talk to her from the very first day.

Touch
Babies begin by "feeling" the shape and texture of objects with their lips and tongue and then explore with their hands.

Taste and smell
Newborns have a complete set of tastebuds and can recognize their parents' smell. They only like sweet tastes and smells, which is why they love breastmilk, but they gradually accept different tastes and make their likes and dislikes known.

Nerve and muscle development

WHAT DEVELOPS	HOW IT DEVELOPS	WHAT IT MEANS FOR YOUR BABY
Nerve connections to limb muscles	Nerves grow slowly from the brain and spine to reach the different muscle groups in the limbs. In a newborn, connections between these nerves have not been formed so movements are uncontrolled and crude. As the nerves grow and forge connections, movements become finer and more precise.	Your baby progresses from picking something up with his fist at four months to picking up objects with his finger and thumb by ten months. As nerves grow outwards and down from the brain and spine, your baby will achieve head control and then sit, crawl, and stand, before finally walking.
Nerve connections to bladder muscles	It takes at least 18 months for nerves to grow as far as the bladder. Prior to that your baby can't have any control over how his bladder works – so don't expect it.	Once nerve connections to the bladder are in place, your baby has to "train" the bladder muscles to hold urine and then let go. This takes several months and can't be hurried.

Cleaning her teeth
Encourage your baby to clean her own teeth from an early age – she'll enjoy it!

How your baby's teeth develop

A first tooth is an exciting milestone. Teeth usually start to come through from six months, but the age varies from baby to baby (a few babies are born with a tooth already through, while others are still toothless on their first birthday). During teething, your baby may be more irritable and more wakeful than usual (see p. 109).

Preventing problems

You can help prevent your baby developing any teething problems:

■ Buy your baby a small, soft toothbrush and get him into the routine of brushing his teeth in the morning and at bedtime.

■ Don't give him drinks and snacks that contain added sugar. Give him plain water to drink instead of juice sometimes.

■ Never add sugar to fruit juice, and always give him undiluted juice in a beaker rather than bottle.

How teeth come through

■ The first tooth to appear is usually a lower incisor, followed straight away by its neighbour.

■ Next come the upper incisors, followed first by the upper lateral incisors, then by the lower lateral incisors. There may be a delay before the first molar appears.

■ After the two first molars come the canines, and finally the second molars appear.

The order teeth appear
The age when teeth are cut varies, but they always come through in the same order: incisors, first molars, then canines.

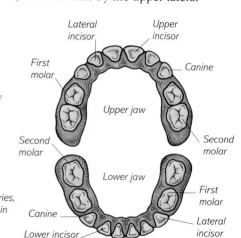

Lateral incisor
Upper incisor
First molar
Canine
Upper jaw
Second molar
Second molar
Lower jaw
Canine
First molar
Lower incisor
Lateral incisor

Developmental checks

You'll be asked to take your baby for a developmental check periodically, for example, at six to eight weeks and perhaps once again later in your baby's first year. As well as discussing any issues with you, the health worker will weigh your baby, measure his length and head circumference and then a doctor will check the baby's general health and carry out specific medical checks (see charts below).

What is the purpose of the checks?

Many health professionals feel that "testing" babies at certain stages to see whether they are "up to the mark", is crude; now they are much more interested in the well-being of the whole child. When you're invited to go to a clinic, or perhaps meet a health worker at your home, you'll be asked a series of questions to establish how you're all getting on together, how you are managing and whether you've noticed any specific problems with your baby. You should think of it as an opportunity to discuss any aspects of your baby's life (not just his development) or of your life with him that seem relevant: baby checks aren't, or at least they're not supposed to be, just about ticks in boxes.

Preparing yourself before you go

Make a list of questions and concerns you'd like to discuss. For example, you may have problems feeding or difficulty coping with sleepless nights. Don't be afraid to highlight problems – being a new parent is not easy for anyone and you should take the opportunity to get expert advice.

What if my baby has a problem?

It's worrying to have doubts cast over your baby's development (see p. 124). If you have any concerns or a problem is found:

■ Ask for time to sit down and talk through exactly what is wrong with your baby. Ask as many questions as necessary, especially if it isn't clear what the doctor is saying. Don't be fobbed off by being told the health worker hasn't got time at the moment or that you are worrying for no reason.

■ Don't accept that you should "wait and see" – if there's any question of a problem, your baby should be referred for tests or to see a specialist straight away.

■ Get a second opinion if you're not satisfied or are still concerned.

6–8 week check

CHECK	WHY IT IS DONE
Heart and lungs	The breathing rate and heart rate are checked, particularly to rule out a heart murmur.
Palate	The palate is checked at birth, and now, for completeness and to test the sucking reflex.
Vision	Your baby will be tested to see if he can follow movement and look towards light.
Hearing	Your baby will have had his hearing tested before the 6–8 week check in the newborn hearing screening programme.
Mobility	Your baby's hips are checked for displacement and any correction needed. Head control is checked.
Testes	If you have a baby boy, the doctor will check to ensure that his testes have descended.

Later in first year

CHECK	WHY IT IS DONE
Speech	Your baby should be making a range of sounds by now and his ability to do this will be noted.
Vision	Any problem should have become apparent, but the doctor may check for a squint.
Handling	The doctor will give your baby a toy to hold so that he can check his handling skills.
Mobility	The doctor will check that your baby can sit up and is able to stand supported.
Testes	The testes may be checked again. If they haven't descended, an operation may be needed later.

Baby development

0–1 month

	What to look out for	
WHAT DEVELOPS	HOW SHE PROGRESSES	HOW YOU CAN HELP
Her mind	■ She can see clearly at a distance of 20–25 cm (8–10 in). ■ She will respond to your voice by moving her eyes and turning her head. ■ She will gaze at you and recognize you. ■ She will become quiet when you speak soothingly and distressed when you are loud.	■ When talking to her, hold your face 20–25 cm (8–10 in) away from hers. ■ When you speak, let her see your mouth moving. Smile and make eye contact at 20–25 cm (8–10 in). ■ Use your voice: speak in a sing-song voice, sing lullabies, and laugh a lot.
Her mobility	■ She will turn her head: this control is the first step towards learning to walk. ■ By the end of the first month, the most she may be able to do is lift her head about an inch off the surface when lying on her tummy.	■ Do gentle exercises to make her aware of her body (see p. 61). ■ Her neck and back muscles are too weak to lift her head so give her something to look at when she is lying on her back.
Her handling skills	■ Your baby is born with "the grasp reflex", which means she will keep her fists tightly closed and grasp anything put into her fingers (see above). ■ If she's startled, she'll spread her arms, fingers, and legs to protect herself.	■ Your baby can't purposely hold on to anything until she loses the grasp reflex. ■ Gently open her fingers one at a time. ■ If she grasps your fingers, she'll take her weight if you pull her up a little way.
Her social skills	■ Your baby is born ready to love other people and asks for love. She longs for company and takes immediate delight in you. ■ She'll respond instantly to your voice and your smell. She is upset by a harsh-sounding voice.	■ Let her have contact with other people from when she's very young. ■ Be physical: make skin-to-skin contact with your baby; use your body to express love; rock, sway, and dance with her.
Her speech	■ She "mouths" if you speak to her at a distance of 20–25 cm (8–10 in) because she is trying to imitate your gestures and expressions. ■ She's born longing to communicate and will start to make little burbling noises as a mark of contentment.	■ Talk to your baby all the time so she gets used to your voice. ■ Make facial expressions to match what you're saying.

Stimulating play
■ Stimulate her senses with songs and by talking to her. Hold her where she can see you, ideally at 20–25 cm (8–10 in) (see left).
■ Move your fingers or a colourful toy through her line of vision so that her eyes and head follow your movements and put a mobile over her cot.
■ Do gentle knee bends and straighten her legs when you're changing her nappy; this will encourage your baby to straighten out her body.
■ Place a small mirror or a clear, cartoon-style drawing of a face in her cot where she can see it when she is lying down.

Baby development

1–2 months

What to look out for

WHAT DEVELOPS	HOW HE PROGRESSES	HOW YOU CAN HELP
His mind	■ Your baby begins to smile at you from a distance and bobs his head when you talk to him (see above). ■ He starts to be interested in his surroundings, looking in the direction of sounds and staring at objects as though "grasping" with his eyes.	■ Prop him up slightly with cushions or put him in a baby chair. Place lots of brightly coloured toys within his view. ■ Put a mobile over the cot – it's good if it makes a sound or has a musical box.
His mobility	■ He can raise his head to 45 degrees when he's lying on his tummy. ■ By the end of this month he can support the weight of his head if you hold him upright with your hands around his chest.	■ Hold a coloured toy close to his head so that he has to lift his head to see it. ■ To teach your baby about balance, hold him upright on your knee so his legs take his own weight for a second.
His handling skills	■ Your baby will no longer have a grasp reflex. ■ His fingers are open most of the time and he's starting to become aware of them.	■ Touch, tickle, and massage his hands. ■ Give him toys and encourage him to bend his fingers over them.
His social skills	■ He's starting to notice people, but knows you from all others. ■ He smiles from a distance at six weeks and moves his whole body with excitement when he sees you.	■ Make sure you give your baby frequent skin-to-skin contact and maintain eye contact when you're talking to him and, more importantly, when feeding.
His speech	■ He will begin by answering you with small throaty sounds and by the end of two months he'll make grunts, cries, and move his whole body in his desire to communicate with you. ■ He knows your voice – and your partner's – and turns his head and neck when he hears you.	■ The more your baby is stimulated to talk by being talked to and encouraged to respond, the earlier he'll learn to talk and the better his quality of speech. ■ Talk non-stop, be theatrical with your conversations and ask questions.

Stimulating play

■ Sing and make eye contact (see right). Sway while you hold him.

■ Show him his hands and demonstrate how to wiggle his fingers. Play "This little piggy".

■ Gently rub a soft brush over his hands and fingers, especially at the tips.

■ Sit him up supported at an angle of 45 degrees – this helps to increase his concentration span. Use cushions or a bouncing baby chair on the floor. Let him touch toys or objects of different textures and shapes.

■ Dangle, kick, or bat small soft toys quite close to him, within striking distance of his hands.

■ Every day have a special walk, talk, and sing time with your baby. Carry him in a sling (see p. 77).

Baby development

2–3 months

What to look out for		
WHAT DEVELOPS	HOW SHE PROGRESSES	HOW YOU CAN HELP
Her mind	■ She's becoming familiar with her own body, staring at her fingers and then moving them. This is her first lesson in cause and effect. ■ She has a repertoire of responses to you: she smiles, mouths when you speak to her, nods, squeaks, yelps, and blows raspberries.	■ Show your baby her fingers so that she can study them. ■ Answer her with responses that are theatrical and larger than life. ■ Reward her attempts to relate to you with hugs, kisses, and squeals of delight.
Her mobility	■ She can keep her head up steadily now when in a standing or sitting position or while lying on her front, but not for long (see above). ■ When she's lying on her tummy, she can hold her head in line with her body.	■ Encourage her to reach out for soft toys, especially when she's on her tummy. ■ Teach your baby about balance: hold her in a standing position with your hands around her chest, for a few seconds at a time.
Her handling skills	■ She begins to discover her hands – she keeps them open and looks at them. ■ She'll hold a rattle for a few seconds if you place it in her hand.	■ Encourage her to look at her fingers and to hold a rattle. ■ Put toys over her cot or give her a baby gym to encourage her to reach out.
Her social skills	■ She turns her head to your voice and smiles because she is happy to see you. ■ She expresses her joy in you by waving her arms and kicking her legs.	■ Keep eye contact with her when feeding – it's heaven for her to have food and your attention at the same time! ■ Respond positively to her overtures.
Her speech	■ She will begin to make simple vowel sounds, such as "oh", "ah" and "uh". ■ She has a repertoire of easily recognized cries to express how she is feeling: hungry, tired, frustrated, lonely, angry, impatient, or just wanting to be left alone.	■ Imitate all the sounds she makes back to her. ■ When your baby cries, it's her way of communicating with you – always respond to it (see p. 104).

Stimulating play

■ Introduce her to small toys with different textures and say out loud to your baby how they feel (see left).

■ Act out nursery rhymes and play pat-a-cake.

■ Play lots of simple physical games, such as gentle jerks, knee bends, arm pulls, and tickling feet.

■ Lie on the floor opposite her while she lies on her tummy and looks at you – this will encourage head control.

■ Encourage her to reach out for soft objects.

■ Take her into the bath with you and encourage her to kick and splash. Make her aware of her hands by splashing them in the water.

Baby development

3–4 months

What to look out for

WHAT DEVELOPS	HOW HE PROGRESSES	HOW YOU CAN HELP
His mind	■ He's curious and wants to join in. ■ He can recognize places and faces as familiar. ■ He loves the breast or his bottle and shows it. ■ He'll laugh by the age of four months.	■ Offer a wide range of toys. ■ Explain everything you see and do. ■ Pin photographs of yourselves in his cot with a safety pin.
His mobility	■ He loves sitting up now with a little support from you or cushions. ■ If you gently pull him into a sitting position, he will bring his head up in line with his body. ■ If he is lying on his tummy, he can look straight at you now.	■ Sit him up with cushions for support. ■ Pull him gently up into a sitting position to strengthen his back and neck muscles. ■ Play games that make your baby swivel from the waist and offer toys that he is able to reach easily.
His handling skills	■ He's starting to control his hands and feet and will start reaching for his toes (see above). ■ He moves his hands and feet together. ■ He crosses his feet and puts a foot on the opposite leg.	■ Put toys in his hands when he reaches for them or he will overshoot. Make him reach for things in every position. ■ Give him rattles so that he can make noises with his hands.
His social skills	■ He looks at and smiles at people who talk to him – he hasn't learned shyness yet. ■ He knows you and your partner and people he sees regularly, such as grandparents. ■ He loves company and cries when left alone for long. He knows warmth, love, and the opposite.	■ Encourage his sense of humour. Laugh with him, share the joke, and imitate everything he does. Don't be afraid to over-act all your responses. ■ Encourage emotional development: laugh when he laughs and cry when he cries.
His speech	■ He'll squeal with pleasure. ■ He's learning all the basic tones of voices. ■ He says "m", "p", and "b" when unhappy and "j" and "k" when happy.	■ Repeat sounds back at him – "M, m, m you're not happy are you". Speak in a tone of voice that is appropriate.

Stimulating play

■ Gently pull him up when he is lying on his back (see right).

■ Play "peep-bo" and hiding-your-face games. When playing "peep-bo" stay slightly to one side so that your baby has to swing his trunk to find you.

■ Put objects on a string over his cot and pram so that he can examine them – one day he'll reach out and knock one.

■ Amplify his experiences by talking to him about what you see and do.

■ Place a rattle in your baby's hand and shake it a few times. He will be intrigued by its texture and by the sound that it makes.

■ Play tickling games to encourage his laughter.

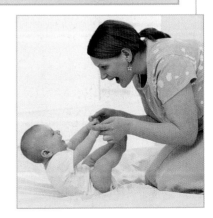

Baby development

4–5 months

What to look out for

WHAT DEVELOPS	HOW SHE PROGRESSES	HOW YOU CAN HELP
Her mind	■ Your baby loves games – she learns skills from them by copying what you do. ■ Her concentration is expanding. She spends a long time examining things. ■ She smiles at herself in the mirror. ■ She moves her arms and legs to attract you. ■ She pats her bottle when feeding.	■ When she attracts your attention respond to it; this will encourage good behaviour. ■ Turn your body theatrically towards her. Let her know you're attending to her by focusing on her: move towards her, bend down and make eye contact. ■ Call her by her name all the time.
Her mobility	■ She has now mastered full control of her head. Although it's quite steady, it may wobble if she moves suddenly.	■ Give her plenty of rocking motion. This will promote head stability and aid her when she begins walking.
Her handling skills	■ She puts things into her mouth, such as toys, her fist, her feet, as it's the most sensitive area (see above). ■ She grasps large toys with both hands and begins to use the little finger side of her hand to grip things. She sometimes can't let go.	■ Don't try to stop her putting her hand in her mouth – it's natural. ■ Play with her toes and guide them to her mouth. ■ Play give and take games with toys.
Her social skills	■ Your baby is beginning to be shy with strangers (this is the first sign of her emerging "self"), but she still smiles at people she knows.	■ Introduce her to all visitors so that she gets used to strangers and the concept of friends.
Her speech	■ Her language is very colourful: she tries to "talk" by blowing, babbling, squealing, laughing, and she says "ka" in an attempt to sound like you. ■ She uses facial expressions to communicate.	■ Imitate all her sounds with changes of pitch and volume. If she listens, stimulate her with new sounds and name them.

Stimulating play

■ Play rocking games while she is sitting on your lap (see left).
■ Play lots of games with her, especially those that involve clapping.
■ She loves crumpling paper – give her sheets of old lining paper or lots of tissue paper that crackles.
■ Hide her face under a towel for a second then whisk it away and say "peep-bo" – she'll squeal with delight.
■ Look out for your baby holding her hands up and her arms wide – this means that she wants to play.
■ Encourage her to open her fingers by playing giving and taking away games. Always give her the object when she reaches out.

Baby development
5–6 months

What to look out for

WHAT DEVELOPS	HOW HE PROGRESSES	HOW YOU CAN HELP
His mind	■ He gets excited if he hears someone coming. ■ He expresses his discomfort or insecurity. ■ He makes lots of attention-seeking sounds and raises his arms to be picked up.	■ Respond to his call as soon as you hear it. Shout out that you're coming, then go towards him and say his name. Hold out your arms as you approach him. ■ Keep using his name every time you speak to him.
His mobility	■ He's now strong enough to take the weight of his upper half on his arms. ■ He can sit for a few minutes supported on the floor with lots of cushions (see above).	■ Play bouncing games with your baby. Get a baby bouncer if he likes it. ■ Lie next to him on the floor and crawl around. It will encourage him to copy.
His handling skills	■ He now has the ability to transfer objects from one hand to another. ■ Holding one toy in his hand, he'll drop it to take hold of another. ■ He'll hold his bottle.	■ Show him how to let go and drop things and how to pass a toy from hand to hand. ■ Play give and take games – this will also encourage him to share.
His social skills	■ He starts to make assertive advances: pats your cheek, scratches, and slaps. ■ He explores your face with his hands – it means "hello", so say "hello" back and smile. ■ He's possessive of you and may be very wary of people he doesn't know.	■ Show your baby new gestures, stretch out your arms to him and he'll lift his too. ■ Make expansive gestures and pitch your voice to match. He will copy you. ■ Avoid leaving him in a room with strangers.
His speech	■ He blows bubbles (this is his first real speech). ■ He now says "ka", "da", and "ma" all the time and a new sound emerges: "ergh". ■ He seems to understand a bit of what you say.	■ If he appears to understand you, ask if he does, repeat what you said and praise him.

Stimulating play

■ Play weight-bearing games: these encourage him to take more and more weight on his legs, which helps to strengthen them. Hold him on your lap or on the floor, gently bounce him up and down and you'll feel him push off (see right).

■ Demonstrate cause and effect. Push a ball to him while he's sitting up and say "the ball is rolling".

■ Blow "raspberries" on his tummy when you're changing his nappy – encourage him to copy the different noises you make.

■ Reward him for holding out his arms by playing lifting games – squeal with delight as you lift him and swing him around.

Baby development
6–7 months

What to look out for

WHAT DEVELOPS	HOW SHE PROGRESSES	HOW YOU CAN HELP
Her mind	■ She starts off conversations and you'll understand many of her own sounds. ■ She knows her name and who she is. ■ She may want to feed herself. ■ She anticipates repetition and imitates you.	■ Encourage her sense of self by showing your baby her reflection in the mirror and repeating her name over and over "That's Oona, that's you". ■ Have conversations with her.
Her mobility	■ She can now bear weight on one hand when she is lying on her tummy (see above). ■ She can lift her head when lying on her back. ■ When you hold her up she can take all her own weight on straight legs and hips.	■ To encourage her to take her weight, play lots of standing games. ■ Place a toy above her while she's on her back and encourage her to lift her head to reach out for it.
Her handling skills	■ She reaches out for objects using only her fingers now. ■ She holds on to a toy if she reaches for another. ■ She bangs the table.	■ Let her try to feed herself from a dish with her own baby spoon. ■ Give her plenty of toys that are easy for her to hold.
Her social skills	■ Your baby loves other babies and stretches out to them in friendship. ■ She may cry if she's left with anyone other than you or your partner, especially if it's someone who she doesn't know.	■ Give her physical affection; she can't be loving to anyone (including herself) if she doesn't have a bank of love to draw on. ■ Keep introducing her to strangers and give her time to adjust.
Her speech	■ She now has very clear syllables with actions, "ba", "da", and "ka". ■ Cries have high and low pitches and a nasal sound has appeared.	■ Make every sound back to her to make her feel important.

Stimulating play

■ Play touching games: use every opportunity to touch your baby and let her touch you; she'll love it if you let her explore your face (see left).
■ Encourage her sense of self by playing games with her things and using her name: say "That's Oona's dress" and "Whose teddy is this? It's Oona's".
■ If she's wary of strangers now, introduce them gradually.
■ Develop her sense of humour with simple jokes like tickling; play "Round and round the garden, like a teddy bear".
■ To encourage her to pull her tummy off the floor, play at aeroplanes. Lay side by side on your front and lift your arms and body – and your baby's – off the floor.

Baby development
7–8 months

What to look out for

WHAT DEVELOPS	HOW HE PROGRESSES	HOW YOU CAN HELP
His mind	■ He's showing signs of determination; he'll keep going after toys he can't quite reach. ■ He concentrates hard on discovering what he can do with his toys – he's learning all the time about the properties of various objects.	■ Encourage him to retrieve a toy for which he has to stretch. ■ Play water games in the bath. ■ Give him plastic containers to pour, empty, and fill over and over.
His mobility	■ He'll sit rocking his body backwards and forwards to try to reach a toy. ■ He loves standing when supported. If you stand him on your lap, he'll jig about. ■ Lying on his front, he'll try to wriggle forwards.	■ While he's sitting, sit a little way from him and hold your arms out. He'll try to shuffle along on his bottom to reach you. ■ Hold him upright as much as possible. ■ Get him to reach a toy while on his front.
His handling skills	■ He loves making any noise by banging. ■ He'll try to copy you if you clap. ■ He can hold any toy firmly in his fingers. ■ He'll point to objects – this is the first stage of him learning the finger-thumb grasp (see above).	■ Give him spoons, pan lids, or a toy drum so that he can use his hands to bang and make a noise. ■ When he's sitting on the floor or in his cot, make sure that he has lots of toys to reach for, pick up, and explore.
His social skills	■ He will respond fully to sociable games such as "Pat-a-cake" or "This little piggy". ■ He doesn't like it when you're angry and will respond accordingly. ■ He's clear what "no" means and responds to it.	■ Make him feel valued by using his name in every situation. This will help him to develop a sense of himself. ■ When you need to say "no", say it firmly and use a different tone of voice.
His speech	■ He plays games with his mouth and tongue, blowing "raspberries" and smacking his lips. ■ He may combine two syllables such as "ba-ba" and "da-da", though not with meaning.	■ Play sound games to convey meaning – "quiet" (whisper) or "loud" (shout).

Stimulating play

■ Hold a mirror up so he can see himself, and say his name (see right).

■ Play and sing word games to encourage him to vocalize. Say rhymes over and over again always with the same emphasis and move your body; he'll start to copy you and use his.

■ Play with all kinds of safe household items as toys – for example, plastic or wooden spoons, pans, and brushes. Banging games will be huge fun.

■ Always answer his needs and cries; this breeds self-confidence and self-esteem.

■ Sit with your baby on the floor and encircle your legs around him. Fill the circle with his favourite toys.

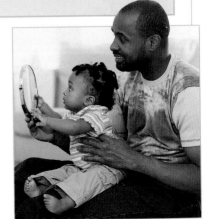

Baby development
8–9 months

What to look out for

WHAT DEVELOPS	HOW SHE PROGRESSES	HOW YOU CAN HELP
Her mind	■ Your baby loves familiar games and rhymes and laughs at the right times. ■ She can anticipate movements. ■ She will turn her head to her name and hold out her hands to be reached.	■ Help her to understand life on a day-to-day basis by explaining all routines. ■ Use meals and bath times as cues for special activities – "Now it's time for lunch", "Now it's time to have your bath".
Her mobility	■ She can take her weight on her legs, if supported. ■ She can sit for ten minutes, lean forwards and sideways, and stay balanced. ■ She can roll from side to side, but can't get up from a sitting position to stand.	■ Help her to stand from a sitting position, bend her hips and knees for her. ■ Help her to cruise round the furniture by having pieces close together. Encourage her to hold on to a low piece of furniture.
Her handling skills	■ Her movements are becoming more refined. ■ Her fingers are used for exploring – she puts things in her mouth much less. ■ She has the ability to lean forwards and pick up small things easily (see above).	■ Show her how to stack bricks on top of one another or side by side – she's learning about volume as well as fine movements. ■ Give her a soft cooked pea to pick up between her finger and thumb.
Her social skills	■ She's shy with new faces and may be reluctant to be picked up by people she doesn't know. ■ She remembers people she has got to know well, even if she hasn't seen them for a few days.	■ Talk to her on the telephone if you have to be away from home at all. ■ Get her a toy telephone to play with. ■ Help her get to know the babysitter.
Her speech	■ She's understanding more and more of what you say so repeat "Yes, that's what daddy means: it's cold outside, brrrr". ■ She'll start to add "t", "d", and "w" sounds. ■ She might make one animal sound if you do.	■ Repeat words that start with t, d and w. ■ Repeat all her sounds back to her. Name everything. ■ Read animal stories and make the noises.

Stimulating play

■ Get lots of noisy toys (wooden spoons, metal pots and pans, or a toy drum). It helps her to understand how to exert some control over things and herself and develops her understanding of cause and effect (see left).

■ Read a book or magazine. She'll love a commentary from you.

■ Name parts of your body and ask her to copy.

■ Crawl beside your baby and imitate her movements to encourage her to do the same.

■ Show her how you can put one brick on top of another. It takes great skill and she won't achieve it by herself for at least another month or so, but she'll enjoy knocking the bricks over and scattering them about!

Baby development
9–10 months

What to look out for

WHAT DEVELOPS	HOW HE PROGRESSES	HOW YOU CAN HELP
His mind	▪ Your baby is getting used to rituals; they order his life and make him feel secure. ▪ He'll wave bye bye. ▪ He'll put his foot out for a sock – he's longing to be helpful! ▪ He knows teddy and dolly. ▪ He'll look around corners for a toy.	▪ Try to keep to some sort of routine so that your baby can get used to it. ▪ Show him how to dress and undress, so that he begins to understand the concept of a daily routine. ▪ He should have toys such as teddies or dolls that are "like baby".
His mobility	▪ He's discovered mobility. ▪ He moves forward on his hands and knees and loves changing positions (see above). ▪ He can twist his trunk around quite confidently.	▪ Hold out your arms, call his name, and encourage him to crawl to you. ▪ Offer your fingers for him to pull himself up on, then lift his foot on and off the floor.
His handling skills	▪ He reaches for objects with his index finger and will master picking up something small, such as a raisin, with his thumb and index finger. ▪ He'll let go of objects deliberately. ▪ He can build a tower of two bricks.	▪ Point to objects for him. ▪ Put toys on the tray of his high chair and encourage him to throw them over; you can tie them on. ▪ Ask him to roll a ball to you.
His social skills	▪ He shows affection by pressing his face and head against yours and hangs on to you tightly. ▪ He'll give you a toy if you ask him for it, but become angry if you take it away.	▪ Teach about hugs – let's both have a hug together – he's learning reciprocity. ▪ Teach sharing: ask him for a bit of food and show him how nice he is for sharing it.
His speech	▪ Your baby begins to make lots of consonant sounds. ▪ He chatters away in the rhythm of speech, without any meaning.	▪ Name absolutely everything. ▪ Face your baby when you speak to him so that he is able to read your lip movements.

Stimulating play

▪ Read to him each day: read real story books and point out pictures. He'll learn to look at pictures the right way up and begin to recognize pictures of objects (see right).
▪ Rock him on your knee and pretend to drop him – he'll enjoy "falling".
▪ Play hide and seek by hiding yourself or a toy.
▪ Give him bath toys – plastic jugs, beakers, sieves, boats, and ducks.
▪ Give him a doll and teddy and show him how to dress and undress it.
▪ Give him squeaky toys, horns, and bells.
▪ Stack blocks or cubes of the same size on top of one another and side by side for him to see.

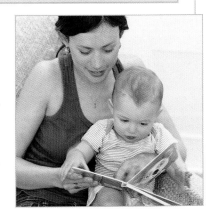

Baby development

10–11 months

	What to look out for	
WHAT DEVELOPS	**HOW SHE PROGRESSES**	**HOW YOU CAN HELP**
Her mind	■ Your baby will point things out to you. ■ She loves dropping toys off her high chair, then looking for them. ■ She asks to be picked up. ■ She learns through opposites: keep showing her examples, such as in and out, here and there, and over and under.	■ Read different kinds of books and magazines to her. ■ Encourage her concentration span by telling her a simple storyline. ■ Pick her up if she reaches out to you. ■ Keep demonstrating cause and effect, by pushing over bricks or splashing water.
Her mobility	■ She's crawling or shuffling at great speed. ■ If you support her standing, she'll lift one leg. ■ She's completely balanced while sitting.	■ Place a toy right behind her to make her twist around – it's okay, she's got the skill. ■ Position her so that she can crawl or shuffle.
Her handling skills	■ Your baby loves taking things out of containers and putting them back (see above). ■ She will hold something out to you if you ask for it.	■ Play giving things to each other and then taking them away, but don't force her to relinquish something. ■ Take her hand and point to objects.
Her social skills	■ She knows her name and knows who Mummy and Daddy are when you use the words. ■ She's got a wonderful sense of humour: play little jokes all the time and laugh at her attempts to make you laugh.	■ Use laughter to show your approval and silence to mean the opposite: this is gentle baby discipline and she'll soon catch on. ■ Demonstrate social rituals, such as kissing and waving goodbye.
Her speech	■ Your baby is now beginning to imitate real speech sounds. ■ She may start to attempt one word with meaning – "Dada" when Daddy appears is often the first.	■ Keep saying "Mama". ■ Repeat "Dada". Use association, for example: "Dada has gone to work".

Stimulating play

■ Play games with bricks: she will attempt to make a tower of bricks and you can demonstrate cause and effect by knocking them down and saying "all fall down" (see left).

■ Play games using the hands, such as "Incy-wincy spider" and "Jack and Jill" – buy a book that shows you the movements.

■ When reading, name several items on each page and go over them in the same order each time you read. Let her turn the pages.

■ Encourage her to practise putting in and taking out by giving her a wooden spoon and bowl or bricks and a basket.

■ Encourage her to pull herself up to standing by holding a favourite toy just out of reach.

Baby development
11–12 months

What to look out for

WHAT DEVELOPS	HOW HE PROGRESSES	HOW YOU CAN HELP
His mind	■ He loves jokes and will do anything for a positive response like a laugh – this will make him feel good about himself. ■ He knows about kissing and wants to kiss you.	■ Laugh when he finds something funny. ■ Let him kiss you, but don't ask him to kiss strangers. ■ Talk enthusiastically about your activities.
His mobility	■ He can walk if you hold one hand. ■ He'll walk if he pushes a sturdy trolley, or he'll hold on to furniture to steady himself.	■ While he's cruising, encourage him to launch off by calling him. ■ Make sure the furniture is steady.
His handling skills	■ He is getting better at feeding himself (see above). ■ He can rotate his hand to turn toys over. ■ He loves throwing things away. ■ He makes lines with a crayon. ■ He holds on to two things in one hand.	■ Keep putting two blocks into his hand. ■ Encourage self-feeding of soft but non-runny food with a spoon. Give him his own special dish and spoon. ■ Give him crayons and paper.
His social skills	■ He knows who he is. ■ He becomes quite possessive of his toys and resents them being removed. ■ He loves social gatherings as long as you or someone he is familiar with carries him. ■ He'll give you things if you ask for them.	■ Introduce him to lots of babies. ■ Encourage him to share. ■ Encourage affection by cuddling his doll. ■ Leave him with a babysitter occasionally. ■ Sit him in his high chair at the table or playpen in the room in which you're sitting.
His speech	■ He follows conversation and makes sounds in the gaps. ■ He may say one word, such as "dog", with meaning. ■ He can make you understand he wants something and what it is.	■ Teach him "thank you"; he may be able to say "ta". ■ Congratulate him when you understand what he's saying.

Stimulating play

■ Give him non-toxic coloured crayons and large sheets of plain paper on the floor, to encourage him to draw (see right).

■ Read simple stories about animals and their young to encourage his interest in other "babies". All babies love this.

■ Encourage him to stand unaided by holding him steady, then letting go for a second or two.

■ Concentrate on the names of objects and name parts of the body. Point to parts of your body and he'll copy.

■ If he uses the furniture as support to get around, place it slightly further apart to encourage him to bridge the gap. Be ready to help.

Going back
to work

No sooner than you've settled into being a mother and found a routine that's right for all of you, you may find yourself thinking about returning to work. For many women, this is a financial necessity and for some it's a relief after months of nappies and baby talk! Going back to work requires some reorganization and a change of priorities, and it's sensible to consider all the options quite soon after your baby is born. Try to decide as a family what arrangements suit you best. You may, for example, have the option to return part-time or work from home some days, or your partner may decide to give up work to care for your baby, especially if you earn more money. If you both work full-time, you'll have to arrange childcare and accept that on weekdays you're only going to see your baby for a couple of hours in the morning and evening. This is never ideal or easy, but as long as you maintain your baby's routine, and she has your undivided attention while you're with her, she won't suffer from having working parents.

Work and parenting

When is the right time?

Aside from legal requirements (see p. 184), your baby's needs and your feelings will, to an extent, dictate when you return to work:

■ If you want to continue breastfeeding, practise expressing enough milk for your baby's needs (see p. 80). If you intend to stop breastfeeding, you need to introduce the bottle in good time.

■ Think carefully about whether you feel ready – physically and emotionally – to return to work.

Work options

Look at all your options.

Part-time/job-sharing
Part-time can be the best of both worlds, as you have time with your baby and the stimulation of work, but you also have the pressure of both. If you can job-share, you may be better able to continue to build your career.

Working from home
You need to be self-disciplined and arrange some childcare (see p. 172), as you're likely to be distracted if your baby is at home.

Career break
You may decide to have a career break. Make sure this is what you really want and that you've thought about all the implications.

Father at home
If you want to return full-time, it may be an option for your partner to be the main carer (see p. 176).

Make the return to work easier for you all by ensuring you've made good childcare provisions and deciding how you'll adjust your routine. Remember that the changes may be unsettling at first, especially for your baby.

Making the decision

You may decide while you're pregnant that you want to return to work at the end of your maternity leave (see p. 184). Once the baby is born, however, it's normal to feel unsure about leaving him, especially as this is likely to coincide with the time that you're just settling into being a mother. On the other hand, you may find that you actually miss work and are ready, after a few months, to take a break from the domestic routine and return to an adult environment. Of course, there may simply be no decision for you to make – financially, you may have to work.

What to consider

Whatever you decided while pregnant, it's important to look at your financial and domestic situation once the baby is born and for you and your partner to talk about work options:

■ What type of childcare can you afford? Have you checked what is available in your area?

■ After covering the cost of childcare, does your salary leave enough extra to make it worthwhile? (Don't forget to take travel costs into account.)

■ Is it feasible to return to your old job as it was and also devote enough time to your baby? For example, does your job involve lots of overtime or travel away from home?

Concerns

For the past few months you'll have been focused on preparing for the birth and then looking after your new baby. Once you have to think about returning to work, you're likely to have concerns and mixed feelings.

Feeling guilty You may feel guilty (especially if you can't wait to get back to work), but don't. Just because you're a working mother doesn't mean you're a bad mother. There's no point in staying at home with your baby if it doesn't fulfil you – it will be more beneficial to him if you're happy and contented when he does see you. Also, don't forget how your baby will benefit from the additional income.

Losing your confidence After a few months at home with your baby, you may doubt your ability to readjust to a working environment. Try to ease yourself back into work mode by catching up on what's been going on and by talking to colleagues. Nearer the time, go into the office (by yourself, if possible) so that it isn't such a shock when you return. You'll soon realize that not much has changed while you've been away.

When you're back at work

It may take a few weeks to settle back into work. You'll just about have worked out a routine with your baby at home and then suddenly have to adapt to a different timetable and concentrate your mind on a different set of priorities. You'll also, for the first time, be doing your job while having to handle added pressures and responsibilities at home.

Making the transition

AREA OF CHANGE	HOW TO MAKE IT EASIER
Preparing your baby	Introduce your baby to the childminder, starting with a couple of mornings each week and gradually building it up, or take him to the nursery for a trial run. You should also start to adapt his feeding routine in good time.
Adapting to a change of routine	Trying to juggle work and looking after your baby can be difficult. Establish a routine in the mornings and evenings so that you are sharing the baby care and chores equally. You'll soon find a routine that works.
Coping with tiredness	No one who is consistently deprived of sleep can be expected to cope adequately with a job, so you must take it in turns to care for your baby during the night. If one of you is in part-time work, still organize a pro-rata arrangement.
Focusing on work	It's an acquired skill not to think about your baby while you're at work. If you've made the best arrangements you can for his welfare, any energy you now dispense on worrying is wasted and sells you and your employer short.
Settling your baby	The fact is your baby will have to settle and he will. What you can do is prepare yourselves for his reaction and, during the time he's with you, be reassuring and comforting to him. Make sure he has whatever comfort object he loves.

Career considerations

People often assume that a woman's first priority will be her child and, in some situations, they're right – when push comes to shove, it's quite often the mother's employment that takes the strain and not the father's. If your partnership is different, you're probably going to have to demonstrate this several times before it's recognized.

How your career is affected may also depend on your employer's attitude – set the ground rules early on by talking to your manager and telling him or her that you're committed to your job, but that your responsibilities at home mean you'll need some flexibility. Explain that you need to leave on time (although, ideally, collecting your baby should be shared equally with your partner), but that with sufficient notice you're prepared to work extra hours, if necessary.

Father

The routine at home will change if you're both working full-time and it'll help if you prepare yourself for this.

How you can help

■ Be supportive. Your partner is likely to find going back to work a strain and may be distressed by leaving the baby. Try to plan in advance as much as possible and give her time to adjust.

■ Share the responsibility. Don't assume that your partner will sort out childcare problems. The carer or nursery should have telephone numbers for both of you (including mobiles), so that you can easily share the responsibility if a problem arises.

■ Share the chores. Your partner may have been doing most of the chores while she was at home, but now she's back at work this should be more equal. Alternate doing the domestic work, getting up during the night, and collecting your baby from the childminder.

Emergencies

Talk about a strategy for emergencies, such as your baby or the childminder being ill. If you don't have an alternative carer, one of you will need to take time off work to care for your child. If either of you feels strongly that your job takes priority, try to agree this in advance. This can save a lot of arguments.

Childcare

Trial period

It's worth having a trial period before you return to work, so that you can settle your baby gradually:

■ Your baby will have time to become familiar with her new surroundings and her new carer.

■ You'll have an idea of the impact on your baby and be able to find ways of soothing her if she becomes unsettled.

■ You'll be able to sort out any practical hitches.

■ If you introduce your baby to her new carer gradually, the emotional impact should be less once you actually return to work.

If things go wrong

If the childcare situation doesn't work out, it can be disappointing and problematic, especially if your carer lives with you. Try to treat the problem professionally:

■ It's best if issues are dealt with quickly; ignoring problems will only make matters worse and lead to resentments building up.

■ Talk to your carer and try to reach a compromise. Agree to see how things go and, depending on the problem, set a time limit. If, after this period, the matter isn't resolved, it may be better to terminate the employment.

■ Decide on a set notice period. This benefits both of you and if your carer decides to leave, you won't be left in the lurch.

Finding and choosing a carer is mainly dictated by practical and financial considerations, but there are also emotional issues. It's hard to leave your baby with someone new so you need to be as happy as possible about the care and carer you've chosen.

What to look for in a carer

Once you've decided on the type of childcare you'd prefer, you need to look around for the best carer. If you plan your childcare well in advance, you'll have more choice. If you leave it too late before you finish maternity leave, you may be restricted by what is available. Ask the person or institution that you're considering lots of questions to find out the type of care that will be provided, and thoroughly check the facilities. If you're unhappy or unsure, follow your instincts and look elsewhere.

Qualifications and references A nanny or nursery nurse should have accredited training with a proper qualification (for example, NNEB in the UK). If you're using a childminder or a nursery, check that the person or institution is registered with a local authority. Remember, au pairs are not professionally trained. Ask a potential au pair for the name of another employer and at least two written references. Try to talk to the referees on the telephone to get a better idea of the person's suitability.

Level of care Check how many babies are looked after at one time and the carer to child ratio. Even if your baby will not be receiving individual care (with a nursery, creche, or childminder), she should still be given enough care to be stimulated and to encourage her development. Check the space and resources available, such as the kitchen and sterilizing equipment, the play area and the types of toys offered. With all types of care, ask what kind of activities your baby will be involved in on a day-to-day basis.

Interaction with your baby Always invite a potential carer to spend time with your baby so that you can see how they interact. Watch to see what she says while holding your baby and how your baby reacts. Ask questions, such as her thoughts on discipline to check that they match your own.

Commitment It can be confusing and distressing for a baby to have a change of carer. Check that the person or institution will be able to provide relatively long-term care. An au pair may only be available for a short time and is likely to have other commitments while she is staying with you.

Your relationship with your carer

However sure you are about employing your carer, it's advisable to discuss and agree on all aspects of caring for your baby from the outset:

■ A trial period before you agree to a full contract is a good idea.

■ Write down your requirements so that you can agree some ground rules; especially with regard to telephone use and visitors for live-in carers.

■ Find out the carer's thoughts or the institution's policy on discipline.

The carer's relationship with your baby

Leaving your baby with a carer is likely to come at a time when you've just settled into being a parent and feel particularly close to your son or daughter. Your carer will also form a close relationship with your baby, but this doesn't mean you're any less important and you're by no means replaced. Your baby is capable of being close to – and accepting the attention of – more than one person; in fact it's beneficial if this happens because the more love, attention, and stimulation she receives the better she'll develop. Babies often go through periods of time when they favour certain people (see p. 131); if your baby seems closer to her carer it's probably only a phase. Your baby may also seem unsettled now and then, but don't read too much into this. However, if it continues for more than a week or two, spend time with the carer and your baby together to try to pinpoint any problems.

Hidden costs

When thinking about the cost of childcare, it's worth considering:

■ Are there transport costs?

■ Are your baby's meals provided?

■ What are the additional costs associated with a live-in carer?

■ If you have twins, would it be cheaper to employ a nanny?

■ Are there hidden emotional costs, such as feeling indebted, if you're using a friend or relative?

Childcare options

TYPE OF CARE	DESCRIPTION	ADVANTAGES	DISADVANTAGES
Relative	You may decide to leave your baby with a member of your family, such as a grandparent. Encourage him or her to involve your baby in outside activities, such as a playgroup.	■ Usually a cheaper option. ■ Your baby is with someone who loves her. ■ You're less likely to have strict time restraints, but don't abuse this.	■ It can be difficult if there are disagreements. ■ You may worry more about your baby forming a close relationship with that person.
Registered childminder	A childminder looks after several children at one time in her own home. She is likely to be very experienced, especially if she has her own children.	■ You can often pay by the hour to suit your budget. ■ Your baby will mix with lots of children, which will help to develop social skills.	■ No professional qualification required. ■ May have limited resources. ■ You can't take your baby if she's ill.
Nanny	A nanny cares for your baby at home and may live with you. Interview a prospective nanny together – you both have to get on with her and observe her with your baby.	■ A nanny is professionally trained and qualified. ■ Care takes place at home, which will help your baby to settle and is more convenient for you.	■ A nanny is expensive (you're responsible for her tax and insurance), but consider a nanny share. ■ Beware of domestic tensions if the nanny lives in.
Day nursery or creche	There are very few local authority nurseries, so you'll probably have to pay for private care. If you're lucky, an all-day creche may be available at your workplace.	■ Your baby is with other babies and care is based around developing skills. ■ Nurseries and creches must be registered and often employ qualified carers.	■ Can be expensive and there will be limited places. ■ You'll have to collect your baby at an agreed time. ■ You can't take your baby if she's ill.
Au pair or mother's help	This is a student from another country who lives with you as part of the family. She will probably want to attend language classes and is only suitable if you work part-time or from home.	■ Care is provided in the home, which is convenient. ■ Cheaper than a nanny. ■ When your baby is older, the au pair may be able to teach her a second language.	■ Not professionally qualified, and not suitable for the full-time care of a baby. ■ Works limited hours. ■ There will be additional live-in costs.

Special time with your baby

Mother

Remember, play doesn't have to involve toys; often just being with you is fun for your baby.

What you can do

■ When you get home, make a habit of picking your baby up straight away and holding him as you walk around doing things.

■ Exaggerate your pleasure at seeing him, talk to him, make eye contact, laugh a lot, play little jokes, and enjoy each other.

■ Try to spend ten to 15 uninterrupted minutes playing with your baby each evening.

■ Read the paper or a book together so that you both relax. Read out items and show your baby pictures to involve him.

■ If you're really tired have a bath together. A skin-to-skin soak is good for both of you.

An hour a day

An hour spent playing with your baby each day is rewarding and fulfilling for all of you. A baby who gets the undivided attention of his parents for an hour a day acquires self-esteem and self-confidence and becomes a generous, loving, and well-adjusted child. It doesn't have to be a solid hour – in fact, your baby won't concentrate for this long; it could be two half-hours or four quarter-hours as long as he has all your attention.

If you're working parents, the time spent at home as a family becomes not just important, but precious. Play is essential to your baby's mental and physical development, and he'll love the attention from you both while he plays.

The importance of play

As well as being a parent, you are your baby's playmate; this is especially true in his first year when he may not have had much opportunity to interact with other children. Every game you play with him is magical and every lesson becomes worth learning, so time spent in games, no matter how simple, ensures that your baby is avidly learning and acquiring skills. Don't underestimate how important play is to your baby: it's his full-time job; a job that requires great concentration and expenditure of energy. It's harder than most adult work because everything is new and fresh lessons are learned all the time. These lessons, however, are made easier and are more fun if he can enjoy them with his favourite playmates – his parents.

Why play is essential

■ Your baby investigates his world through play.
■ It stimulates and excites him and is the best use of his time.
■ For the first few years of his life it is the only way he learns.
■ It is an integral part of his physical and mental development.

Getting the most out of play

Make the time to join in activities with your baby and encourage him in play that will stimulate his development.

Investing time Formal play isn't necessary, but some planning does reap dividends so try to make play a part of your morning, evening, and weekend routine so that your baby is getting at least an hour of playtime in total from both of you each day (see left). A baby has a very short attention span so don't expect him to sit playing happily while you cook the dinner. Fifteen minutes invested in playing with your baby before you begin a task will pay off; if you only give him five minutes of your time he's more likely to become attention seeking when you're busy doing something else.

Stimulating development Babies start acquiring skills from the very moment of birth. These mental and physical milestones (see p. 146) emerge at particular stages as your baby's brain and body develops. It follows that these are optimum moments for you to introduce games that encourage particular skills to flourish, so make sure you vary the activities that you play with your baby; for example, physical games encourage mobility; singing helps to develop speech; playing with toys, such as building blocks, helps your baby to become more dextrous.

Maximizing your time

If you work full-time, try to take advantage of any spare moments you have to spend time with your baby. It helps if you're organized and can prioritize. If you're both in high-pressured jobs it's easy to let work take over and work an extra hour at the beginning or end of the day, but this hour is invaluable time you could be spending with your baby.

Weekends

Don't bring work home with you; if it's not there you can't do it, which means you can spend time with your baby without feeling guilty. Try to get out as a family at least one of the days at the weekend; if you're in the house, you're more likely to get distracted with other things. Keep to your baby's weekly routine as much as possible – at around nine months he'll begin to understand that certain things happen at certain times.

Mornings

Most babies do wake up early so use this opportunity to spend time together. If you don't have time for proper play, sing and talk to your baby as you change and dress him, and sit down to breakfast with him.

Evenings

Working full-time will make you tired in the evenings. Try to establish some sort of routine for when you get home because as well as having time with your baby, it's important that you both have time to yourselves and time together as a couple (see p. 134).

Leave work on time Try to leave work on time. It's unfair on your partner and the baby if either one of you is always home late. Don't take advantage of the childminder – an extra hour in the evening is a lot when she's been looking after the baby all day.

Divide the chores One of you should cook and the other wash up so that you both have time to spend with your baby.

Choose relaxing activities It will be difficult to get your baby to bed if he's very excited. Read or sing to him to calm him down before you put him to bed.

Relaxing together
Play doesn't always have to be energetic. Settle into a comfortable chair in the evening and read a story to your baby. This is a relaxing and enjoyable activity for both of you.

see p. 95

Father

Your baby will look forward to you coming home in the evenings. Shower him with attention and show him how special he is.

What you can do

■ Develop a special routine for when you get home from work. It could just be holding out your arms for your baby to walk or crawl to you, or picking him up immediately, walking around with him, and telling him about your day.

■ Try to find time each evening to spend ten or 15 minutes playing a game.

■ If you read the paper in the evening, read to your baby and give him some paper to crumple.

■ You and your baby can relax with a bath together (see p. 95) before getting him ready for bed.

■ If you don't have much time on weekday mornings, try to make time to dress him and give him breakfast at the weekend.

Time-saving tips

To give yourself more time with your baby in evenings:

■ Try to prepare some weekday meals at the weekend.

■ Record any early evening TV programmes and watch them once your baby has gone to bed.

■ Save any long telephone calls until after your baby's bedtime.

■ Eat mid-afternoon sometimes so that it's possible for you to wait later for your evening meal.

Fathers at home

Mother

Being the breadwinner while your partner stays at home can lead to conflicting emotions.

How to help yourself
In general, society still pressures women to be the main carer and it's difficult not to be affected by this. You may feel guilty, and envy other women who have more time at home. Try to be confident in your decision or accepting of your predicament and spend as much time as possible with your baby. Being the breadwinner can be stressful, so find ways to relax and try not to feel resentment.

How to help your partner
Make sure he has time out to relax, see his friends, and spend time with you (see p. 134). Try not to leave all the chores to him.

Reactions

Full-time dads are more common now, but you will get some flak. Some traditionally-minded men find it threatening that the "house husband" is independent and strong enough to flout the more traditional social conventions – they like to hang on to these conventions because it gives them security. But if you're a man who's strong enough to have made the decision to be a full-time parent, you'll no doubt be strong enough to take the flak!

It suits some couples best for the mother to return to work and be the breadwinner, while the father is a stay-at-home dad, caring for the baby and running the home.

Making the decision

For many couples, the decision to reverse roles is made because they feel that their baby will benefit from having a full-time parent at home. If the mother is earning more, it makes sense for the father to be that person – especially if his work is something he can do from home. When a parent stays at home full-time, a couple will be financially worse off than if both work, but this is often compensated for by an improvement in their quality of life and is seen as a worthwhile investment in their child. A man may be forced to stay at home due to a job loss; even if this is only short-term, it can often be an invaluable opportunity for him to spend time with his child and take on the role of primary carer.

A learning process

Those people who make a stand on the traditional roles of father and mother as being "natural" are missing the point and to divide parental labour along the lines of gender is completely redundant. Looking after a baby is a learning process for all new parents, whether they're male or female, so don't let anyone tell you otherwise. Remember the following:
■ Women are not born with an innate ability to change nappies and dress babies. Possibly, they appear more confident at it because they're made to feel that they should know what to do.
■ Looking after and nurturing a baby is a learned skill and to begin with it's as difficult for a mother as it is for a father.
■ Men are not at a disadvantage when it comes to caring for a baby. If you're a father who has decided to stay at home to be the main carer, you have as much chance at being good at it and raising a happy, confident, and intelligent child as your partner.

Parenting

If you're a couple who have chosen the father-at-home option, you are hopefully committed to parenting in general rather than fathering or mothering (see p. 11). It's only sensible to base your family set-up on your mutual strengths rather than be captive to stereotypes that may well conflict with your personalities.

The advantages

As a father who chooses to stay at home, you'll form a close bond with your baby and have a chance to watch and enjoy her development at an age that most men miss out on. This role will enable you to express your affection and feelings in ways that are difficult when you're in the more traditional male role. Being the carer lets you change your priorities and releases you from the pressures of being the main provider for your family. This leaves you with more of yourself to offer your baby and partner, which can be hugely beneficial to the family as a whole.

How your child is affected

To a baby, her mother and father are interchangeable. The baby only knows parental love and care – it doesn't matter who is doing the giving. The advantage of a man being the main carer is that he can offer a positive role model to his children free from the commonest kind of stereotyping. A son will grow up feeling comfortable with the emotional side of his personality and he'll follow his father's lead in having an independent spirit unpressured by prevailing social mores. A daughter, of course, will seek out the same well-balanced kind of men as her father – and that's no bad thing.

Being the lone man

The main problem for most full-time parents is isolation and since a large proportion of people are working during the day, adult company can be found largely with others looking after children. As these are usually women, this can cause a problem for the full-time father. It's pointless to pretend that people interact with the opposite sex in the same way as with their own, but it's likely that a man with enough flexibility and confidence to become the main carer in the first place will move fairly easily into this predominantly female world. While some mothers may be surprised to find their ranks as full-time child carers joined by a man, few will be hostile. The surprise at the "house-husband" is usually a bit of a nine-day wonder whose presence is very shortly taken for granted. Most men are welcomed, although some are the victims of maternalism of the "let-me-help-you-love" variety, which can be as irritating as the "leave-that-to-me-darling" paternalism practised by some men.

Being accepted
Over time, a full-time father will stop being the token male and become just another parent, who shares the same pleasures and problems of parenthood as his female friends.

An equal share

Some couples decide that they'll both work part-time or one or two days at home, so that they both have a mix of parenting and work. This is possible if the job can be done part-time or at home – new technology is making it even easier to do this. It may mean that both of you put your careers on hold, but many feel that it's the right choice. At least it prevents either person having to give up their career altogether. The advantages include:

■ Both of you have real quality time with your baby, which will mean you'll form an equally close bond with her.

■ You'll both have a strong appreciation of the frustrations involved in being in sole charge of your baby and the problems of juggling work and home.

■ The baby benefits from building a close relationship with you both.

■ You become a real team by sharing things equally, and prevent the resentments that often build up when one parent is at home.

Looking to the future

Your constant role

Your role as nurturer means respecting your child, and offering support without foregoing your own principles. It takes many forms.

Comforter
You can only help your child to cope with emotional or physical pain by acknowledging it, and offering comfort when it's needed.

Playmate
Play is a serious business for your child, and the best play is with other people, the most important of whom are his parents.

Limit-setter
The first limits you set for your baby will be to prevent him from hurting himself; later, these limits will prevent him from hurting others as well. Never be apologetic about consistently setting reasonable limits, but try not to do so in a punitive or accusatory manner. Rather than saying "no" all the time, help him to understand your reasons.

Teacher or role model?
The role of teacher is crucial for any parent; but it isn't formal teaching: you do it by example. Your child learns about life from you, so you can't shrug off responsibility for an errant school child or a truculent teenager.

Authority figure
Don't confuse authority and power: power results from the use or threat of force; authority comes from a person who has influence over, and receives consent from, others without force. Your child will accept your authority if he also sees that you are fair, competent, loving, and reasonable.

Your baby has now completed his first year of life; he's beginning to communicate with language, he's mobile, he's feeding himself, and asserting his personality as a full member of the family. He's growing up, so your role as parents will be changing too, and it'll continue to change as he progresses on to school and ultimately to adolescence and adulthood. Under your care he'll become more and more independent, but he'll always need you both as his permanent bedrock of security, sympathy, friendship, and love.

Your baby grows up
The main change you'll see, and must be prepared to accept, is that your baby is becoming a person in his own right, with personality, preferences, and a will of his own. He will gradually acquire a sense of place in the family, a sense of independence, and, most importantly, a sense of self-worth. Not all these changes are straightforward for you. On the one hand, they are all signs of growing maturity and so should be welcomed. On the other hand, some aspects of his growing up may lead to clashes with you and could result in a battle of wills that needs careful handling. Then again, his frustration at wanting to out-perform his ability may express itself as tantrums that leave you bewildered, perplexed, and sometimes helpless (see p. 182). Tantrums, though, are a crucial milestone; he can't become a reasonable, self-controlled child without experiencing them.

A hierarchy of needs
Keep in mind the basic needs that will help your child to grow and develop normally. Health, of course, is a pre-requisite, but you also have to try to provide the right sort of environment for him to reach his full potential – physically, emotionally, socially, and intellectually. All children have a hierarchy of needs,

Self

Actualization

Self-esteem

Belonging

Safety

Survival

Building confidence
These fundamental building blocks help your child reach his full potential.

starting from the very basic need for survival. You could think of your child's needs in terms of a pyramid: the solid base is the provision of the food, drink, and shelter needed for survival; then comes safety: protection from harm; a sense of belonging: your child feels wanted and secure, leading to self-esteem: no one can feel good about himself if he feels unloved. Near the top of the pyramid comes actualization: understanding his place in the world – with a fully-developed sense of self as the pinnacle that can't be achieved without the rest in place.

Becoming independent

Your child's burgeoning spirit of self-reliance is more important than you may think because so many good things can flow from it. Without a secure feeling of independence, a child can't relate to others, share, be reasonable, outgoing, and friendly, have a sense of responsibility, and eventually respect others and their privacy. Many other qualities stem from his belief in himself – curiosity, adventurousness, being helpful, thoughtful, and generous. With such qualities people will relate well to him and he'll automatically get more out of life. What you pour in as love, expresses itself as self-worth and belief in himself. Love, of course, is not the only spur; you can encourage him practically as well.

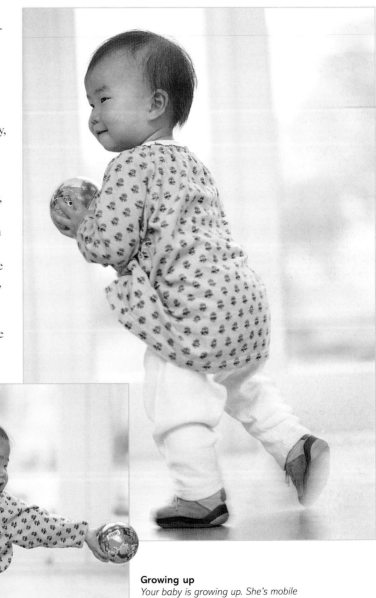

Growing up
Your baby is growing up. She's mobile and is beginning to know her own mind. As she gains independence, physically and emotionally, your role is also changing.

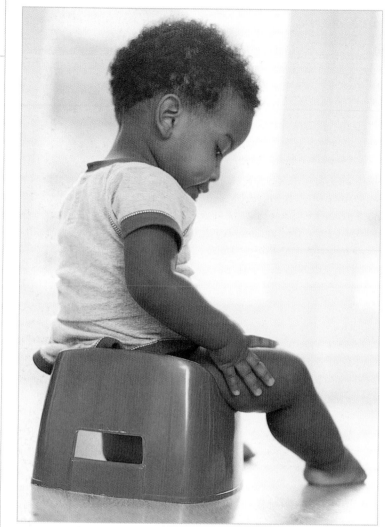

"Potty training"
There's no need for "potty training". Let your baby develop at his own rate and he'll achieve bowel and bladder control as soon as he's ready.

Helpfulness Ask her to fetch things for you, such as the shopping bag or the dustpan, so that she can help and feels useful.

Decision-making Give her small decisions to make, like which toy to play with or which cup to use, so that she can use her judgment and rely on it.

Sense of identity Ask questions about her preferences, solicit her opinion to give her a sense of identity and importance.

Physical independence Give her slightly more and more difficult tasks – like jumping up and down, throwing or kicking a ball, so that she can feel pleased with the strength and coordination of her body.

Emotional independence Show her that she can trust you: you always come back after leaving her, you always comfort her when she's hurt, you always help her when she's in difficulties.

Toilet tips

Here are a few tips that you might find helpful:

■ Let your child develop at her own pace. There is no way you can speed up the process, just be there to help your child along.

■ Let your child decide whether or not to sit on the potty. Never force the issue.

■ Praise your child and treat her control as an accomplishment. Always forgive and ignore any accidents.

Cooperation "We can do it together" is a motto that you should keep repeating – it breeds faith in your baby's own efforts. When she overcomes an obstacle or succeeds in a task on her own, she'll experience the thrill of achievement – especially if you heap praise on her.

Achieving control of her body

Many parents believe that they can set a clock for their baby to achieve bowel and bladder control. Those parents are doomed to frustration. Your baby's timetable has nothing to do with your expectations – only with her speed of development. Bowel and bladder control are undoubtedly important milestones between dependent baby and independent child, but they can't be reached until other areas of development have been achieved. This is why I dislike the label "potty training"; no child can control her bowel or bladder until her muscles are strong enough, no child can do something until she's ready for it and, once ready, no child needs training.

When she'll be dry

At around 18 months and no earlier, your child might start to tell you that she can feel herself passing urine. She can't hold it, she can't wait, she has no control over it. She'll give you a sign; she'll point to the nappy and vocalize to draw your attention to it. Then, and only then, do you start a gentle programme of encouragement. Your daughter will probably have achieved bladder and bowel control by the age of two, and be dry at night by three; it may take your son longer. Being dry all night can take some children a long time – it's quite normal for a boy not to achieve full control until he is four or five. Never scold your child for wetting the bed, or having an accident during the day, especially if she's been "dry" for a while. It could be a sign of illness or emotional distress, so think about the underlying causes. Being angry with your child for something over which she hasn't much control will just upset her and make the problem worse.

Playing together
Help your child to understand sharing. Invite her friends to the house so that she can play group games and share play materials.

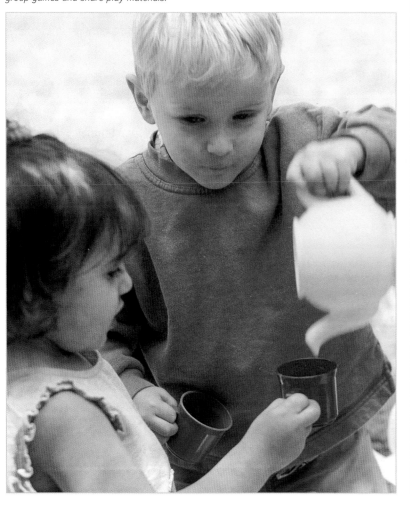

Being reasonable

This heading disguises a few personal comments on discipline in young children. I have to disguise it because what I believe to be good discipline has little to do with the usual punitive interpretation of the word.

Re-defining discipline
Good discipline has nothing to do with a parent forcing a mode of behaviour on a child; it's about encouraging reasonable behaviour from a child. Your aim should be to create a desire to behave well most of the time, rather than to conform to an arbitrary adult code out of fear, weakness, or resignation.

Encouraging good behaviour
Praise good behaviour rather than penalizing poor behaviour.

Start from the beginning
It's easier if you start how you mean to finish; discipline doesn't just happen at, say, three years old. It's been building from birth and is based on reasonable behaviour expressed by you.

Parental responsibility
Children are born with an overwhelming desire to please; if they lose that desire, my view is that we parents must take responsibility. If you think you're doing everything right, but still have a difficult child, you may be being too easy on yourself. Look at what you think of as "right", and ask yourself if it is right for your child.

Being consistent
Work out your joint attitude to discipline, and be consistent in your response. A child who gets different reactions from each parent will be confused about what her limits really are, and her behaviour will reflect this.

Temper tantrums

By the time he's about two, your child's will is well developed, but his ambitions far outreach his capabilities. The resulting combination of stubbornness and frustration can be explosive, resulting in the classic temper tantrum. There are ways to cope:

■ Accept temper tantrums as normal. Better still, see them as a cry for help. Having your child throw a fit of screaming, kicking, and crying is upsetting, but if you're firm, gentle, and have a steady nerve, you'll nurse him out of them; remember that he's not being wilfully naughty – he simply can't control himself.

■ Don't shout, smack, or get angry. He needs you to help him regain control. A temper tantrum means he's saying, "Help me. Protect me from myself." Your very quietness should calm him down.

■ A really upset child can frighten himself by the sheer strength of his emotions, so cuddle him close; be firm – he will struggle.

■ Be businesslike; he's trying to elicit a dramatic response, but he'll calm down if you're cool.

■ If this doesn't work, say you're going to leave the room or walk where he can't see you, but you can see him. Do as you promised and the screaming will stop; it usually does without an audience.

■ Try to stay where you can see him as much as possible, and be ready to prevent him from hurting himself or others.

Caution
Some children develop breath holding attacks that may be frightening, but most are brought to an abrupt end by a firm tap between the shoulder blades.

Gender differences in development

It's clear from the previous page that bladder and bowel control is one obvious area of development where there may be a marked difference between boys and girls (although there will always be exceptions to the rule). However, many gender differences are imposed on boys and girls by adults' own prejudices about what boys or girls are expected to be like (see p. 148), and so it's not always clear whether the recognized differences are solely due to nature or nurture. However, differences in the rate of development of certain skills between boys and girls throughout childhood and into adolescence have been measured by researchers (see chart below). Being aware of these differences may help you to understand your children better, which can then enable them to move forward at an appropriate rate and also help overcome any difficulties before they become problems. It can also help to avoid the sort of gender stereotyping that doesn't allow girls to be adventurous or boys to show affection.

Widening horizons

As your child grows and develops, he'll become increasingly sociable and need contact with other people in order to develop natural curiosity and intellectual growth. He'll get these from the everyday interaction he has

Some developmental differences

GIRLS	BOYS
As toddlers, girls are better at hopping, rhythmic movement, and balance.	At school age, boys are usually better than girls at running, jumping, and throwing.
Girls are slightly faster than boys at some aspects of early language ability. They learn to read and write, and grasp grammar and spelling, earlier than boys.	Most boys talk later than girls, and take longer to make complicated sentences. They have more reading problems by adolescence, and are less adept at verbal reasoning.
Girls are more emotionally independent than boys and are also more sociable and form close friendships from an earlier age.	Boys are more emotionally dependent than girls, and tend to have more behavioural problems before and during adolescence.
There's little difference in strength and speed between girls and boys until puberty, but from that time fat to muscle ratio is greater in girls.	At adolescence, boys become stronger and faster than girls and have more muscle and bone, less fat and larger hearts and lungs.
Physical growth is faster and more regular; girls mature at adolescence earlier than boys.	Physical growth tends to go in uneven spurts; boys reach puberty later than girls.
Girls may be slightly better at arithmetic than boys before they reach adolescence, after which the trend reverses.	At every age boys are better at spatial visualization and, from adolescence, tend to be better than girls at mathematical reasoning.
In early childhood, girls generally appear to be more willing to obey adults' requests.	From toddlerhood, boys are more aggressive socially, and more competitive than girls.

with you, your friends, and their children, with grandparents and other relatives. But it's also a good idea to let him meet other children of his own age with you at a creche or parent-and-toddler group, and later to think about playschool or nursery as a way of preparing him for formal schooling in the future. Although your child may not start to form strong attachments – real friendships – until he's approaching three years old, he'll enjoy playing alongside other children. This will enable him to start finding out about giving and sharing, and to begin exploring the enormous potential for creativity in joint imaginative play.

Extending your family

Once you're settled as a family with one child, it's natural to think about whether or not you're going to extend your family and, if so, how long to wait. As with all family matters, there's no hard and fast rule about this. It suits some couples to wait until their first child is old enough to attend a nursery, or even until he's at full-time school. For others, a smaller gap seems better, but bear in mind that children have been found to benefit from a minimum gap of two and a half years. You also need to take into account work commitments and financial considerations, as well as your own health; a mother who had a strenuous labour and birth, or perhaps a Caesarean section, would probably want to feel that her body is completely back to normal and has had time to become "hers" again, before embarking on another pregnancy. Age also has significance, although nowadays this doesn't have much bearing on the ability to bear and look after children. However, biology is against you: the older you are, the longer it will take you on average to conceive again (see p. 18), so you may not want to wait too long before trying for another baby.

The impact on your child

Whatever the length of time between the two (or subsequent) births, it's important that you think carefully about the impact on the older child, and that you introduce the idea to him sensitively and in good time. Even a teenager can feel displaced by the arrival of a new baby, something that may well happen if you've entered a new relationship and one of you already has children (see p. 142). Your decision to extend your family must always be inclusive: your first child is a fully paid-up member of your family unit and deserves to be treated as such, whatever his age.

A final word

Long after your child can cook himself a meal, iron his own clothes, and has set off on his own path in life, he'll still need both his parents to nurture him. True nurture caters not only for his material wants, but also offers continuing and unconditional love, and it's a lifelong commitment. If this unconditional love is combined with reasonable limits and guidelines, you'll both help him to mature into an individual who is sensitive to the needs of others, but remains independent of mind, confident and open to all the possibilities that life can offer.

Sibling rivalry

Jealousy is a normal emotion for a small child to feel if his security appears threatened by the arrival of a new baby. Although you can't guarantee to avoid some jealousy, the best way to help him cope is to prepare him for the new arrival and to keep on showing him that his place in your affections is quite safe.

Before the birth
Talk to him about the new baby as soon as your tummy looks really swollen. Let him touch your tummy whenever he wants to, but especially to feel the baby kick. Refer to the baby as his baby, and ask if he'd like a brother or a sister to get him involved. If you know the sex in advance, tell him so he can start to identify with the new baby. Get him to show love and affection openly by reading parent and baby animal books together, by encouraging him to be gentle with other babies, and by exchanging lots of cuddles.

After the birth
When he visits you in hospital for the first time, make sure you aren't holding the baby – have your arms free for him and wait for him to ask to see the baby. Give him a present from the baby. Share bath and feeding times so that he can show you how helpful he is and be praised by you. Put aside at least half an hour a day when you give him your full attention. Keep telling him how much you love and treasure him.

The father's role
Reassure your elder child that you still love him. You're ideally placed to arrange special treats and activities. With your attention and love, you'll enable your first-born to negotiate the choppy waters of sibling rivalry and you'll have cemented a lifelong friendship.

Useful information

Minimum rights

Regardless of how many hours you work or how long you've been employed, you're entitled to:

- Working conditions that are safe for your unborn child – any risk must be removed, or you removed from it, if necessary by moving you to a suitable alternative job or suspending you on full pay.

- Time off work without loss of pay to attend antenatal appointments and classes.

- The right to keep your job; you cannot be dismissed as a result of your pregnancy.

- Minimum maternity leave and pay, subject to length of service and salary criteria (see right).

Benefits

You may be eligible for other benefits to help you support yourself and your baby:

- If your income is low, enquire about the possibility of Income-based Job-seeker's Allowance, Income Support, a Maternity Grant, Housing and Council Tax Benefits, Tax Credits.

- Once your baby's birth is registered and you've got a birth certificate, you can claim for child benefit.

- The government provides a "Child Trust Fund" for every child born after 1 September 2002. The money goes into a savings account and will stay there until your child turns 18.

This section provides information on the resources and benefits available. It also includes a summary of the health care procedures and recommended immunization schedule for your baby, and details of specialist organizations that offer help and support.

Finding out your maternity rights

The important thing is to start making enquiries and getting help from the appropriate bodies early on in your pregnancy – don't leave it until you're 35 weeks pregnant, or you may find yourself losing out. Many women have additional maternity rights provided by their individual employer. It's a good idea to read your contract and staff handbook, especially if you work in a large company, so that you can check your entitlements. If you're confused about anything, make an appointment with your personnel officer and talk it through to find out exactly what is offered by your company. To qualify for maternity leave and pay you need to obtain the appropriate forms from your midwife, GP, or local Social Security office and apply by the deadlines (see chart, opposite).

Maternity leave and pay

You have the right to 26 weeks minimum maternity leave, and extended maternity leave if you've worked for your company for a certain period. When you return to work you're entitled to return to the same job. You need to write to your employer at least 15 weeks before your expected week of childbirth, stating that you are pregnant and giving your estimated delivery date and when you intend to start maternity leave. If your employer requests it, you must provide a copy of your maternity certificate (form MAT B1; in Northern Ireland, form MB1), which you can get from your midwife or doctor.

An employee who wants to return to work before the end of her maternity leave needs to give her employer 28 days' notice of the date she wants to return to work. If you've worked for your current employer for 26 weeks continuously at the 14th week before your baby is due, you're entitled to take a further 26 weeks' additional maternity leave. When you return to work you are entitled to return to the same job on the same terms and conditions.

Maternity pay

If you have worked for the same employer for at least 26 weeks by the end of the 15th week before your baby is due, you are entitled to Statutory Maternity Pay (SMP). This is paid for a maximum of 26 weeks starting when you leave work. You can decide how soon you want to stop work, and hence how early you start your maternity pay – week 11 before your estimated date of delivery is the earliest you can start getting SMP, and you can, if you wish, work right up to the week of your baby's delivery. SMP is 90 per cent of your average pay for the first six weeks; after that it's paid at a basic rate for up to 20 further weeks. However, many companies offer better deals for women taking maternity leave.

If you do not qualify

If you aren't entitled to SMP, but have paid National Insurance contributions for at least 26 of the 66 weeks before your baby's estimated due date, you can get Maternity Allowance. This is paid for up to 26 weeks starting any time between 11 weeks before your baby is due and the day after your baby is born. If you don't qualify for SMP or Maternity Allowance, but have paid some National Insurance contributions, you may be entitled to Incapacity Benefit, a benefit paid from six weeks before the birth until two weeks after.

Paternity rights

Eligible employees can take either one week or two consecutive weeks' paternity leave. To qualify for this leave you should be the child's biological father, responsible for its upbringing, or be the mother's husband or partner. Most fathers will be entitled to Statutory Paternity Pay (SPP) from their employers.

Registering the birth

You are legally required to register the birth within 42 days (21 days in Scotland). A registrar may be available in the hospital; otherwise you will have to go to a Registery Office. If you were married at the time of the birth, either parent may register. An unmarried mother must attend, and if the father wants his details entered he must accompany her. You need to give various details; the baby's names; parents' names, addresses, occupations, and dates of birth; the number of previous children; and marriage date. You'll be given a copy of the short certificate (you may buy further copies), and a medical card so that you can register your baby with a doctor.

Rights and benefits summary

WHEN	WHAT YOU NEED TO DO	WHY YOU NEED TO DO IT
When pregnancy is confirmed	If you're working, inform your employer. If you're not entitled to SMP, find out about Maternity Allowance (MA).	To establish eligibility for SMP and so that you can organize paid time off for antenatal visits.
15 weeks before your baby is due	Confirm to your employer, in writing, when you intend to stop work.	By confirming your intentions to your employer, you protect your right to return to work and to get SMP.
15 weeks before your baby is due	Inform your employer that you intend to take paternity leave, stating when the baby is due and when you expect to take leave.	To establish eligibility for paternity leave and for paternity pay.
15 weeks before your baby is due	Ask your doctor or your midwife for a maternity certificate (form MAT B1; in Northern Ireland, form MB1).	The maternity certificate must be given to your employer to confirm your right to maternity leave and pay.
11 weeks before your baby is due	This is the earliest date that you are allowed to finish work, start your maternity leave, and receive SMP.	You are entitled to claim your SMP or Maternity Allowance once you have stopped work.
After the birth to six weeks	You have to register the birth by the time your baby is aged six weeks (three weeks, in Scotland). You can claim child benefit.	Register to get a birth certificate, and start claiming child benefit. After three months, child benefit won't be backdated.
28 days before returning to work	If you want to return to work before your maternity leave ends you should write to your employer at this time to inform him or her of the actual date that you intend to return to work.	Again, writing to your employer with your return date protects your right to return to work.

Healthcare professionals

You'll be looked after by a series of professionals.

General practitioner (GP)
If you're not registered, sign up with your GP as soon as you find out you're pregnant. She'll confirm your pregnancy, if needed, and refer you to the hospital.

Midwife
The midwife is responsible for your antenatal care. She'll be with you during labour and delivery, and she'll monitor you and the baby for about two weeks after the birth.

Health visitor
A health visitor is a qualified nurse with specific training in childcare. She advises on your baby's health and development and arranges any further help. She visits you at home from about ten days after the birth to answer any questions you have and examine the baby. She is also available on the telephone or at the clinic if you need additional help.

Health benefits

During pregnancy and for the first year you will be eligible for health benefits, qualifying for more if you are on a low income:

▪ You are entitled to free NHS dental care and free prescriptions while you are pregnant and for a year after your baby is born, regardless of your income.

▪ If you are on a low income, your entitlements may also include free eye tests, vouchers towards spectacles, assistance with travel to your hospital, as well as milk tokens and vitamins. Contact your Social Security office for details.

Health information

Your baby's health will be closely monitored so that any problems can be picked up as early as possible. To protect your baby from certain illnesses, you will be advised to take her for a series of immunizations.

Healthcare records

A record of your pregnancy, labour, and delivery is kept as well as anything from your medical history – or your family's – that could affect your child. Once the baby is born and the birth is registered, you will be given a NHS form to fill in so that you can register your baby with your doctor (see left). Details of your baby's growth and development are recorded and updated at the regular checks (see p. 155).

Immunizations

Some parents are anxious about the possible side effects of immunization. If you have concerns, talk to your GP and health visitor. The risk of complications in all cases is extremely small; the risk of harmful effects from the diseases themselves is much more serious. Your baby will not be immunized if she was premature or has a fever. If she has had side effects from a previous vaccination, the GP may delay or stop further immunizations, depending on the severity of the reaction.

First immunizations

AGE DUE	VACCINATION	HOW GIVEN	POSSIBLE SIDE EFFECTS
Two months	▪ Meningitis C	▪ One injection	▪ Redness and swelling at injection site, mild fever; irritability, headache
	▪ Diphtheria, tetanus, pertussis, (whooping cough), polio and Hib	▪ One injection	▪ A slightly raised temperature; sickness and/or diarrhoea, a small lump at the injection site that will disappear in a few weeks
Three months	▪ Meningitis C	▪ One injection	▪ As above
	▪ Diphtheria, tetanus, pertussis, (whooping cough), polio and Hib	▪ One injection	▪ As above
Four months	▪ Meningitis C	▪ One injection	▪ As above
	▪ Diphtheria, tetanus, pertussis, (whooping cough), polio and Hib	▪ One injection	▪ As above
Around 13 months	▪ MMR (measles, mumps, rubella)	▪ One injection	▪ Fever; rash; slight risk of high fever and convulsions

Useful addresses

Labour and birth support

The Active Birth Centre
25 Bickerton Road
London N19 5JT
0207 281 6760
http://www.activebirthcentre.com/
Runs classes and workshops to prepare you for pregnancy, birth, and parenthood.

Independent Midwives Association
1 The Great Quarry
Guildford, Surrey GU1 3XN
01483 821 104
http://www.independent
midwives.org.uk/

Support for you as parents

Association of Breastfeeding Mothers
PO Box 207
Bridgwater, Somerset TA6 7YT
0870 401 7711
http://www.abm.me.uk

Association for Postnatal Illness
145 Dawes Road
Fulham, London SW6 7EB
020 7386 0868
http://www.apni.org/

BLISS
68 South Lambeth Road
London SW8 1RL
020 7820 9471
http://www.bliss.org.uk/
Help for parents with special care babies.

British Agency for Adoption and Fostering
Skyline House, 200 Union Street
London SE1 0LX
020 7593 2000
http://www.baaf.org.uk/

Contact a Family
209–211 City Road
London EC1V 1JN
020 7608 9700
http://www.cafamily.org.uk/
Advice and support for parents whose children have special needs.

Cry-sis
BM Cry-sis
London WC1N 3XX
08451 228 669 (helpline)
http://www.cry-sis.org.uk/
Help and information for parents with a baby who has crying or sleep problems.

Gingerbread
7 Sovereign Close, Sovereign Court
London E1W 2HW
020 7488 9300
http://www.gingerbread.org.uk/
Help and advice for one-parent families.

La Leche League (Great Britain)
PO Box 29, West Bridgford
Nottingham NG2 7NP
0845 456 1866
http://www.laleche.org.uk
Advice for women who are breastfeeding.

National Childbirth Trust (NCT)
Alexandra House, Oldham Terrace
Acton, London W3 6NH
0870 770 3236
http://www.nctpregnancyand
babycare.com/

National Childminding Association
8 Masons Hill
Bromley, Kent BR2 9EY
020 8290 8973
http://www.ncma.org.uk/

Meet A Mum Association (MAMA)
7 Southcourt Road, Linslade
Leighton Buzzard, Beds LU7 2QF
0845 120 6162
http://www.mama.co.uk
Support for new mothers and mothers to be.

Parentline Plus
520 Highgate Studios
53–79 Highgate Road
London NW5 1TL
020 7284 5500
http://www.parentlineplus.org.uk

Twins and Multiple Births Association (TAMBA)
2 The Willows, Gardner Road
Guildford, Surrey GU1 4PG
0870 770 3305
http://www.tamba.org.uk/

Maternity rights

Association for Improvements in the Maternity Services (AIMS)
5 Ann's Court, Grove Road
Surbiton, Surrey KT6 4BE
0870 765 1433 (helpline)
http://www.aims.org.uk/

Maternity Alliance
Third Floor West
2–6 Northburgh Street
London EC1V 0AY
020 8490 7638

http://www.maternityalliance.org.uk
Information and advice about welfare and employment rights, and benefits.

Special needs

Association for Spina Bifida and Hydrocephalus (ASBAH)
42 Park Road
Peterborough PE1 2UQ
01733 555988
http://www.asbah.org/

National Children's Bureau
8 Wakley Street
London EC1V 7QE
020 7843 6000
http://www.ncb.org.uk/

Cystic Fibrosis Trust
11 London Road
Bromley, Kent BR1 1BY
020 8464 7211
http://www.cftrust.org.uk/

Down's Syndrome Association
Langdon Down Centre
2a Langdon Park
Teddington TW11 9PS
0845 230 0372
http://www.downs-syndrome.org.uk/

The National Eczema Society
Hill House, Highgate Hill
London N19 5NA
020 7281 3553
http://www.eczema.org/

MENCAP
123 Golden Lane
London EC1Y 0RT
020 7454 0454
http://www.mencap.org.uk/

National Deaf Children's Society
15 Dufferin Street
London EC1Y 8UR
020 7490 8656
http://www.ndcs.org.uk/

Royal National Institute for the Blind (RNIB)
105 Judd Street
London WC1H 9NE
020 7388 1266
http://www.rnib.org.uk/

Scope
PO Box 833
Milton Keynes MK12 5NY
020 7619 7100
http://www.scope.org.uk/

Index

Acknowledgments

Art direction for photography:
Sally Smallwood

Medical consultants for new edition:
Dr. Sarah Reynolds, Lizzie Ette

Index: Hilary Bird

Picture library: Romaine Werblow

The publisher would like to thank the following for their kind permission to reproduce their photographs:

Alamy: Chad Ehlers 29. **Corbis:** Cameron 47. **Getty Images:** Stockbyte Platinum 16–17. **Mediscan:** Shout/Medical-on-line 28. **Mother & Baby Picture Library EMAP:** 43, 48, 52. **Robert Harding Picture Library:** BananaStock 8–9. **Science Photo Library:** BSIP/Keene 150; Ruth Jenkinson/MIDIRS 44; Horacio Sormani 63.

All other images © Dorling Kindersley. For further information see: www.dkimages.com

The publishers would also like to thank:

For help in producing this book:
Lucy Heaver for proofreading; Talia Krikler for assistance with props and photography; the National Stepfamily Association and the British Association for Adoption and Fostering for advice.

For modelling:
Kim Davidson with Carla and Georgie Rabin; Lawrence and Nicola with Eddie Clarke; Deborah Seitler with Hannah Stanton; Deborah Golend, David Pratt with Anya Golend-Pratt; Seemah Burgess with Findlay Nahome-Burgess; Megan with Millie Aslan; Susu Lawrence with Anna Lawrence-Wasserberg; Shirley and Sharnah with Rohan Karper; Annabel with Amelia Lermer; Nicole with Glisha Izsak; Terumi Ehara with Mirei Kong; Tsega with Elud and Lamek Neftalem; Julie with Charli Pactor; Anna Josse with Elijah Lifton; Afsheen with Layla Foroozan; Ian Shapiro, Katie and Maya Wiseman; Keith with Shana Horwood; Jez with Jake Goswell; Pooja, Sanjive, Shey and Saanvit Sethi; Jodie Clarke with Jack Lipsey; Marta Bird with Max Brusniak; Jo and Tim with Gracie Wright; Mel Hastings with Millie Gibon; Michelle with David Horam-Cashmore; Deborah Tammer with Ruby Katz; Sam with Edie Josephs; Jo and Nick Einhorn; Andy Harvey; Laura Compton-Bishop, David with Milo Petrie; Mr and Mrs Gahir; Anna Tobin with Ella Plasett.